DEADLY DEEDS

MURDER IN CANADA

Robert Silverman
Leslie Kennedy

UNIVERSITY OF ALBERTA

Nelson Canada

Published in 1993 by
Nelson Canada,
A Division of Thomson Canada Limited
1120 Birchmount Road
Scarborough, Ontario M1K 5G4

Canadian Cataloguing in Publication Data

Silverman, Robert A., 1943–
  Deadly deeds : murder in Canada.

Includes index.
ISBN 0–17–603527–3

1. Murder – Canada. I. Kennedy, Leslie W., 1951–
II. Title.

HV6535.C3S54 1992   364.1'523'0971   C92–094433–7

Acquisitions Editor   Dave Ward
Supervising Editor   Nicole Gnutzman
Developmental Editor   Cynthia Boylan
Art Director   Bruce Bond
Cover Design   Bruce Bond
Cover Illustrator   Michael Herman
Text Design   Matthews Communications Design

Printed and bound in Canada
1 2 3 4   WC   96 95 94 93

To
Marvin E. Wolfgang

Elaine, Jason, and Michael
Ilona, Alexis, Andrea, and grandparents

Contents

Foreword

Deadly Deeds: Murder in Canada is the first in a new series of Canadian criminology books from Nelson Canada. The titles in this collection will include, among others, corporate crime, robbery, family violence, and homicide. Until now, discussion of Canadian criminality has appeared only in journal articles, sets of collected readings, and books written about specific types of crime. Therefore, this series is the first to compile an up-to-date review of crime in Canada, guided by the principle that we must discuss crime in terms that are understandable and accessible to all. The series, however, does not promote a single, unified perspective, governed by one school of thought that is distinctly Canadian. Rather, all volumes of the series are eclectic in inspiration and ideas and are bound together by a common desire to better comprehend the Canadian experience through the study of local examples and data drawn from Canadian sources. Each volume in this series will focus on conceptual, theoretical, empirical, and policy issues; and each will view all of these issues as vital to a comprehensive understanding of crime.

In *Deadly Deeds*, Silverman and Kennedy present a comprehensive review of the explanations of the most violent of all crimes, drawing from a detailed data set that presents all occurrences of murder in Canada over the last thirty years. This book emphasizes explanations that focus on the situational dimensions of interpersonal conflict as the determining factors in precipitating murderous outcomes. A central element in understanding most murders, Silverman and Kennedy argue, is the relationship that exists between the victim and offender. A great deal of attention is paid in the book to the differences that characterize killings in domestic situations from those that occur between friends or strangers.

There is, as well, detailed discussion of those events that catch the greatest amount of public attention—serial and mass murders—which sets them into context as low occurrence crimes in Canada. The book ends with a review of ameliorative strategies that could be adopted to remove the conditions that foster murder.

It is our hope that this book and the others in the series will add to our collective understanding of crime in Canada and will serve as an important, up-to-date, reference source to inform public debate on these issues.

Leslie W. Kennedy, University of Alberta
Vince Sacco, Queen's University

Acknowledgments

The authors would like to thank David Forde for his assistance in the preparation of the theoretical sections of this book. David has collaborated in a number of research papers from which we have drawn in the development of our approach to the study of homicide. Where appropriate, reference will be made to his specific contributions. Other work we have done over the past five years is integrated into the body of the book and is also cited. This book is a compilation, synthesis, and extension of ideas developed during five years of homicide research. Here we attempt to describe and discuss many aspects of homicide as it has occurred in Canada during a thirty-year period.

We are grateful to Steve Baron (University of Alberta) for reading an early version of the manuscript and for organizing our reprint files. Thanks to Bill Meloff who agreed to permit use of parts of the article published with Silverman on kids who kill. Others who read and commented on the manuscript and have our thanks include Ezzat Fattah (Simon Fraser University), David Forde (University of Manitoba), Vincent Sacco (Queen's University), A. Ron Gillis (University of Toronto), and Marc Riedel (Southern Illinois University). Many of their comments and corrections have been incorporated into the current text. They gave us detailed comments and stimulated us to write a better book. J.C. Levy (University of Calgary) made us face the precision of the law in defining culpable killing. We are indebted to all who contributed.

Frank Avakame provided valuable aid as a research assistant for parts of our work, and Dorothy Burgess patiently did first drafts of much of the manuscript. Others at the University of Alberta who deserve thanks include: the late Pamela Jarvis, who, while not directly involved in the book, effectively managed the Department of Sociology, allowing Silverman the time to work; Kerri Calvert, Librarian for the Population Research Library, who provided necessary census data to complete our analysis; and Bruce Elman, Faculty of Law for providing insights into the "battered woman defence."

Without the cooperation, encouragement, and support of Dr. Sange DeSilva, Director, Canadian Centre for Justice Statistics, Statistics Canada, we would not have been able to complete the book. The Canadian Centre for Justice Statistics (CCJS) provided the data upon which the core of the book is based. We would like to thank those at CCJS who were most responsible for the generation of the data—Jacques Bazinet, Bob Blais, and Ron Kearney. We are especially grateful to Gail Cole for coordinating the effort and making sure that our many requests were answered. Glenda Sullivan facilitated various aspects of communication among those involved.

Special thanks to Ray Enright who both read the manuscript and allowed us access to research files he has amassed for a book about individuals serving life sentences for murder.

This research was supported by the Solicitor General of Canada Contributions Grant, through the Centre for Criminological Research, University of Alberta. The Department of Sociology at the University of Alberta provides an environment and facilities that have fostered and enhanced our efforts to complete this task.

We are especially pleased with our association with Nelson Canada. Dave Ward has been enthusiastic, encouraging, helpful, and, most important, patient. We are grateful for all of the help we have received and hope that the result is an informative and accurate account of culpable killing in Canada.

R.A. Silverman
L.W. Kennedy
Edmonton, March 1992

Introduction

Jeffrey Dahmer said he was sorry. His apology added a some-what surreal end to a trial which depicted acts of violence and murder that horrified a public already overwhelmed with tragic tales. Dahmer's crimes included seventeen slayings over a period of fifteen years, made more heinous by the fact that after he killed his victims, he butchered them. Indeed, his arrest came after neighbours complained about the foul smells that emanated from his Milwaukee apartment. The police uncovered parts of bodies and a long history of sexual abuse and violence (*Newsweek* 1992).

Following the discovery of these grizzly remains, there were admissions by neighbours that they had been suspicious of Dahmer's actions. On one occasion, the police had even been called to deal with a problem between Dahmer and a teenager who had fled his apartment naked. Assuming the "problem" to be a gay lovers' quarrel, the police returned the victim to Dahmer; the teenager is probably among the dead.

Dahmer received a total of seventeen consecutive life sentences with no eligibility for parole for 936 years. He escaped the death sentence because Wisconsin does not execute people for first-degree murder. In his apology, Dahmer said that he wanted to be executed, and that medical explanations about his sickness had given him some peace (*Edmonton Journal* 1992b): cold comfort for the relatives of his victims and a public traumatized by his actions.

The Jeffrey Dahmer case focuses attention on murder as the most feared and one of the most disturbing crimes, particularly when committed to satisfy sexual appetites. We are bombarded by stories of serial killers and mass murderers that stoke our anxieties not only about our own safety and that of our family but also about a society in which such crimes can occur. Despite their riveting nature, however, the actions of a Jeffrey Dahmer constitute only a very small portion of fatal crimes.

Murder is, in reality, not one type of crime. Varieties of criminal killing are determined by the motives of the offender, the circumstances of the event, and the interaction between offender and victim. Even with no background in the study of murder, it should be easy to understand that killing which takes place during a robbery is fundamentally different from serial murder or from spousal murder. In this book, we explore varieties of homicide, major explanations for homicide, and some remedies. Our analysis is far from complete and our research continues, but this text offers an overview of patterns and distribution of murder in Canada that has not been previously available. We hope to educate the reader about the nature of killing and thereby set cases like Dahmer's into their proper perspective.

In this chapter, we begin by examining the interest that the public and press have in fatal crime. The rest of the book is devoted to an analysis of the nature of the crime, its explanations, and its remedies. Along the way, we address some of the questions that are typically raised by the press and public.

THE PUBLIC VIEW OF HOMICIDE

As the Dahmer case so readily illustrates, homicide attracts a great deal of attention. The act of murder instills fear in the public and a desire for quick apprehension of the offender. Further, it demands explanation. It is not enough for people to be told that the crime occurred and that the offender has been apprehended. They want to know what provoked the crime and, more importantly, what can be done to prevent further such crimes from occurring. The spectre of killers stalking neighbourhoods looking for victims generates fear. "Who will be the next victim? Will it be me?" There is a sense of unease in society about the disorder that murder represents. The more we read about it, the more concern arises for the state of health of our community. We are riveted by talk about murder and inundated with descriptions of it in the daily media.

On July 29, 1990, Edmonton recorded its eighteenth murder of that year. This put the murder rate ahead of the pace set in previous years, suggesting a record number of murders by the end of the year. Not having read the morning paper, we became quickly aware of the anticipated record from the sudden deluge of telephone calls from newspaper reporters and radio disc jockeys trying to meet their employers' demands that they find a criminologist (or anyone else with "credentials") who could provide an explanation for these record numbers.[1] Our first response was: "Talk to us in November when we can judge better if the trend holds or if there is a drop back to the trends of previous years."

Individual events such as murders do not always occur according to a consistent pattern discernible in a short period of time. A clustering of murders may be followed by a time when none occur at all. Overall, though, the annual numbers may remain the same from year to year. The time frame used for trend comparisons is important in determining whether or not the problem has become worse, stayed the same, or improved. The media appreciate these distinctions but reflect the public's desire to know about the "evil" spreading through our society that causes such nastiness to rear its ugly head.

As will be seen, however, a few cases can make a big difference in a population the size of Edmonton. As criminologists, we are acutely aware of the hazards of rate calculations. We are also wary of taking specific cases and drawing general conclusions from them that may be isolated or unrepresentative of what is really going on in the community. Depending on the population that is being studied and the ways in which we count victims, a small change in numbers of murders can have an astounding effect on the rates generated. For instance, assume that a city has a population of 500,000 and twenty-five murders in one year. The annual rate is 5 per 100,000 population. Now, suppose that one man kills his family of five. The city then has thirty killings for the year and a rate of 6 per 100,000. No doubt, this rate would make the city the "killing capital of Canada." The fact is, one very disturbed individual can force us to generalize unfairly and inaccurately about the social conditions in this community.

For several years, Edmonton was "the murder capital of Canada," even though it has under thirty murders per year in a metropolitan area of somewhat over 600,000 individuals. (By way of comparison, the Bronx, a borough of New York City with a population of about 700,000, has close to 400 murders per year.)

Another consideration in presenting our case on the extent of murder in a community involves improper use of the simple percentages that are reported. Percentage differences from year to year can appear large when using small numbers. For example, an increase in crimes from ten to fifteen is a 50 percent increase but hardly, when the absolute numbers are considered, a reason for panic.

In our discussion with the media, we face their insistence that the numbers speak for themselves. The trend is upward. What explains this, they ask. In response, we try to put these events into context. We explain the reasons for their occurrence by referring to the problems of inner-city living where abuse of drugs and alcohol along with poverty and broken families combine to create the tensions that develop in intimate relations that turn sour. We explain that murderous events require a variety of explanations depending on circumstances. A killing during a robbery bears little resemblance to a husband killing a wife or a homicide that results from a drunken bar brawl. In fact, the only thing the three events have in common is extreme violence and at least one dead body.

What can be done about the problems that give rise to murder? We have mentioned the difficulties with explaining individual events using general theories. It is necessary, we argue, to see beyond individual events, which seem to require immediate reaction, to the larger issues which may create the tension and conflict that results in fatalities. We conclude that the direct action of social agencies, including the police, is needed to remove the causes of social breakdown that sometime lead to fatal conclusions. However, we also point out that the urgency in dealing with the immediate threats often overwhelm these agencies in their attempts to confront fundamental social problems.

RESPONDING TO MURDER

The public's impatience for immediate solutions is shared by some criminologists. James Q. Wilson (1983) points out that, although there is probably some relationship between changes in social structure (such as increases in unemployment) and crime, it requires major efforts to bring about changes in the economic structure to remove the factors that create unemployment. These changes do not happen overnight. In the meantime, Wilson argues, we have to attack the problem right now. We cannot afford to wait for long-term solutions.

The escalation of violence in the drug wars in the United States is testament to the upward cycle of conflict and harm that comes from violent confrontation. But some would argue that the response to drug crime may itself be more dangerous than the crime itself. This is not to say that we should not confront crime, especially violent crime, in our attempts to deter it. What is needed, though, is an approach that acknowledges the social dynamics of the events that precede fatal attacks and proposes ways in which these events can be short-circuited into harmless outcomes.

In our discussions with the media about rising violent crime, we attempt to unravel complex social behaviour in terms that are easily understood by reporters, practitioners, and the public. We are often left with the frustration of being unable to provide the media with the simple answers that they would like to offer their listeners and readers. But these crimes need to be understood in all their complexity, especially when it comes time to plan ways of preventing their occurrence. We will present as full a description of the murder nexus as we can in this book. We have a distinct advantage in this task as we will be using a comprehensive data set that includes all murders recorded by police in Canada between 1961 and 1990. This data set is invaluable in identifying the different types of murders, offenders and victims, circumstances, and methods. It provides an important basis upon which we can identify the extent to which murders occur and the people affected by them.

The concerns about rising violent crime have repercussions throughout society, creating fear, distrust, and apprehension. Based on exposure to the U.S. situation (through the media), many Canadians believe our level of crime is much higher than it actually is (Doob and Roberts 1982). The chaos of random killings experienced in the large U.S. cities are making Canadians assess their own vulnerability. Will these same levels of violence soon be visited on us?

The mesmerizing effect on the community of well-publicized murders, such as those committed by Jeffrey Dahmer and others like him, should be evident. What is needed is an attempt to decipher the factors that can contribute to their occurrence. We need to learn which social factors are likely to coexist in the context of particular types of murders and which groups of people are most vulnerable to specific circumstances. Our efforts to explain the murder event require that we take the individual experiences as a whole and compare and contrast them across time and across location.

We attempt this analysis recognizing that it lacks some of the glamour of murder mysteries or the violence of Hollywood police movies. Yet these too provide important background to our analysis. It is clear that society regards murder and violence with fear, but also with curiosity and fascination. Violence that is depicted in movies seems safe and satiates our desire to explore the underside of the human psyche. But this violence sometimes seeps out to pervade the society. Some researchers have argued that murder is connected to a climate of violence. Research conducted by Baron and Straus (1988) indicates that variations in the level of tolerance (measured independently of the murder rate) that people have to violent events, either depicted in movies, in sports, or in daily life, is related to the amount of murder that occurs in these environments. They indicate that the differences in violence in the different regions in the United States (with higher tolerance levels in the South and the West) is directly correlated with higher levels of homicides in these areas. In Canada, the cultural differences across regions are not as great as they are in the United States, but it is clear that there are similar elements tolerant of violence, if only because we are exposed to so much of the American media and sports. The problem of understanding the emergence of murder in violent societies is a difficult one, as single acts of violence may seem unique and unrelated to one another. In fact, as with all social phenomena, there are patterns in motives and circumstances that allow us to identify commonalities in these events.

RESEARCH ON MURDER

Modern sociological murder research began with Wolfgang's 1958 *Patterns in Criminal Homicide*. Wolfgang illustrated the value and importance of describing the phenomenon in precise detail (Cheatwood 1991). In examining Wolfgang's contribution, Margaret Zahn wrote:

> There are a number of things that homicide research needs to do: (1) trace the volume of killing over time in various geopolitical units; (2) delineate clearly the types of homicide that exist, for homicide is indeed a multidimensional, not unidimensional, phenomenon; (3) specify the particular populations affected by these different types; and (4) determine the causes of increasing volume over time. Accomplishing these four objectives will allow us to reach the ultimate objective which is the development of social policies that can impact this lethal phenomenon.

In the following chapters, we attempt to address all of these issues as they relate to murder in Canada. While the data do not always lend themselves to hypothesis-testing, we do introduce readers to various explanations that have been offered for homicide commission, and in later chapters test some of the hypotheses that have been generated by these theories.

THE PLAN OF THE BOOK

Chapter 2 offers legal definitions and exceptions to charges of homicide. Having defined homicide and murder, we illustrate the temporal patterns of homicide that have occurred in Canada. It must be noted that throughout most of the book the data we discuss refer to murder (leaving out manslaughter and infanticide)—the distinction should become clear in Chapter 2. However, in some instances, we do refer to those two crimes (manslaughter and infanticide) in which case homicide is the appropriate term. Adding to this possible confusion is the fact that most of the research we discuss refers to "homicide," even though the precise definition will vary with the jurisdiction being covered. In fact, we find that most criminological literature is not concerned with the precise definition. Most use "homicide" to refer to culpable killing, no matter what specific types of acts are being considered. We have tried to be more precise here. Chapter 2 makes it clear that "homicide" is the broader term and "murder" the more narrow.

Following our discussion of homicide patterns and definitions, we turn to theoretical approaches or explanations for the act in Chapter 3. These focus on both individual and societal causes and the multi-level factors that contribute to the conditions that lead to murder.

Chapters 4 through 8 present and analyze Canadian murder data. Chapter 4 examines the importance of relationships, demographic differences, and opportunities in contributing to fatal outcomes. Chapter 5 focuses on crime-based murder (especially theft and sex crimes), considering, as well, the special cases of serial killers and mass murderers. Chapter 6 looks at special groups of offenders—women, the young, and the elderly. Victim groups of special contemporary interest—children, the elderly, and women—are dealt with in Chapter 7, while Chapter 8 deals with the role of Canadian Indians (as opposed to native peoples as a whole) as murder victims and offenders. Finally, in Chapter 9, we examine the responses that have been offered, from punishment to training in conflict management, to deal with the problem of containing violent behaviour that becomes fatal.

The perspective offered in this book is that homicide can occur when a series of factors coincide to bring about conditions that are conducive to this act. Homicide, of course, does not always result from these factors. We argue that murder can be better understood by examining the importance of these factors in the etiology of killing. Using this perspective, we can focus on these conditions as not only conducive to fatal outcomes but as factors that need to be addressed in reducing the probabilities that such outcomes will occur.

We hope also to put the high-profile cases of murderous behaviour that attract so much attention, like the Dahmer case, into context. While the extreme depravity depicted in the Dahmer case is morbidly fascinating, the vast majority of murders are far more mundane in their details.

CANADIAN HOMICIDE DATA AND THEIR LIMITATIONS

While the theory and speculation about causes and patterns lead us in one direction, it is not always possible to obtain data that allow us to check these insights or hypotheses. The data used in this book come from a variety of sources, each with its own unique characteristics. Wherever possible, we point out specific sources and limitations of the data.

The information that we use to present profiles of Canadian murder is provided through police reports compiled by the Canadian Centre for Justice Statistics, a division of Statistics Canada that gathers information from summary police reports about murders around the country. These data are a rich source of information about the circumstances of the murder, including the characteristics of the offenders and victims, their relationships, the location of the offence, and the means of killing. They do not, however, provide us with much information about the factors that lead up to the murder. Motive is recorded by the police based on their assessment of what occurred previous to the murder. Hence, while the information is invaluable, it does not provide us with everything we would need to examine other interesting aspects of homicide. Because we are using police-generated information, it is important to keep in mind that those we call "offenders" are really suspects at the time the information is collected. Some of them are found not guilty and others are found guilty on reduced charges.

In order to produce trends, we have had to use multiple sources of data. These are not always fully comparable but they do give a fair idea of long-term homicide trends. This is especially true in Chapter 2 where we combine data from a historical document with those generated by a contemporary data set produced by Statistics Canada (Relative Trends). The data that refer to post-1961 material cover all murders, based on numbers of victims.

Much of our earlier published work has been based on single offender/single victim homicide events. For this book, we include all incidents of murder but only analyze the relationship between the socially closest victim and offender. This gives us a slightly larger data set. Some research literature argues that single victim/single offender cases may differ from multiple victim/multiple offender cases and should therefore be analyzed separately. An examination of the trends and patterns generated by the data set we used in this book reveals that, in terms of important trends and relationships, the proportions produced rarely vary by more than 1 or 2 percent from the earlier findings. Hence, we have decided to continue to use "incident" as the unit of analysis, regardless of the numbers of victims and offenders.

Tables for this data set were produced by the Canadian Centre for Justice Statistics to our specifications and for the most part refer to a series between 1961 and 1990. The one exception to that, in Chapters 4 through 8, is that any information referring to Canadian Indian offenders and victims is available only to 1989; the lack of one year will have no effect on trends or proportions revealed.

One warning to the reader is that the numbers generated by this data set will not correspond directly to published data (by Statistics Canada) that use "victim" as the unit of analysis. Our data set includes a total of 12,828 victim-incidents between 1961 and 1990. Not all of these can be included in every table or graph because of missing values for subsets of information. Percentages are generated without missing values. When there is a large number of missing cases, we usually do not display or discuss the variable. When appropriate, we reveal the proportion of missing cases. Approximately 16 percent of all homicides are unsolved. Hence, there is no suspect information for analysis. These are treated as missing values and deleted from the tables, graphs, and charts.

Finally, at some points in the text, stated proportions for a phenomenon will vary from stated proportions at another point in the text. The reason for the differences is the context for looking at the variable, either the source of data or the unknown category in the specific context.

In Chapters 4 through 8, we present victim, offender, and offence profiles—in the form of charts—for each subgrouping of homicide. The variables included in each table are (more or less) consistent for each subgroup and should provide a convenient comparison point. Profiles at the beginning of each section describe the data, so readers can see at a glance significant characteristics of the group to be discussed. *The profiles are not always fully discussed in the text.* Further, the variables chosen for display are the most common elements available. The profiles show percentages within groups of variables. At the bottom of each chart, the total number of known cases for that variable and subgroup is shown.

Information about the effects of social and economic conditions comes from statistical data produced by Statistics Canada, drawn mainly from census material. The homicide data files are time-dated and geographically coded, which allows us to identify temporal and regional characteristics that relate to the homicide incident. The links between social conditions and individual behaviour are not always direct. However, as have other researchers, we suggest that the insights provided by the descriptive statistics and the explanations that can be culled from the analysis of the relationships between social and economic factors and homicide help to provide a larger view of the problem.

It is our strong contention that we cannot understand homicide solely as a product of interpersonal breakdown or solely as a result of social disintegration. Both the individual and social forces in society must be considered in any assessment of murder. The relationship between individual and social "causes" of murder can be terribly confusing. More important, it seems far removed from the media image of the body lying on the floor or pavement. The criminologist examines crime from the perspective of abstract categories that help to explain observed patterns of behaviour. This does not mean that we go out of our way to obscure the horror of the real event, although this is sometimes an inadvertent consequence of an arms-length analysis.

While we may talk about the correlation between homicide and social inequality, unemployment, age relationships or gender, no one was ever directly killed because of social inequality. Murder takes place in emotionally charged environments or during the course of another crime. Economic frustration may be an indirect precipitator of one individual's actions against another, but no offender says, "The economy is in a tailspin; therefore, I will kill my wife." Instead, frustrations with the economy may lead to psychological distress, which results in feelings of futility, which lead to drinking alcohol, which leads to violence (often serial), which culminates in killing. The best that the criminologist can do is say that, in certain circumstances, downturns in the economy will lead to the direct forces that influence the occurrence of homicide.

MURDER IN CANADA: A BRIEF OVERVIEW

In this section, we have taken the aggregate data for murders that occurred between 1961 and 1990.

SUSPECTS

Profile 1.1a shows that murders in Canada are committed mainly by young, single, male Caucasians. Eighty-seven percent of suspects are male, 40 percent are under 25, 45 percent are single, and 76 percent are Caucasian. Other information is available for only a part of the suspect population. For instance, we have information about educational achievement for about one-half of the suspects. Forty-three percent of those attained a Grade 8 (or less)

PROFILE 1.1a

SUSPECT CHARACTERISTICS, MURDER IN CANADA, 1961–1990

Suspect's Gender

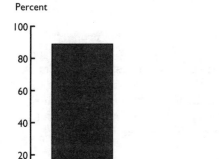

N = 11,586.

Suspect's Age

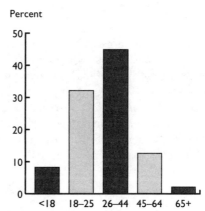

N = 11,561 (excludes unknowns).

Suspect's Marital Status

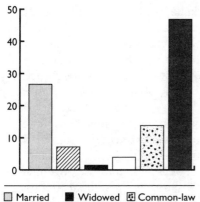

☐ Married   ■ Widowed   ▦ Common-law
▨ Separated   ☐ Divorced   ■ Single

N = 11,331 (excludes unknowns).

Suspect's Race

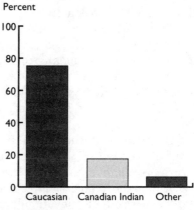

N = 11,150 (excludes unknowns).

education, while another 30 percent achieved a Grade 9 or 10 level. Similarly, occupational data are available for about two-thirds of the suspects, one-third of whom are labourers. Because of the missing values, in the rest of the text we tend to avoid those variables. Finally, 87 percent of the murders are committed by a single offender and another 9 percent involve two offenders. Hence, only 4 percent involve three or more offenders. The four variables noted in Profile 1.1a are the variables with which we are most concerned in Chapters 4 through 8.

VICTIMS

Victims are more often male than female, but the proportions contrast with those for suspects. Females make up 37 percent of murder victims over the thirty years. Like suspects, most victims are young (31 percent are under 25), though somewhat older than offenders, single (42 percent) and Caucasian (80 percent). There is little other information available about victims in the data set. However, some of the offence information is relevant to victim characteristics.

OFFENCES

Murder most often takes place in the home of the victim (49 percent) or suspect (9 percent), or some other private place (16 percent) that would include other people's homes. Only about 20 percent of the murders occur in public venues. For the most part, murder is an indoor activity.

The most common method of dispatching of a victim is by gun (38 percent), followed by stabbing (25 percent) and beating (21 percent). Other means constitute 16 percent of the murders and include strangulation, suffocation, arson, drowning, and any other means. When guns are used, over two-thirds are long guns (rifle, shotgun, sawed-off shotgun) while about 30 percent are handguns.

Police identify the motive in these crimes as robbery/theft in about 13 percent of the cases, and as a sexual crime in under 5 percent of the events. About two-thirds of the cases are considered to be the result of anger, arguments, jealousy, or revenge. Only 7 percent of the offenders are classified as mentally ill. About 10 percent of murders are followed by the suicide of the offender. In the chapters that follow, we use suicide as an indirect measure of remorse on the part of the offender.

Unfortunately, the data set does not offer a clear indication of alcohol involvement in murder. The research literature referred to later clearly indicates a strong link between alcohol and vio-

PROFILE 1.1b

VICTIM CHARACTERISTICS, MURDER IN CANADA, 1961–1990

Victim's Gender

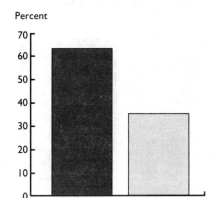

N = 12,828.

Victim's Age

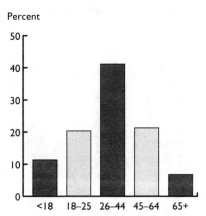

N = 12,814 (excludes unknowns).

Victim's Marital Status

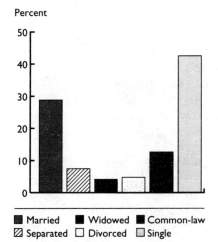

■ Married ■ Widowed ■ Common-law
▨ Separated ☐ Divorced ☐ Single

N = 12,666 (excludes unknowns).

Victim's Race

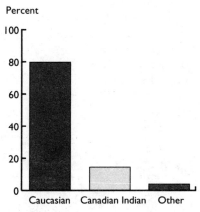

N = 12,221 (excludes unknowns).

PROFILE I.Ic

CHARACTERISTICS OF MURDER EVENTS, IN CANADA, 1961–1990

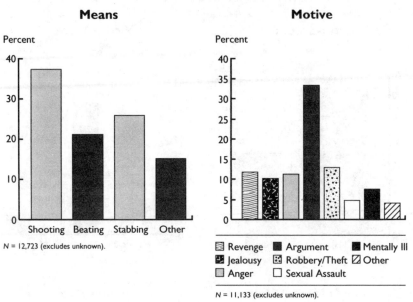

Means

Percent

Shooting   Beating   Stabbing   Other

N = 12,723 (excludes unknown).

Motive

Percent

▦ Revenge   ■ Argument   ■ Mentally Ill
▨ Jealousy   ▥ Robbery/Theft   ▨ Other
▢ Anger   □ Sexual Assault

N = 11,133 (excludes unknown).

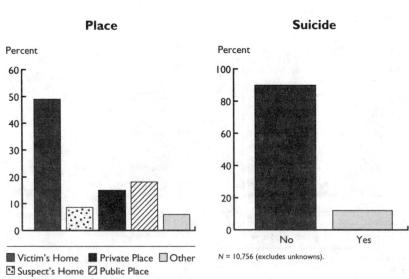

Place

Percent

■ Victim's Home   ■ Private Place   □ Other
▥ Suspect's Home   ▨ Public Place

N = 11,919 (excludes unknowns).

Suicide

Percent

No   Yes

N = 10,756 (excludes unknowns).

lence. Our data show that police record alcohol involvement in 30 percent of the cases and drugs in 33 percent. However, the category that shows no involvement is really an "unknown" category. Hence, percentages are difficult to calculate. As a result, we are not able to make definitive statements about the amount of alcohol involvement in Canadian murders.

SOCIAL RELATIONSHIPS

PROFILE I.Id

SOCIAL RELATIONSHIP BETWEEN VICTIMS AND SUSPECTS, MURDER IN CANADA, 1961–1990

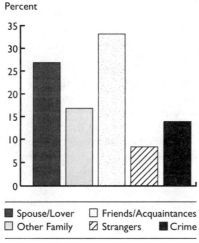

Percent

■ Spouse/Lover   □ Friends/Acquaintances
□ Other Family   ▨ Strangers   ■ Crime

N = 10,756 (excludes unknowns).

A large part of this book is concerned with the social relationships between victims and offenders as that relationship has a great deal to do with the particular kinds of interactions that lead to violence. Profile 1.1d shows that over the 30-year period about 45 percent of all murders take place within the family. Twenty-seven percent are spouses (including common-law) and lovers killing each other, while 17 percent are other family members such as parents, brothers, sisters, cousins, aunts, uncles, grandparents, or any other family relationship that is nonspousal. Friend/acquaintance relationships account for one-third of the murders. Strangers are involved in only 8 percent, while murder during the commission of another crime accounts for 14 percent.

Overview

The charts and other information presented here serve as a starting point for discussion of murder in Canada. In a way, this description represents the average kind of murder. Chapters 4 through 8 focus on various subgroups within the murder-committing population. In those chapters, we dissect the average to cast light on specific types of murder in Canada. The information presented later in the profile charts can be easily compared to the "averages" presented here.

The reader should be aware that there have been dramatic changes over time in some of these relationships, and the average often does not accurately represent the situation in the later years of the series. The distributions of some of the variables examined vary dramatically depending on the subgroup being examined.

N O T E S

1. We gained an interesting insight into the focus of the local press when, in March 1992, it was announced that homicide had gone up by 14 percent in Canada between 1990 and 1991. We did not receive one call about this phenomenon—we presume that the silence resulted from the fact that there had been no increase in Edmonton's homicide rate. (Most of the rise was accounted for by increases in three major Ontario cities.)

Definitions and Trends

Homicide is the killing of one person by another. A number of factors influence the ways in which we classify those acts that result in death as either criminal or noncriminal. There are different forms of homicide, according to the law, depending on the intent of the perpetrator. Of course, the courts spend considerable time trying to determine that intent. We will review the legal definitions of homicide, including the ways that killing can be defined either as murder or as a noncriminal act. While it may at first seem obvious that any form of killing is unacceptable, there are instances in which killing is exempt from penalties and is even sometimes considered acceptable within a particular society. For instance, killing the enemy during war is considered acceptable by most people, while killing someone in self-defence is considered to be a necessary (if lamentable) act.

Homicide is defined by section 222 of the Criminal Code as follows:

222. (1) A person commits homicide when, directly or indirectly, by any means, he causes the death of a human being.

(2) Homicide is culpable or non-culpable.

(3) Homicide that is not culpable is not an offence.

(4) Culpable homicide is murder or manslaughter or infanticide.

(5) A person commits culpable homicide when he causes the death of a human being,

(a) by means of an unlawful act,

(b) by criminal negligence,

(c) by causing that human being, by threats or fear of violence or by deception, to do anything that causes his death, or

(d) by wilfully frightening that human being in the case of a child or sick person.

(6) Notwithstanding anything in this Section a person does not commit homicide within the meaning of this Act by reason only that he causes the death of a human being by procuring, by false evidence, the conviction and death of that human being by sentence of the law.

Some theorists point out that the law is very specific in the kinds of killing it bans and the kinds it ignores. For instance, when through negligence manufacturers cause the death of those who purchase their products, the criminal law is not equipped to deal with them (Box 1981), although they may suffer penalties through civil procedures. While the law is capable of finding criminal negligence in such cases, the criminal justice system is not geared to investigating them.

Despite the exceptions, there is general agreement about which acts are culpable killings. The basic components of the legal definition of culpable homicide come to us from common law and are a part of the definition of murder in virtually all Western nations. The way in which particular behaviours come to be defined as criminal homicide informs most other aspects of the study of homicide. The specific types of behaviour that are defined as criminal homicide by the Criminal Code of Canada are the focus of this book.

LEGAL DEFINITIONS

Because this book deals with murder as defined by the criminal law of Canada, we present the verbatim definitions of homicide, murder, manslaughter, and infanticide as they appeared in the Criminal Code as of 1990–91. By the time you read the section, the law may have changed. The law regarding murder (and many other laws) is subject to revision by legislation and by interpretations of Canadian courts, and ultimately the Supreme Court of Canada—especially with regard to issues involving the Charter of Rights and Freedoms. For instance, notions of "constructive intent" (discussed below) were struck down by the Supreme Court of Canada in 1990. An equally dramatic decision occurred in early 1992 when an Alberta provincial court judge ruled that a couple should stand trial for the murder of their 3-year-old foster child, even though the child was still alive. The child had been beaten and his upper brain was "technically no longer alive" (*Edmonton Journal*, 1992a). The court has since decided to proceed with charges of aggravated assault. However, this case illustrates that if the couple had been convicted of first- or second-degree murder, the decision would have given a new meaning to the definition generally applied to murder. These changes in the law do not affect the data that are analyzed in the following chapters.[1]

How does the Criminal Code define culpable homicide?

Culpable homicide is murder

229. (a) where the person who causes the death of a human being
  (i) means to cause his death, or
  (ii) means to cause him bodily harm that he knows is likely to cause his death, and is reckless whether death ensues or not;
(b) where a person, meaning to cause death to a human being or meaning to cause him bodily harm that he knows is likely to cause his death, and being reckless whether death ensues or not, by accident or mistake causes death to another human being, notwithstanding that he does not mean to cause death or bodily harm to that human being; or
(c) where a person, for an unlawful object, does anything that he knows or ought to know is likely to cause death, and thereby causes death to a human being, notwithstanding that he desires to effect his object without causing death or bodily harm to any human being.

Planned and deliberate murder—Contracted murder—Murder of peace officer, etc.—Hijacking, sexual assault or kidnapping—Second degree murder

231. (1) Murder is first degree murder or second degree murder.
(2) Murder is first degree murder when it is planned and deliberate.
(3) Without limiting the generality of subsection (2), murder is planned and deliberate when it is committed pursuant to an arrangement under which money or anything of value passes or is intended to pass from one person to another, or is promised by one person to another, as consideration for that other's causing or assisting in causing the death of anyone or counselling another person to do any act causing or assisting in causing that death.
(4) Irrespective of whether a murder is planned and deliberate on the part of any person, murder is first degree murder when the victim is
  (a) a police officer, police constable, constable, sheriff, deputy sheriff, sheriff's officer, or other person employed for the preservation and maintenance of the public peace, acting in the course of his duties;
  (b) a warden, deputy warden, instructor, keeper, jailer, guard or other officer or a permanent employee of a prison, acting in the course of his duties; or
  (c) a person working in a prison with the permission of the prison authorities and acting in the course of his work therein.
(5) Irrespective of whether a murder is planned and deliberate on the part of any person, murder is first degree murder in respect of a person when the death is caused by that person while committing or attempting

to commit an offence under one of the following sections:

(a) section 76 (hijacking an aircraft);

(b) section 271 (sexual assault);

(c) section 272 (sexual assault with a weapon, threats to a third party or causing bodily harm);

(d) section 273 (aggravated sexual assault);

(e) section 279 (kidnapping and forcible confinement); or

(f) section 279.1 (hostage taking).

(6) [Repealed R.S. 1985, c.27 (1st Supp.), s.35.]

(7) All murder that is not first degree murder is second degree murder. R.S. 1985, c.27 (1st Supp.), ss.7(2), 35, 40(2).

In defining most crimes, there must both be an act and an intent to do the act. Murder is no exception. The criminal law clearly states that "murder is first degree murder when it is planned and deliberate." Planned and deliberate refers to intent.

Except for the rather turgid legalese that makes up its definitions, the law seems clear enough concerning what constitutes murder. However, not every act in which one individual kills another results in a clear ability to define whether or not offenders committed the act in a planned and deliberate manner. In fact, in murder cases, the courts spend much of their time trying to determine whether the act is planned and deliberate under the terms of reference of the law.

Considering the penalties, it makes a great deal of difference whether the court finds an offender guilty of the planned and deliberate type of murder (first degree) or second degree ("All murder that is not first degree murder is second degree murder"). The reader should realize that second-degree murder is not clearly defined. It is a residual category. Hence, if a defence attorney can "prove"[2] that a client was not guilty of first-degree murder, and if that client is not guilty of manslaughter, then she or he is likely to be tried for second-degree murder. The sentence for both crimes is life in prison, but in the case of first-degree murder the offender is not eligible for parole before serving twenty-five years in prison, while for second-degree murder the offender must serve ten years before parole eligibility.[3]

In the case of homicide, the act (*actus reus*) itself is rather obvious. The *actus reus* is the act of one person killing another— that is, the act is a homicide.[4] In the most direct case, this may involve an offender pulling the trigger of a gun that he or she has pointed at the victim; or the offender could see the victim crossing the road and deliberately run over him or her with an automobile. The point is that the offender does something that directly results in the death of the victim. The act therefore results in a *consequence*, which is the death of the victim. This, too, is a part of the definition of the act. And it is important that the conduct of the accused be at least a contributing cause of the consequence (the death). Hence, the law states that one cannot be convicted of culpable murder if the death of the victim does not occur within a year and a day of the "... last event by means of which the person contributed to or caused the death" (section 227).

Indirect cause complicates matters a good deal, and is to a large extent dealt with by the three sections of the Criminal Code reproduced below. For instance, an offender stabs a victim; the victim is taken for treatment to a hospital where he or she contracts an iatrogenic[5] virus and dies. One argument is that the victim would not have died if the stabbing had not taken place— therefore the offender is guilty of manslaughter (at least). A second argument is that the contraction of the virus is so significantly a new circumstance that it operates as an intervening circumstance, relieving the original actor of responsibility.

224. Where a person by an act or a mission does anything that results in the death of a human being, he causes the death of that human being notwithstanding that death from the cause might have been prevented by resorting to proper means.

225. Where a person causes to a human being a bodily injury that is of itself of a dangerous nature and from which death results, he causes the death of that human being notwithstanding that the immediate cause of death is proper or improper treatment that is applied in good faith.

226. Where a person causes to a human being a bodily injury that results in death, causes the death of that human being notwithstanding that the effect of the bodily injury is only to accelerate his death from a disease or disorder arising from some other cause.

The *actus reus* is usually the easy part of the event to prove. It is the *mens rea* with which the courts find difficulty. In essence, proving *mens rea* means you have to know what was going on in the offender's mind to determine whether he or she intended the act. Even when the offender confesses to the act, the courts may find that the individual did not have the mental capability of forming intent. These are the issues over which juries struggle.

While intention is difficult to prove, motivation (which is what most observers believe to be a major component of the law) is irrelevant. The confusing thing is that lawyers often use motivation to attempt to show intention. The fact is that one can do bad acts with good motives. Hence, the terrorist believes he is assassinating a political leader with very good cause. His motive is noble (according to him) but, if he intends to do the act and it is planned and deliberate then he should be found guilty of first-degree murder in Canada.

As an example, in the late 1980s the Ayatollah Khomeini of Iran instructed his followers to kill the author Salman Rushdie, who was residing in England. Rushdie's would-be assassins believe their cause is just, noble, and a God-given duty, but were they to perform the act in a Western country, the intent rather than the motive would drive the jury deliberations. As indicated earlier, a murder must include both intention and an act. The intention itself is not a crime and the act itself is not a crime if there is no intention.

Knowing that one has been convicted of first-degree murder does not necessarily mean that the individual performed a planned and deliberate act which, as such, would be defined by common sense or common usage. A real case example illustrates the point.

> An individual enters a bar in a Canadian city and proceeds to order drinks. He is drunk but his drunkenness is not obvious. He does not slur his speech and seems to be able to walk without being shaky. After four doubles, he swears, "Oh, fuck!" A bartender says he can't talk that way in here and after a verbal altercation orders him cut off and out of the bar. The patron settles his tab. He tells the bartender he will "blow him away." He repeats this to the person who escorts him from the bar. His tone is not angry but "matter-of-fact." He goes to his truck, which is located in a distant part of the parking lot, and gets his shotgun. After being in the sunlit parking lot for about five minutes, he returns to the entrance-way of the bar and shoots twice into the darkened room. One of the shots hits and kills a 19-year-old waitress standing at the back of the bar at the entrance to a darkened storage room.

The defence lawyer argued that the defendant had an inability to form intent due to alcohol consumption and temporary insanity.[6] The defendant argued that he never intended to kill anyone, even though he verbally stated that he would "blow away" the two bartenders. It was reasonably obvious that he did not aim at the bartenders or at anyone else in particular. Other parts of the physical evidence (e.g., the line of fire) support the argument that he was not aiming at anyone. Of what was the offender convicted? Every time this question is asked, whether to undergraduates or to police officers in a training seminar, the majority split between second-degree murder and manslaughter. In fact, the individual was convicted of first-degree murder and is spending twenty-five years in a Canadian maximum-security institution. The logic of the court is not difficult to figure out, though it is not entirely obvious from the definition presented above. First, even though there is evidence of copious alcohol consumption on the part of the offender during the day of the shooting, he did not display obviously drunken behaviour; therefore, the judge did not accept the mitigating circumstance of drunkenness. Second, the offender stated that he was going to "blow away" the bartenders and, even though he did not aim at them, a prudent person knows that shooting into a darkened room is dangerous and someone could be hit. Therefore, the offender should be culpable for the killing. More important, in the time between leaving the bar, getting the gun, and returning, the offender had time to think about the consequences of his act (form intent) and he had stated his intent. From a legal point of view, this is enough to make the event planned and deliberate, resulting in a conviction of first-degree murder. Even if one argues on the basis of the physical evidence that the offender deserves to be culpable for murder, because it was clear that he did not aim to kill, he should have been convicted of second- (not first-) degree murder. If there is a lesson here, it is twofold. First, when the circumstances are not crystal clear, it is the court that decides what happened (even when that is not what really happened). Second, lawyers can make a big difference in determining the outcome of a murder case when those fuzzy circumstances exist.[7]

Murder in commission of offences

230. Culpable homicide is murder where a person causes the death of a human being while committing or attempting to commit high treason or treason or an offence mentioned in section 52 (sabotage), 75 (piratical acts), 76 (hijacking an aircraft), 144 or subsection 145(1) or sections 146 to 148 (escape or rescue from prison or lawful custody), section 270 (assaulting a peace officer), section 271 (sexual assault), 272 (sexual assault with a weapon, threats to a third party or causing bodily harm), 273 (aggravated sexual assault), 279 (kidnapping and forcible confinement), 279.1 (hostage taking), 343 (robbery), 348 (breaking and entering) or 433 or 434 (arson), whether or not the person means to cause death to any human being and whether or not he knows that death is likely to be caused to any human being, if

(a) he means to cause bodily harm for the purpose of

   (i) facilitating the commission of the offence, or

   (ii) facilitating his flight after committing or attempting to commit the offence, and the death ensues from the bodily harm;

(b) he administers a stupefying or overpowering thing for a purpose mentioned in paragraph (a), and the death ensues therefrom;

(c) he wilfully stops, by any means, the breath of a human being for a purpose mentioned in paragraph (a), and the death ensues therefrom; or
(d) he uses a weapon or has it on his person
   (i)   during or at the time he commits or attempts to commit the
         offence, or
   (ii) during or at the time of his flight after committing or attempting to
         commit the offence, and the death ensues as a consequence. R.S.
         1985, c.27 (1st Supp), s.40(2).

As previously stated, in 1990 the Supreme Court of Canada
struck down the notion of *constructive intent*, but until that time
it was a valid component of the law. "The law wishes to hold able,
but negligent, people to account and it does so by inventing the
idea of constructive intent, a term that stretches intent to cover
the unintended, injurious consequences of some of our behaviour.
A person is deemed reckless when she is aware of the probable
harmful consequences of her act but nevertheless takes the
risk—whether or not she intended the bailful outcome" (Nettler
n.d.).

Constructive intent also includes those acts such as murder
in the commission of other offences. The law holds culpable of
murder those individuals who would undertake serious offences,
whether or not the offender intended death. Previously, the law
stated in effect that if you put people at risk then you are guilty
of the offence, even if you had no intention of committing the
offence. The Supreme Court felt that such a construct violated
the Charter of Rights and Freedoms and struck down its legality.
Hence, unless the law changes again, killing during the course of
another crime is no longer automatically considered to be first-
degree murder. Rod Martineau, an accomplice in a robbery-
killing in 1985, recently had his conviction for two second-degree
murders reduced to two manslaughters because the court had to
prove "intent to kill" rather than simply showing that he was
involved in the robbery. In spite of the nature of the crime, the
prosecution could not generate enough evidence to prove intent
(*Edmonton Journal* 1991b).

**Murder reduced to manslaughter—What is provocation—
Questions of fact—Death during illegal arrest**

232. (1) Culpable homicide that otherwise would be murder may be reduced to
manslaughter if the person who committed it did so in the heat of passion caused by sudden provocation.
(2) A wrongful act or insult that is of such a nature as to be sufficient to
deprive an ordinary person of the power of self-control is provocation
for the purposes of this section if the accused acted on it on the sudden

and before there was time for his passion to cool.

(3) For the purposes of this section, the questions

    (a) whether the accused was deprived of the power of self-control by the provocation that he alleges he received, are questions of fact, but no one shall be deemed to have given provocation to another by doing anything that he had a legal right to do, or by doing anything that the accused incited him to do in order to provide the accused with an excuse for causing death or bodily harm to any human being.

(4) Culpable homicide that otherwise would be murder is not necessarily manslaughter by reason only that it was committed by a person who was being arrested illegally, but the fact that the illegality of the arrest was known to the accused may be evidence of provocation for the purpose of this section.

The law allows certain defences against conviction for murder. That is, the law recognizes that full intent cannot always be formed and further accepts the fact of legitimate reasons for killing. Murder[8] is excluded from certain excuses allowed for other offences, for example, duress, coercion, or compulsion.

The excuse of mistake of fact[9] suggests that the accused was acting under a misapprehension about circumstances of the event when he or she killed the victim. Even if the court does not believe the accused's version of events and misapprehension, the court must accept that version until it is satisfied beyond a reasonable doubt that the accused's version is untrue. As long as the accused's version is the operant version (i.e., the Crown has not proved beyond a reasonable doubt that the accused's version is untrue), the court will treat the misapprehension as if it were the fact.

For example, suppose an individual is awakened from his sleep by sounds of breaking glass. He gets his gun and proceeds to the location of the sounds. When he arrives at the location, an intruder raises an object that looks like a gun. The accused shoots and kills the intruder. The victim was not an intruder but a relative who had lost his keys to the house and had broken a window using a broomstick. The broomstick was mistaken for a gun. This act is not culpable killing.

Duress, Coercion, or Compulsion

The Criminal Court excludes the use of this defence in murder, attempted murder, and several other crimes (Parker 1987:258). These three terms have somewhat different meanings but refer to similar circumstances. Either by some inner force or by pressure from another individual, you are forced to kill another person. In effect, exclusion of this defence means that if someone "forces" you to kill someone else, or if you cannot resist the compulsion to kill someone, you cannot use that as a defence against the crime.

Self-Defence

This is one of the oldest defences. In the case of homicide, one kills to prevent one's self from being killed. Problems arise in the use of this defence in situations in which the court believes that killing was an overreaction to the actual threat. The law (probably unreasonably) requires that individuals use the "minimum" force necessary to defend themselves in a given situation. For example, if someone slaps you, it is unreasonable to defend yourself by shooting them through the head with the gun you keep in your house. Or is it? If you are a frail 80-year-old individual and the person doing the slapping is a 240-lb., 6-foot-3-inch, 20-year-old male, does the victim not have a reasonable fear of bodily harm? This shows how complex the issue of self-defence can be.

When the force in self-defence is considered reasonable by the court then no crime has taken place. For instance, if V shoots at D and misses during an attempted robbery and D shoots back and kills V, no crime has taken place. Shooting is used to defend against shooting. The dilemma occurs when "unreasonable" force is used. Should the defendant be found guilty of second-degree murder, manslaughter, or something else when a mild assault is countered by a lethal assault? The Law Reform Commission of Canada has suggested that one way around the dilemma is to leave self-defence as no excuse when excess force is used but allow the aggression of the victim to be used as a mitigating factor in sentencing.[10] But, as the commission points out, this only works if the mandatory sentence for second-degree murder is dropped (Law Reform Commission 1982).

Provocation

Provocation is a partial defence that has been used to reduce murder to manslaughter (Parker 1987). The offender claims that his or her actions were provoked. Or, according to section 232 (see above), a crime of passion has taken place. For instance, the accused returns home from a hunting trip to find his spouse in bed with her lover. In his rage he raises his gun and kills them both. The court may find the circumstances to be mitigating and the act to have been provoked. This is the classic "crime of passion" in which the offender is so overwrought with emotion in finding the "love nest" that he loses all his normal self-control and shoots. In fact, in some jurisdictions this is taken for granted. For instance, in Texas until recently a man's killing of his adulterous wife was considered justifiable—therefore lawful—homicide (Lundsgaarde 1977).

Because there are fixed penalties for first- and second-degree murder, there cannot be any mitigating circumstances in sentencing. Hence, murder has to be reduced to manslaughter before provocation can be taken into account. Here the law deals with the myth of the "ordinary person," i.e., would the actions of the victim be such that any ordinary person would be provoked by them? The provocation must be so obvious that an ordinary person would lose his or her normal self-control.

Infanticide

233. A female person commits infanticide when by a wilful act or omission she causes the death of her newly-born child, if at the time of the act or omission she is not fully recovered from the effects of giving birth to the child and by reason thereof or of the effect of lactation consequent on the birth of the child her mind is then disturbed.

This section relates to diminished responsibility against the charge of murder. Introduced in 1948 and assuming its current form in 1955, this concept is based on antiquated medical thinking and a practical consideration that jurists did not want to have mothers who killed their young children charged with murder.[11] We deal with the issue of infanticide to some extent later in the book (see also Silverman and Kennedy 1988). For the moment, suffice it to say that the infanticide provision as currently formulated does not belong in a contemporary criminal code.

Manslaughter

234. Culpable homicide that is not murder or infanticide is manslaughter.

Manslaughter is unintentional but still culpable homicide. It requires either criminal negligence or an unlawful act. As noted in section 232, it may be a crime of passion. It is probably worth noting, again, that all of the categories we discuss refer to charges by police, legal outcomes of judicial deliberations, or, at an earlier stage, the charge by prosecutors. At best, they are only approximations of "what really happened"—the actions, behaviours, perceptions, and motivations of the individuals involved.

Punishment for murder—Minimum punishment

With the conviction, there are prescribed sentences that attach to each type of homicide.

235. (1) Everyone who commits first degree murder or second degree murder is guilty of an indictable offence and shall be sentenced to imprisonment for life.

(2) For the purposes of Part XXIII, the sentence of imprisonment for life prescribed by this section is a minimum punishment.

Conviction for first-degree murder carries with it a sentence of twenty-five years nonparolable.[12] For second-degree murder, it is ten years nonparolable (section 742). The public often finds the parole section of the sentence confusing in light of the "life sentence." In essence, the sentence is for life but it is not necessarily all spent in an institution. Time on parole counts as part of the sentence, and, in the case of first- and second-degree murder, the time on parole lasts for the individual's lifetime after his or her release from an institution.

Punishment for manslaughter

236. Everyone who commits manslaughter is guilty of an indictable offence and liable to imprisonment for life.

The important thing here is that life imprisonment is not necessarily the minimum sentence for this offence, and, further, that even individuals given life imprisonment as a penalty have normal eligibility for parole.

Punishment for infanticide

237. Every female person who commits infanticide is guilty of an indictable offence and liable to imprisonment for a term not exceeding five years.

Exemptions

The law provides for certain exemptions to individuals who cannot be held accountable for their actions because of their age or their mental state. Section 13 of the Criminal Code states that no child under the age of 12 can be convicted of an offence. Therefore, age itself is a defence against conviction for any crime, including various types of homicide.

The age provisions are not generally controversial, although there has been concern about teenagers who have committed murder while still under the age of 18. The Young Offenders Act provides that individuals who are at least 12 but under 18 cannot be sentenced to longer than three years in custody for first-degree murder. Attempts have been made to lengthen this term, or to use provisions in the act that allow certain dangerous individuals to be tried by adult court.

Insanity as a defence is usually the most controversial. Often the meaning of insanity becomes technical and legal rather than scientific. The court may decide prior to a trial that the accused is suffering from a mental disease and is unfit to plead, in which case there will be no trial (Parker 1987).

The defence of insanity is complex. Unfortunately, good data on the use of the defence in Canada are not available. In essence, though, the insanity defence suggests that the offender was suffering from a mental disease and did not know the nature and quality of the act he or she was performing at the time of the killing. The defence is controversial because many members of the public assume that it is often used by accused persons to "get away with" a crime for which they should be punished. But it is also controversial because it brings into question the definition of "mental disease"; the ability of the court to distinguish between the mad and the bad; and the use of "experts" in courts (Saunders and Mitchell 1990). Defining mental disease or insanity is a difficult task. Nettler (1982) suggests that "insanity" is an embarrassment to a legal profession that prides itself on precise terminology. In some jurisdictions (e.g., Netherlands and Norway), insanity is simply what psychiatrists say it is in court testimony (Nettler 1982).

At various times and places, the law has suggested that the insane could not form intent and therefore were not guilty of the crime. Now, however, it seems to be accepted that many killings by insane people are planned, deliberate, and effectively executed. They are rarely "motiveless." "The special legal status of the insane ... is not based on their lack of intent or lack of knowledge but rather on the theory that their unconsciously caused impairment somehow results in or contributes to their wrongful act" (Saunders and Mitchell 1990:492).

The public view seems to remain that individuals use the insanity plea to escape prison terms, preferring instead to spend their time in a mental institution where their confinement may be much shorter and more "comfortable." Many lawyers believe that for every three "experts" the prosecutor can get to say a defendant is sane, three will say that the defendant is insane (Nettler 1982). They cancel each other out. Particularly in homicide cases, a psychiatrist will argue that the accused would have to be insane to commit his or her offence. But the legal definition is a narrow one that is often not consistent with the psychiatrist's medical model. In a later chapter, we briefly discuss the case of Kenneth Bianchi—the Hillside Strangler—who lured, tortured, and killed young girls using increasingly bizarre and cruel methods with each killing and dumping the bodies by the roadside. While the public may believe that one would have to be "crazy" to behave this way, according to the narrow legal definition, Bianchi was legally sane at the time of the acts and able to stand trial.[13]

Culpable homicide offenders can be convicted of four different types of crimes: first-degree murder, second-degree murder, manslaughter, and infanticide. When the police and the Crown prosecutor have made a prior decision to pursue a charge of first-degree murder and when the prosecution is able to prove that there was a premeditated intent to murder, the verdict will be first-degree murder. Murders that are not first-degree are second-degree. If the Crown cannot prove the requisite intent for murder, the accused may be convicted of manslaughter. When an individual's actions lead to a death in which there is not necessarily an intent to kill, that person may be charged with manslaughter. In such a case, killing committed during the commission of a crime might qualify as a first-degree murder, but unless intent can be shown the act is no longer considered first-degree murder. Infanticide is a totally different form of homicide and is treated differently by the courts.

Exemptions can be made in considering each case of culpable killing. It is clear that there is no prescribed way in which the courts act that would lead one to predict the outcome of a trial. A number of factors can mitigate guilt, including provocation, self-defence, and insanity. Also, there are provisions for dealing differently with cases of infanticide[14] and with cases of murder committed by individuals under age 18.[15]

It is important for the student of culpable killings to be aware of the impact that legal definitions, and changes in these, can have on the operation of the criminal justice system. Beyond the consideration of the complex issues surrounding guilt and innocence in each case, legal responses are heavily influenced by public opinion and by current views about the effectiveness of punishment in deterring this crime (a point that will be reviewed in detail in Chapter 9.) But legal responses are accompanied by extralegal reactions that work to remove the opportunities for crime and reduce the possibility of violent outcomes. The legal response cannot operate without some sensitivity to the ways in which the community deals with violence. At the same time, the legal structure is highly vulnerable to the moral outrage that notorious cases can evoke. In a study done in the U.S. on cases handled by prosecutors, it was found that those that attracted the greatest amount of public attention were the ones least likely to result in a plea bargain, in which the prosecutors offer a lesser charge to individuals in exchange for a plea of guilty (Pritchard 1986). This finding further illustrates the emotionally charged character of murder and its consequences for the criminal justice system and the community at large. These themes will be discussed in Chapter 3, which examines the etiology of homicide and theoretical perspectives that attempt to explain the social dynamics of murder.

COUNTING MURDERS: AN OVERVIEW OF TRENDS AND PATTERNS IN CANADA

Now that the reader has a good idea of how various forms of culpable killing are defined, it is appropriate to provide an overview of the extent of these crimes in Canada. In previous sections, we defined homicide with a good deal of precision, but the definitions we offered were contemporary. For purposes of this section, suffice it to say that historical data on homicide do not define the phenomenon precisely, and that the definitions used before and after legal changes do not always correspond one to the other. In a general way, we are dealing with death from criminal causes, but the specific meaning of each curve presented in the charts is elusive. We exacerbate this problem as, in trying to show as complete a trend as possible, we have used multiple sources of data that may not be fully compatible. *The reader should view these as gross approximations.*

Data after 1961 represent modern, consistently defined and collected information generated from a statistical package provided by Statistics Canada, Canadian Centre for Justice Statistics (1988).[16] The package only includes data to 1988, which we have supplemented with data to 1990.

Using international data, Adler et al. (1991) have constructed a comparison of homicide rates for males between the ages of 15 and 24 in twenty-two industrialized nations. In that group, Canada ranks sixteenth highest with a rate of 2.9 per 100,000 citizens between the ages of 15 and 24. The rates range from 0.3 in Austria to 5.0 in Scotland for the first twenty-one nations on the list. The highest country is the United States with a rate of 21.9 per 100,000—more than four times the next closest rate. When all homicides, for all age groups, are considered, the U.S. homicide rate is usually 3 to 4 times that of Canada. In recent times, the United States has recorded an average of over 20,000 homicides a year.

Relatively, the Canadian homicide rate is not very high. The relative paucity of homicide is brought home to us when we present our research findings at American professional meetings. Our U.S. colleagues complain that we really do not have enough homicide in this country to do some kinds of analysis. One colleague was so incredulous at the homicide numbers we reported that he questioned their accuracy. It seems that in the United States high homicide rates are expected. At least some American researchers do not realize that the U.S. homicide rate is an aberration among industrial nations, not the norm. The U.S. provides us with a convenient and obvious country for comparison. It is not our goal to compare all aspects of murder in Canada with those in the U.S., but we do present comparisons on a selective basis.

The Canadian Uniform Crime Reporting system (based on the similar U.S. Uniform Crime Reporting) was first implemented in 1962. Statistics Canada is responsible for systematically collecting "uniform" monthly data from major police departments across the country, covering over 90 percent of policing areas. The post-1961 period produces the most accurate crime statistics in Canada. Unfortunately, most of the post-1961 data are not comparable with the pre-1962 data. The change in the system resulted in a different group of crimes being recorded in Canada.

What effect does this have on homicide data? The answer is probably less than other crimes because, as the most serious criminal event, homicide has always been the crime most likely to be accurately recorded. Hence, the homicide data from earlier years that we display in this chapter are likely more precise than similar historical data for other crimes.

The measurement of crime is altered by changes in the law, which can have major impacts on the available data.[17] For instance, before 1961 all murder was capital murder and the penalty was death. After September 1961, the classification of the offence was extended to capital and noncapital murder. Capital murder was premeditated murder, murder of a police officer, prison guard, etc., or murder during the commission of another criminal act. The penalty was death. All other types of murder were noncapital and the penalty was life imprisonment. Murder was defined as capital and noncapital, a classification that is not exactly comparable to our current categories of first- and second-degree murder (Statistics Canada 1983). In 1967, the murder provisions were amended for a five-year trial period.[18] During that time, capital murder was murder of a police officer, warden, etc., and the penalty was death. All other murder was noncapital and the penalty was life imprisonment (Statistics Canada 1983). With the abolition of capital punishment in 1976, murder became first- and second-degree.

We cannot be sure what effect the above changes have had on the trend lines displayed in our graphs given that some crimes are counted only for portions of the period. For instance, infanticide and manslaughter are counted separately only in homicide statistics after 1973. Also, it should be recalled that Newfoundland did not enter Confederation until 1949, so its data would not be included until after that time,[19] and the Yukon and Northwest Territories were not included until 1956.[20] None of these factors has had a dramatic effect on the data.

As we have stated, most of this book is concerned with murder after 1961, but for the sake of comparison and to offer a historical context, we have generated homicide rates for an earlier historical period. Homicide as used here refers to all culpable killings (including what is now called first- and second-degree murder, manslaughter, and infanticide[21]) and thus offers an inclusive view of these kinds of crimes. Murder refers only to first- and second-degree murder.

High numbers of homicides in Canada are a post-World War II phenomenon, one among many extraordinary changes Canadian society went through in that period. However, the most recent trend in the homicide rate has been a decline.

FIGURE 2.1

HOMICIDE RATES, CANADA, 1926–1990

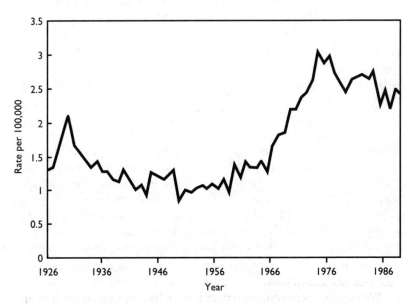

Source: Statistics Canada, 1983; Canadian Centre for Justice Statistics.

Figure 2.1 illustrates the homicide rate per 100,000 population[22] between 1926 and 1990. Homicide rates reach a peak in 1930 (2.1 per 100,000) that is not seen again until 1970. After the 1930 peak, there is a steady decline in the rate until 1944 (.89 per 100,000). What is noteworthy here is that the decline was steady and gradual, not a sudden drop, which might suggest an aberration in 1930. Nonetheless, it is reasonable to suspect that the peak and the subsequent decline was related to the post-1929 stock market crash and the resulting economic depression.[23]

There is a "blip" between 1944 and 1950. For a few years immediately following the war homicide rates rose. One could speculate about the effects of returning service personnel, major changes in family arrangements, alterations in women's roles and so on as proximate causes of this pattern.

The lowest rate of homicide between 1926 and 1990 occurs in 1950. Between 1950 and 1965, there is a gradual rise in the rate of criminal homicide (from .82 per 100,000 to 1.41 per 100,000). Then, from 1966 to 1975, the most dramatic rise in Canadian homicide rates took place (from 1.24 per 100,000 to 3.07 per 100,000), a rise of 250 percent. Since 1975, there has been a rather consistent decline in the homicide rate to 2.4 in 1990 (that is, about the same as the 1970 level). The patterns of shifts in the homicide rates were similar in the U.S. and Canada in the early part of the century (even though the U.S. rate is much higher), but while the Canadian rate has fallen since the mid-1970s, the U.S. rate has continued on a steady rise.

We are observing social phenomena related to the war and immediate post-World War II period, as the tranquillity of the 1950s gave way to disruptive social changes in the 1960s and early 1970s. Despite its economic woes, the 1980s was a socially calmer period.

Since 1962, with the Uniform Crime Reporting system in place, homicide laws have been relatively unchanged. There was an amendment to the law in 1976 with regard to the abolition of capital punishment, but this has little effect on the quality of the data. Homicides and murders are counted on the basis of the number of victims in an event. Thus, if two people are killed in a robbery, two homicides occur, and if forty people are killed in a deliberately set fire, then forty homicides are counted. The latter kind of event can cause significant shifts in the homicide rate.

Figure 2.2 shows that the homicide rate and the murder rate mirror each other. Since 1962, most homicide has been classified as murder. The patterns of the two are virtually identical. Dividing murder into first- and second-degree, we find that those murders classified as first-degree have been rising since 1977, while second-degree murders have fallen. Regarding manslaughter, in *The Last Dance: Murder in Canada* Boyd (1988) observes:

> We must also recognize that most killings are defined by our courts as acts of manslaughter, that is, crimes committed "in the heat of passion caused by sudden provocations." The increase in homicide that we experienced between 1966 and 1975 was primarily an increase in manslaughter—as defined by our courts.
>
> As a consequence, it is more accurate to say that we have experienced a rapid escalation in our *manslaughter* rate than to say we have experienced an increase in our murder rate (1988:4).

FIGURE 2.2

HOMICIDE, MURDER, AND MANSLAUGHTER RATES, CANADA, 1962–1988

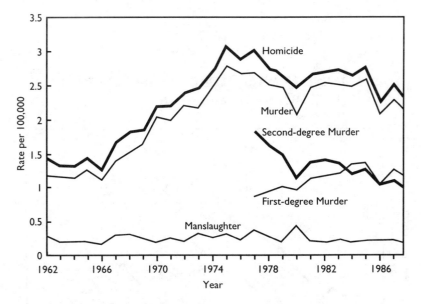

Source: Canadian Centre for Justice Statistics, 1988.

A quick examination of Figure 2.2 reveals a very different picture than that suggested by Boyd. In fact, one could say that the manslaughter rate (as represented by police charges) has remained relatively constant over the thirty years represented in the chart.

The quote from Boyd illustrates the bewilderment generated when court information and police information are confused. Boyd is referring to what happens after the case is taken to court, while our data refer to the classification of the initial event. It is important to remember that all of the data in this book are police-level data. In the case of homicide, murder, and manslaughter, these are counts of events that occurred rather than convictions. Which type of data is likely to represent what really happened? It has been more or less accepted since the 1930s (Sellin 1932) that the police data are closest in time to the act and therefore more accurately represent what happened. Convictions include such mitigating factors as available witnesses, lying participants, and plea bargaining. Because there have been no reliable court data in Canada for at least the last fifteen years, we have to conclude that the kind of killing called manslaughter has been relatively stable, and that the more serious forms of killing have risen between 1962 and 1975.

GENDER AND MURDER RATES, 1962–1988

FIGURE 2.3

MALE AND FEMALE MURDER RISK RATES, CANADA, 1961–1990*

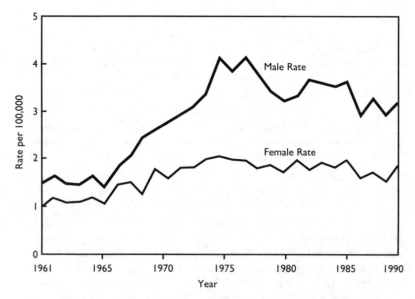

*Data include all victims. Rates based on male and female population.

Males drive the murder rate. Figure 2.3 shows that the male victimization rate for murder reflects the shape of the curve seen in Figure 2.2. It peaks in 1975 and generally is responsible for other ups and downs in the curve. The rate for female victims shows more subtle variations. It rises until 1975 and then begins a gradual decline, while male murder rises again in 1977 and then declines over the next few years. The thing to keep in mind here is that when one compares the male victimization rate with the female rate at both of their peaks, males account for twice the rate of females. For female victims, there is a rise between 1988 and 1989 and then a decline to 1990. That rise is virtually all accounted for by the mass murder of fourteen females at the University of Montreal.[24]

SUMMARY

From a peak in 1930, homicide rates decline to a low point in 1950. From that point the rates rise to a high in 1975 (the most dramatic rise occurring between 1966 and 1975). Since 1975, the homicide rate has been falling. Males have a much higher rate of homicide perpetrated against them than do females, a finding confirmed in many other countries (Nettler 1982). Changes in the pattern of homicide against females has been more subtle than the pattern of rates against males.

The most accurate and consistent data on homicide have been generated since 1961. Examining those trends we see that homicide peaked in the mid 1970s and has consistently declined since that time. This is particularly interesting in light of the fact that other types of reported violence have continued to rise during the period. There is no obvious explanation for the decline. It may simply be that response time for medical care has improved, or it may be attributable to one of the structural theories addressed later in this book to help explain the phenomenon.

Rates and patterns give us only the beginnings of an understanding of culpable killing. Theories generated by criminologists have tended to focus on causes of delinquency and on property criminality. Violence, after all, accounts for only 8 percent to 10 percent of Criminal Code violations in Canada, but violent crimes elicit a much more intense response than either common delinquency (Hagan et al. 1985) or property offences. In the next chapter, we examine explanations that can be best adapted to explain the various forms of homicide.

NOTES

1. When these data were collected and analyzed, constructive intent was part of the law and individuals had been convicted under those statutes. Hence, these homicides are part of our sample.

2. According to legal procedure in Canada, the burden of proof is on the Crown (prosecution).

3. Note that the offenders become eligible for parole only after that amount of time in prison. Even then, parole is not guaranteed.

4. It does not become a murder until the *mens rea* (intention) is added to the equation.

5. Illness caused by the treatment.

6. This raises a major unresolved judicial debate. Some would argue that the correct test is incapacity (inability) to form intent due to alcohol/drugs; others contend that the correct test is whether intent actually was formed in fact. Temporary insanity usually brings into play section 16 of the Criminal Code, which deals with insanity. The lawyer in question chose to link the two elements.

7. The major problem in this case is that the defence lawyer did not argue intent (*mens rea*) which, at least on the surface, seems to be the logical defence against a first-degree charge. As to what really happened, as in many other cases, we will probably never know. The court deals with the evidence presented by the Crown and the defence that the "rules of evidence" allow to be presented. When the evidence is ambiguous, when the Crown does not prove its case, or when the defence mounts a poor case, the outcome may be less than true justice.

8. The exclusion applies only to actual killers, not to parties to the offence (i.e., those who aid and abet under section 21 of the Criminal Code).

9. The excuse of mistake of fact is a common-law defence that is preserved by section 8(3) of the Criminal Code. It is by virtue of this provision that such defences as intoxication exist—reducing murder to manslaughter. Such modern issues as PMS as a defence are also dealt with under this heading.

10. An alternative formulation, which was rejected by the Law Reform Commission of Canada, is represented in the law of Australia. Excessive force in circumstances where some force is justified as a matter of self-defence shall be considered in the context of the accused's intentions and beliefs, and may well justify a verdict of manslaughter. In Australia, this solution is seen as furthering the objective of sentencing flexibility.

11. Some of these considerations are bound up with the implications of capital punishment. Jurists did not want mothers who killed their young children to be subject to that punishment.

12. The twenty-five year parole provision may be reduced during a review that takes place after fifteen years are served.

13. Similarly, as this book was being brought to completion, the insanity defence had been argued in the trial of Jeffrey Dahmer, the serial killer who lured his victims to his apartment, killed them, had sex with their dead bodies, ate the flesh of some of them, and preserved some of the body parts (*Newsweek* 1992). The first psychiatrist to testify said that Dahmer could have stopped the behaviour; hence, he was not insane. In fact, this is what the court decided—Dahmer was not insane from a legal point of view. Most of the public would disagree.

14. Not murder under law.

15. While young offenders may be charged with and found guilty of murder, the sentencing provisions of the Young Offenders Act are different from the Criminal Code provisions.

16. For most purposes, homicide is counted by the number of victims in an incident. This can sometimes skew the data (e.g., when there are forty victims in an arson). In later analysis in this book, we count incidents rather than victims, but in this chapter victims represent homicides that occur.

17. For an example of how legal definitions have changed the measurement of one form of homicide, see Silverman (1990).

18. It is worth noting that even during much of the 1960s and 1970s, virtually all sentences of death were commuted to life in prison.

19. Newfoundland is not included until 1951 in Figure 2.1.

20. These make little difference to the overall counts.

21. Not included until 1974.

22. It is important to distinguish between rates of homicide and absolute numbers. Homicide rates are averaged on the population of the country; by taking into account population fluctuations, they make better comparisons than absolute numbers. This is also true when one examines homicide over time or between regions in the same country.

23. The U.S. homicide rate also peaked in this period (1933) and then declined.

24. Discussed in detail in Chapter 5.

Conceptualizations
of Murder

There are essentially two classes of theory that deal with homi-cide.[1] The first relates to individual social interaction and con-flict. The second deals with larger societal factors and correlates these with homicide rates. Drawing on theories of social control, conflict, and routine activities, in this chapter we review the lit-erature that seeks to explain causes of homicide at the individual level. We also examine homicide trends at the societal level through social disorganization and inequality perspectives. Both individual level and societal level perspectives are needed to fully understand homicide.

Gottfredson and Hirschi (1990) explain that crime is gener-ally committed by poorly socialized individuals who lack self-control. In their view, the nature of criminal acts is fully predict-able. The acts tend, on the whole, to require little foresight, plan-ning, or effort. Between the thought and the deed, little time passes. The carefully planned and executed crime is rare. Crime tends to take place near the offender's residence or where he or she typically "hangs out." Criminal acts are, then, spatially and temporally highly constrained. Targets that provide immediate benefits will be selected over those that may occasion delay. This spontaneity of criminal action leads to crime that produces little in the way of profit. Finally, targets that pose little risk of detec-tion are selected over those that pose greater risk when there is any thought at all given to the relevance of the target (Gottfred-son and Hirschi 1990:13).

According to Gottfredson and Hirschi, crime is often a func-tion of spontaneous action occurring between people who know each other and in locations that they frequent most often. Homi-cide is best explained as an "opportunity" crime rather than one that is carefully and rationally planned. It occurs not at the hands of the cold and calculated killer, as depicted in the mystery novels, but rather most often as an unplanned consequence of events that escalate out of control. Individuals who have limited skills at controlling their anger or frustration are the most likely candidates to direct harm toward others.

As Harries (1990) points out, murder is a *process* crime distinguished from other violence in terms only of outcome rather than means of operation. Murder is, most often, not the intended consequence of the offender's actions. The events that lead up to murder regularly have the character of assaults or seemingly harmless arguments. Differences between homicide and assault are due primarily to variations in the lethality of weapons (Harries 1990:60) The large number of murders that end in second-degree and manslaughter convictions testifies to the rather loose etiology of murder in cases where it is not the explicit intention of the murderer to kill the victim. The typical homicide is most appropriately considered a fatal assault.[2] In other homicides, the fatality is the result of some other event occurring, such as rape or robbery.

Of course, not all poorly socialized individuals kill or even commit other crimes. It is a combination of factors including low self-control, conflict, opportunity, and social disruption that lead to homicide outcomes. Such a depiction of homicide poses some problems in our assessment of its prevention. Gottfredson and Hirschi believe that, in the case of homicide, the penalties of the state are largely redundant, acting more on potential offenders already deterred by previous learning and social sanctions. The spontaneity of the act often makes it an unlikely candidate for deterrence (Williams and Hawkins 1986).

Sherman et al. (1991) address this issue when discussing the predictability of homicide resulting from domestic disturbances. They argue that the police cannot be certain that intervention in domestic disturbances will preclude the possibility that a homicide may occur. In fact, using Milwaukee police data, they report that the argument that there is an escalation of violence in domestic disturbances cannot be supported in homicide outcomes, because reported domestic disturbances were almost never reported prior to the occurrence of a homicide. Sherman et al. (1991) use this argument to suggest that the police are not accountable in homicide cases in which assaults or threats were reported to them but did not lead to an arrest. The police, they believe, are simply not able to predict these outcomes. However, the point that Sherman et al. miss is that the police may have had an impact in deterring escalation of violence to murder through their early intervention in the conflict between partners.

Lack of self-control may be less likely to result in murder if we were to improve the potential offender's skills, reducing the chances of criminal outcome either through conflict management or through a change in lifestyle, a point to which we will return.

Sherman et al. (1989) also point out that homicide is likely to occur in areas that can be characterized as "hot spots," places that generate repeat calls to the same address.[3] Such areas are most often locations containing concentrations of low-income individuals and families. Individuals who experience the stresses of uncertain or inadequate economic conditions are more likely to be involved in violence. These factors contribute to the conditions that enhance the opportunity for crime. Some obvious remedial measures that can be taken include the eradication of social ills such as homelessness and chronic unemployment.

Not everyone agrees that success in attacking social problems is inevitable. Wilson (1983), reports that, although the U.S. crime rate rose following a rise in unemployment, the subsequent decline of unemployment in later years was accompanied by a further rise in crime. Obviously, large-scale economic changes must be studied in the context of other social developments—the rise in drug and alcohol use, the change in family structure, the high levels of internal migration, the age structure of the population, and so on.

It is exactly the point that the outcomes are not predictable that helps in understanding why murderous crimes are so unlikely to occur. A murder is either spontaneous or at least rarely considered lightly. It may be diverted through intervention to reduce the negative effect of individual styles of conflict, opportunities, or the stressors that operate on individuals. In the previous chapter, we talked about a man who shot up a bar after being refused a drink and being told to leave. A myriad of circumstances could have intervened to prevent this event. The offender may have had to have his alcohol problem dealt with but there was not an inevitability to his murderous behaviour.

Sherman et al. (1989) make the point that even if we were to accept the idea that we need to protect individuals who are likely victims of murder (in a model of low predictability), the costs of providing police protection would be prohibitive and could potentially infringe on individual civil liberties. What might be more successful and desirable, they argue, would be to remove the opportunity for crime, including shutting down high-risk locations that promote violence (e.g., notorious taverns) and destroying instruments of violence (e.g., guns). Of course, some locations are easier to control than others. The sanctity of the home environment contrasts greatly with the public nature of commercial establishments. It is interesting to note that in Edmonton's more notorious hotel barrooms proprietors have posted "No Knives" signs in an attempt to curb the violence. It is unclear how effective such actions can be.

Our approach emphasizes, first, the undersocialized individual. Poor socialization can result from a breakdown in social control within the family, school, and peer group. Second, there is the social conflict that emerges in social relationships. The kind of relationship and the skill (or lack thereof) in conflict management predicts differing levels of escalation in the conflict. Third, opportunities for criminal behaviour will depend on the extent to which routines that people follow expose them to circumstances that may be risky. Finally, the factors in the economic and social structure, such as levels of poverty and unemployment, may create a climate of uncertainty that produces reduced levels of self-control and higher levels of interpersonal stress, which leads, in turn, to violence. The combination of circumstances that result in fatalities operates as an overlay that involves ingredients from all four sets of factors.

INDIVIDUAL-LEVEL THEORIES

CONTROL THEORY

Control theory, as first proposed by Travis Hirschi (1969), was offered as a way of explaining criminal behaviour by examining the ways in which social bonds that individuals have to others encourage them to conform to conventional behaviour. Through the same process, the weakening of these bonds contributes to deviance, leading some individuals to become involved in criminality. Social bonds are developed through socialization. Learning through contact with significant individuals, such as parents and teachers, produces a set of prescribed ways for individuals to act. Inner control (see Nye 1958) develops when individuals impose rules on themselves that are consistent with their beliefs about what is right and what is wrong.[4] Outer control develops with an awareness of the fact the rules may be imposed by others, as occurs when parents impose punishment or the police enforce the law.

Control theorists argue that individuals who are poorly socialized tend to have reduced levels of inner control. Further, these individuals are likely to discount the effects of the imposition of sanctions on them from external sources. Individuals with this view of the diminished impact of sanctions tend to have lower levels of attachments to others. Weak attachments to family, friends, or teachers are expressed through a reduced level of respect or affection. Individuals with weak social bonds ignore or minimize the importance of the expectations, feelings, and wishes of others in controlling their own behaviour. They are left with little to deter them from deviant behaviour—action that does not conform to conventional group norms.

Deviance can be seen, then, as an expression of a lack of commitment by individuals to the values of conventional society. Certain types of behaviour can be judged in terms of individual "stakes in conformity" (Toby 1957). Deviant behaviour jeopardizes the individual's stakes or investments in society, resulting in a loss through stigma or punishment. For example, a young adult convicted of a minor crime such as vandalism may encounter great difficulty in working for a financial institution or related industry where employees have to be certified to occupy certain positions; his or her conviction may stand in the way of certification. Thus, control theory suggests that those committed to conventional values will be cautious of legal entanglements. Commitment is important to those who are worried about the loss of reputation, employment opportunities, or advancement in their careers.

Hirschi assumes that individuals who make the effort to be involved in conventional activities are deterred from partaking in deviant endeavours. This view is a longstanding one, reflected in the adage "Idle hands are the Devil's workshop." Participation in organized sports or the regular routine that one follows in going to work preclude the lure of delinquent routines, although they do not completely stop people from taking part in risky lifestyles outside of work or school (Kennedy and Forde 1990a). Involvement in conventional routines limits the amount of time that one can devote to alternative, and potentially deviant, behaviour. Hirschi argues that a reduced level of belief in the common value system increases the likelihood that deviance will occur.

An important aspect of social control theory, as stated by Hirschi, is its prediction that those who have weak social bonds to conventional society will not be deterred from delinquent acts by informal sanctions, as they do not place any value on ties to people or accomplishments. Sanctions lose their effectiveness. It follows, then, that if there is little concern about the stigma that comes from informal sanctions, formal punishment will have reduced effect as it relies on informal sanction for its effectiveness (Baron and Kennedy 1990:6). This is a reiteration of the point made earlier by Gottfredson and Hirschi (1990) about the low deterrence levels of certain types of crime given an individual's low self-control.

According to Gottfredson and Hirschi (1990), individuals with low self-control are unreliable, thoughtless, selfish, and untrustworthy. Low self-control individuals also have difficulty making and maintaining friendships. When these individuals come together in groups, they create unorganized, unstable collections of individuals who may act in undisciplined and erratic ways. It is in this context that conflict can occur and it is in these circumstances that a lack of self-control can lead individuals to violence.

Aspects of self-control can vary by gender. In accounting for the differentials that appear in the rates of delinquency for males and females, Hagan et al. (1985) propose a power control theory that adds interpersonal power factors to control theory.[5] They suggest that, in nonegalitarian families, girls are socialized by their mothers in a way that vastly differs from the socialization of boys. Women, nurtured by their mothers, are more attuned to informal sanctions than men who are raised by their fathers and who respond more directly to formal sanctions (Hagan et al. 1985; Hagan 1989:156). In advanced capitalist societies, the fact that men have been more directly involved in the operation of the economic system suggests that they are more likely to be subject to control by the sanctions of the criminal justice system, which is male-dominated (Hagan et al. 1985; Hagan 1986:78). This focus on formal sanctioning for males has left them less amenable to the forces of stigma and informal shaming that is more pervasive in interpersonal life and more effective in curtailing certain types of behaviour, for example, aggressiveness and violence.

The reliance on informal sanctioning for women makes them more susceptible to the influence of others' opinions and more likely to curtail behaviour that is likely to harm others. A further aspect to this equation is the reduced power to which women have access in managing their lives, which leaves them more likely to be victims of certain types of aggressiveness by males. The criminalization of the violence in aggressive behaviour by men toward women has been offered as a way to limit the damage that is done in violent relationships. It is also seen as a means whereby men, who appear to be unconcerned about informal sanctioning when they are violent, get the message, through formal arrest, that this behaviour is unacceptable.

Power control theory includes, as well, an analysis of the importance of risk-aversion in promoting individual participation in delinquency. As Hagan states it, "... delinquency may involve a spirit of liberation, the opportunity to take risks, and a chance to pursue publicly pleasures that are symbolic of adult male status outside the family" (Hagan 1989:153). One reason why delinquency is fun, he goes on to say, is that it includes more behaviour, both legal and illegal, open to men than to women. Power control theory proposes that the higher likelihood of delinquency among boys than girls, and the subsequent higher levels of criminality among men than women, relates to the expression of gender differences in risk preferences. These preferences result from the different patterns of parental control imposed on daughters compared to sons (Hagan 1989:154). It is further suggested that in families more egalitarian in their makeup, especially in the relative status of husbands relative to wives, differences in parental control over boys versus girls diminish, leaving girls to be less risk-aversive and more likely to become involved in delinquency.

As a refinement of control theory, power control theory is useful in examining homicide, a predominantly male crime. The propositions of power control theory provide us with a link to the importance of socialization in control theory in creating behavioural repertoires that conform to expectations set by adult role models. We would suggest that these repertoires provide a basis for differences in the ways in which individuals learn to manage conflict, and that conflict styles will vary markedly between genders. In addition, it is clear that there are differences in the nature of the risky lifestyles that individuals follow (Gartner and McCarthy 1991).

Thornberry (1987) offers an additional refinement of social control theory in what he calls interactional theory.[6] Like control theory, interactional theory proposes that the fundamental cause of delinquency is a weakening of bonds to conventional society. When bonds are weakened, the individual has more behavioural freedom—in effect, more freedom to act in an unconstrained manner. Interactional theory adds three elements to social control theory. First, it assumes that variation in the bond to conventional society is related to structural variables such as social class position and residential area. Second, it assumes that elements in the causal model vary over the life course. That is, issues that cause a particular behaviour at one point in a potential offender's life may not at another point; behaviour changes over time. Finally, it assumes the possibility of bidirectional effects. Deviant behaviour can be both a cause and effect of the weakening of the social bond.

Hirschi's conceptualization of social control through social bonds, Hagan, Gillis, and Simpson's power control theory, and Thornberry's interactional theory were developed in the context of delinquency. Types of crimes engaged in by the individuals being studied to test the theories run the gamut of misdemeanours and felonies but rarely include homicide. However, these are general theories of illicit behaviour and are readily applicable to more serious crimes. The similarities between Hirschi's initial formulation, Hirschi and Gottfredson's self-control model, power control theory, and interactional theory, are self-evident. They all derive from similar assumptions about behaviour and society. Those who have a weak bond to society will likely lack self-control; the structural conditions predicted by Thornberry will likely effect those who are more likely to exhibit a lack of self-control; they will more likely be male than female. Low self-control leads to volatile reactions, to frustrations, and to a higher likelihood of becoming involved in violent solutions to problems. Those who engage in violence regularly are potential murderers.

CONFLICT AND THE ESCALATION TO VIOLENCE

Individuals who lack self-control and have not learned conflict management techniques will be frustrated by conflict. Conflict between individuals has many origins and takes many different directions, depending on the characteristics of the individuals involved and the circumstances they face. The solutions to conflict are most often peaceful, although there may still be some residual resentment or disappointment, particularly for individuals who feel cheated by the resolution. The resentment that develops may be reduced or even eliminated when the conflict is managed in such a way that all parties feel that the resolution is a fair and equitable one, addressing some, if not all, of each participant's concerns.

Successful conflict management is a product of socializing individuals to handle their own feelings and to be willing to accept certain rules of give-and-take in the negotiation of a settlement. The successful use of these skills will be influenced by personality characteristics. It has been observed that people who are aggressive, dominant, and suspicious will have a greater likelihood of enhanced conflict with others (Terhune 1970) and, presumably, more difficulty managing the conflicts that occur. However, personality factors can be compensated for in conflict situations by the cues that individuals pick up for interaction with others that allow them to take into account these responses in keeping conflict from getting out of control.

Kelley and Thibaut (1978) argue that a combination of personality and situation contributes to an individual repertoire that Hocker and Wilmot (1985) refer to as "conflict style." Individuals use their conflict styles as a guide for appropriate responses in different situations. The consistency that people develop in their conflict styles derives from socialization and through experimentation with different responses over time (Kennedy 1990:19). This routine behaviour makes it easy for individuals to deal with daily interactions without having to relearn or re-establish acceptable standards of behaviour. The routine conflict style serves as a behavioural indicator of norms and values promoted in conventional society.[7]

Not all conflict styles, of course, are acceptable. Some are the product of poor socialization or weak social bonds as described above. Destructive conflict styles often coincide with risky lifestyles that incorporate confrontation rather than negotiation as an acceptable means of dealing with slights to honour or attacks on one's character, as may be witnessed in many of the quarrels that develop in public places, such as bars and lounges (see Luckenbill 1977). Individuals who have not yet developed mediative conflict styles may, when confronted with threat or harm, respond with excessive violence. Similarly, individuals may encounter a situation that unleashes their repressed anger or resentment, leaving them out of control. When routines are changed or when confrontational conflict styles develop unchecked, we are likely to encounter violence and harm.

Alcohol and drugs also contribute to the escalation of conflict and the reduction of inhibition. Destructive conflict styles would appear to intensify with alcohol. Individuals who may find a way to work out a problem while sober (e.g., walking away from the confrontation) may become more aggressive and more violent when drinking. Further, the presence of a third person who promotes confrontational styles may lead to an escalation of violence (Felson and Steadman 1983). At the same time, a third person can be useful in redirecting the anger and frustration and finding a resolution without threat or harm.

An important factor influencing the conflict that occurs is the relationship between the parties who are in disagreement. The closer the relationship, the greater the opportunity for tension and conflict to develop, although it is understood by these individuals that there is more to lose in these situations (Coser 1956). This type of conflict is more intense but also more liable to result in attempts at resolution. Nonetheless, sudden explosions of anger may lead to injury in relationships in which conflict management becomes strained through repeated disagreements over money or sex. Conflict with people less close can be more easily resolved through avoidance, although this is not considered a desirable option when, for example, one's reputation for being tough is at stake. Nonetheless, the ability to elude such situations or to find a temporary solution are not options so readily available to the family relationship, which must be sustained over time.

Straus (1987) describes the family as the place where violence is first learned. Violence that is directed against children (including physical punishment), as well as toward other family members, is likely to mould the child's orientation toward the use of physical force in problem-solving. Hence, the child from a violent home is likely to be violent in his or her own home upon reaching adulthood. According to Straus (1980a), the marriage licence has been used as a hitting licence. The routine management of conflict in certain relationships is violent, involving physical and mental abuse that can lead to serious injury or death of one spouse at the hands of the other. Alternatively, a partner who is subject to sustained abuse might turn on other members of the family to vent frustration, anger, or hurt (Dutton 1980). Mothers who kill may be transferring their feelings to a convenient and perhaps annoying target (Silverman and Kennedy 1988).

The crux of conflict is disagreement, which may reflect major or minor conflict. The intensity of the disagreement is largely a matter of perception. Again, in an individual lacking the socialization that promotes nonviolent solutions, violence comes into play as a conflict-management technique (whether with a mate or the person at the bar who took your ash tray). Conflict styles can be understood as part of one's management of routine activities and the coordination of personality and situational aspects of interpersonal relations across time. It is evident that most individuals are able to manage their life in routines that are safe and free from escalating conflict. Individuals who lead risky lifestyles, on the other hand, are more likely to confront problems that may result in injury or death.

RISKY LIFESTYLES AND DANGEROUS RESULTS

Routine activities theory suggests that people who are alike in terms of lifestyle and age come together in daily routines where, on occasion, there will be "predatory violations" (Cohen and Felson 1979:588–89) and offenders will take the opportunity of circumstance and vulnerability to prey on other individuals. Much behaviour is repetitive and predictable, and, as Cohen and Felson point out, when motivated offenders, accessible and vulnerable targets, and an absence of protectors coexist in time and space, the chance of crime increases.

Hindelang et al. (1978) present a set of propositions about victimization based on repetitive and predictable lifestyles. "Lifestyle refers to routine daily activities, both vocational ... and leisure" (241). They suggest eight propositions that link lifestyle with victimization patterns. (Age, sex, marital status, family income, and race are all bound up with lifestyle and help predict victimization.) First, the amount of time spent in public places, especially at night, relates to victimization. Second, the probability of being in public places varies with lifestyle. Third, social contacts and interactions occur disproportionately among those who share lifestyles. Fourth, the chance of being a victim varies with the extent to which victims and offenders share demographic characteristics. Fifth, the proportion of time spent among nonfamily members varies as a function of lifestyle. Sixth, the probability of personal victimization (particularly theft) increases with the amount of time spent among nonfamily members. Seventh, variations in lifestyles are associated with the ability of people to isolate themselves from those with offender characteristics. Eighth, variations in lifestyle relate to the convenience, desirability, and vincibility of persons as victimization targets (Hindelang et al. 1978:251–64).

This characterization of lifestyle puts emphasis on the interaction that individuals maintain in their day-to-day environments. The lifestyle factor helps individuals to plan routines and to anticipate certain types of outcomes from their actions. When these lifestyles are more risky or leave individuals more vulnerable, the probability of victimization can increase. For example, following certain lifestyle routines raises the probability of being in public places during different time periods (day and night). Miethe et al. (1987), using data from the U.S. National Crime Survey, report that certain demographic groups who are involved in nighttime activities away from home are more likely to report victimization related to property crime. A similar pattern does not appear for victims of violent crime.

Miethe et al. (1987) speculate that, unlike property crime in which the offender seeks to benefit materially from his or her behaviour, violent crime results from interpersonal conflict or disagreement that is spontaneous. Their finding not only contradicts the prediction of routine activities theory that violent offenders are rational, calculating in a reasonable fashion the risks of their crime—it is also at odds with the power control theory prediction that certain individuals, particularly males, will more likely be involved in risk-taking.

Using data from the Canadian Urban Victimization Study, Kennedy and Forde (1990a), refute the Miethe et al. (1987) findings. They identify young, unmarried males who frequent bars, go to movies, go out to work, and spend time out of the house walking or driving around as the group most vulnerable to assault. Kennedy and Forde (1990a) show that public behaviour creates exposure to risk and may lead to dangerous results, including robbery and assault. The potential for risk may spontaneously become a reality when the targets of assault frequent places that are conducive to conflict. We are unable to account for the motivation behind this risk-taking behaviour, but we certainly can understand the dynamics of the event occurring under these circumstances.

The vulnerability of risk-takers may be increased by the fact that they are less likely to be able or willing to turn to the police for protection. The high incidence of assault in locations such as bars that remains unreported provides an example of the reciprocal nature of much of the violence that occurs. The victim may find recourse through retribution more acceptable than reporting to the police (Kennedy 1988). This "street justice" approach provides the ingredients for an escalation of violence that may result in a miscalculation and subsequent fatality. If we believe that a climate of violence can develop, as suggested by Harries (1990), and that homicide is an extension of assault, it would be logical to assume that those living risky lifestyles in dangerous areas are potential victims of murder.

The victim who uses poor judgment in placing himself or herself at risk is not characteristic of all risky situations. Some potential victims are unlucky to be in a dangerous place at a particular time,[8] or they cannot extract themselves from what has become a risky situation. An example is the victim of wife abuse who is so emotionally and economically dependent on her partner that she may feel that she cannot leave the relationship.[9] But her situation is still risky. By staying in the environment in which she is almost surely to be beaten, and by not calling the police, she has placed herself at risk. On the other hand, the more obvious forms of risk that can be avoided include getting drunk in public places and walking home alone on darkened streets. Routine activities theory suggests that some situations are more risky than others. It does not prescribe that all victims can avoid risk at all times.

There is much data to suggest that victims and offenders in violent acts share many characteristics. Risk-taking makes certain individuals more likely to be not only offenders but also, through a process of homogamy, victims of crime (Sampson and Lauritsen 1990). It may in fact be that those who place themselves in risky situations are low self-control individuals. In the case of barroom brawls that result in homicide, there is little to distinguish victims from offenders. On the other hand, the routine of home life coupled with a poorly socialized abusive male partner allows us to predict violent outcomes and the gender of the most likely victim.

In summary, the theories that focus on individual behaviour as it relates to violence concentrate on the interpersonal dynamics that develop between persons in different relationships. The conflict that emerges from these dynamics can be influenced by the routines that individuals use to interact and by their personal styles of managing interpersonal disagreements. In addition, individuals may lead lifestyles that are more risky, increasing the chance of recurring conflict and, possibly, an escalation to violence.

ALTERNATIVE APPROACHES: PSYCHOLOGY, SUBCULTURES, BIOLOGY, AND THRILL

Alternative approaches to explain homicide at the micro-level attempt to account more directly for offender motivations by focusing on propensities within individual personalities to partake in certain types of behaviour. These propensities can operate outside of the influence of social forces. They may be genetically based, or they may derive from an innate search for immediate gratification or "thrill," or they may be the result of a subculture of violence. Such explanations of murder are difficult to test empirically, given their exclusive concentration on the inner drives of individuals, something that is hard to confirm when working with a small group of murderers. The importance of motivation in assessing guilt, though, requires that we address some of the issues raised in this literature, acknowledging that murder can be more than a series of mistakes or circumstances that go wrong.

Daly and Wilson (1988a, 1988b), using a sociobiological perspective, suggest that homicide varies in interaction with age, unemployment, and marital status. For family-based murders, they offer the proposition that there is a greater likelihood of homicide the more distantly related the principals. Also, it is more likely to involve young people (1988b). Family murders evolve, they argue, as a result of genetic predispositions to jealously guard blood relatives while being more violent toward those unrelated to the offender. A focus only on family members, however, leaves us with little insight into the importance of age for other relationships. Further, the analysis done by Daly and Wilson, while purporting to address the contextual elements in the environment that might influence behaviour, focuses only on individual characteristics of victims and offenders, leaving out important macro-level indicators of the social structure in which homicide occurs.

Research on twins and adoptees that searches for genetic predispositions to crime (see, for example, Mednick et al. 1987) has provided compelling evidence on crime trends related to genetic makeup, especially in tracking the differential effects of birth parents versus adoptive parents in intergenerational tendencies to be involved in crime. While there is no gene for criminal behaviour or criminal intent, there may be biosocial inclinations toward precursors to crime, such as differential reaction to alcohol consumption or differential degrees of difficulty in socializing particular individuals.

We are not equipped to explore biological explanations for violence in this volume. There have been many attempts to link aggressive behaviour to violent crime, but a thorough review of the literature reveals little compelling evidence for such explanations. For instance, the XYY chromosome was a popular explanation for violent behaviour for several years. The theory labelled as aggressive, males who had an extra Y chromosome and other physical characteristics that included being tall, lean, and having a poor complexion. But review after review showed that the methodologies attached to the initial studies were badly flawed (Wahlsten 1991).

Other explanations have dealt with biological/constitutional (rather than genetic) elements that lead to violence. The topics are a veritable cornucopia of variables that have been explored as correlates of violent behaviour. Diet, physiological tolerance to alcohol, the lunar cycle, neuropsychology, and many other issues have been linked to aggressive behaviour (see, for example Wolfgang et al. 1981). Again, the empirical support for such explanations is either lacking or very narrow in its potential applications.

While biological influences provide some easy answers to observed behaviour, certain social-psychological explanations seem to be more effective in explaining the actions of killers. According to Levin and Fox (1985), in their study of 364 cases of mass murder from 1976 through 1985 in the U.S., there is a common thread of severe frustration in behaviour among murderers (Levin and Fox 1985:68). Frustration appears as a precursor of a violent attack—a final straw. Usually there is some precipitating event. Further, the killer has few outside contacts with friends and neighbours who might help to reduce their growing rage. The implication of this research is that, in cases of mass murder where the violence is most severe, uncontrolled conflict rather than psychopathology provides the best explanation of the final outcome.

On the one hand, it can be argued that the demented personality finds life too hard to manage and explodes in an inevitable outburst of rage and violence. On the other hand, many people who have violent dispositions are kept from endangering others by the constraints imposed by the social situation. Although they occur infrequently, the evidence is clear, as we pointed out previously, that homicides are most often preceded by interpersonal conflict. Close to three-quarters of the murders committed in Canada from 1961 to 1983 (about 7500 cases where motive is assigned) were a result of revenge, jealousy, anger, or argument. Only about 15 percent were preceded by another crime or a sexual assault (see Silverman and Kennedy 1987). While this does not constitute a fully convincing argument against genetic explanations of homicide, with their emphasis on biological deficiencies that promote criminality, it would seem that genetic problems are not sufficient (nor possibly even necessary) to contribute to a murderous outcome of a serious assault resulting from interpersonal conflict. The certainty of explanation suggested by constitutional theories does not mesh with the uncertainties that typify criminal outcomes, particularly homicide. In summing up their devastating attack on biological positivism, Gottfredson and Hirschi note that "... biological positivism has produced little in the way of meaningful or interpretable research" (1990:61–62); they show that the only possible genetic effects are minuscule.

There is a second view of criminality offered to explain individual motivation that has been used to analyze violent behaviour. In developing the "subculture of violence" approach, Wolfgang and Ferracuti (1967) state that certain groups use violence as a means of continuous control over members. Thus, the escalation of violent behaviour, which can include homicide, results from the subculture in groups that promotes rather than discourages aggression. Violence in this context is seen as a valued goal of the group.

Group power through the advocacy of violence makes individual attempts to seek resolution in interpersonal conflicts more difficult. The promotion of violence may depend on circumstances, however. As Hagan (1985) points out, researchers have been unable to isolate deviant subcultures in which violence is considered an integral aspect of the group's functioning. Nonetheless, Katz (1988) proposes a way of examining crime that relates to the subcultural view. Crime, he argues is a consequence of thrill-seeking rather than biological deficiency or social conflict. In *The Seductions of Crime*, Katz develops an approach to criminality that emphasizes the "... need to comprehend the cognitive states of actors in explaining their behaviors" (Hagan 1990:169). Katz feels that there is a need, when studying crime, to understand the actual experiences of the offence from the point of view of the offender. It is with this view in mind that he offers a view of murder as "righteous slaughter."

Other than crime-based murders, "criminal homicide is an impassioned attempt to perform a sacrifice to embody one or another version of the 'Good.' "(1988:12) Katz sees most murder as the outcome of moral rage. The offender has been wronged and has set out to right that wrong. He may be wronged by a crying child or by an unfaithful wife, but whatever the case the solution is violent death. In his discussion, Katz links frustration, shame, humiliation, and rage as factors that lead to the righteous slaughter.

Katz's point of view is invaluable particularly in the emphasis that it places on the acts of violence from the point of view of those being violent. He examines the homicide interaction from the perspective of the offender seeking to right the wrong of a perceived humiliation. The offender's moral stance is at the centre of the analysis. However, as Hagan (1990) points out, this perspective requires us to disassociate the offender's cognitive state from the historical and structural factors that impinge on his or her behaviour and that of others. Thus, Katz reduces the importance of such factors as unemployment, family disruption, and even self-control in explaining variations in violent crime rates. In his attempt to get into the mind of the killer, Katz ignores the social factors that may have helped influence the way in which the killer thinks and acts. Further, the view of righteous slaughter implies that the life of violence draws with it a willingness to risk the punishment that comes with these offences, which renders the offender effectively nondeterrable (Hagan 1990:176) and only truly harmless when confined.

Katz's approach does offer a qualitative sense to the discussion of murder, highlighting the importance of understanding that the process by which we identify patterns in behaviour is not to imply that all behaviour is rational. Rather, we would argue that it is the combination of situation, interpersonal dynamics, and (sometimes) risky lifestyles that lead to fatal outcomes. Just how often we discover individuals who are seductively attracted to violence and attempting to right a wrong is difficult to assess. It would seem likely, however, that individuals may be attracted to situations that have an aura of risk and violence.

It is the intersection of risky lifestyles with opportunities for crime that seems to be the most important generator of violent behaviour. The connection between the individual experiences discussed by Katz and the structural variables outlined by Hagan would appear to have the greatest impact on the likelihood of violent events occurring. Associated with this connection is the degree to which individuals relate to others through strong or weak social bonds, as discussed in social control theory.

Katz's methods make empirical verification of his assertions very difficult. He concentrates mainly on spousal homicides, but, as will be seen, there are many other types of homicide for whom these arguments are not as compelling. For instance, serial killers seem to be motivated by something other than a compulsion to set things right. Katz does offer other categories of killers into which the serial killer might fall, but there is a certain artificiality in trying to slot these killers. There is too much evidence in the pages that follow that much intimate homicide leads to extraordinary remorse, guilt feelings, and even suicide to entertain Katz's scenario as a major explanation for why people commit murder. The stereotype of the contract killer is that of a cold-blooded professional who feels neither joy nor sorrow in the taking of another's life. The contract killer is merely doing a job. Again, we see no justification for Katz's portrayal of murder as righteous slaughter. There is no doubt that the seduction theme is compelling, but it must be approached with some caution.

Psychology has dealt with violence through theories of aggression and through the study of individual pathologies that result in violent behaviours. Berkowitz (1982) does not believe that subcultural theory can adequately explain aggressive behaviour. He says that aggression takes at least two forms—instrumental and hostile (angry). The former, which is goal oriented, may have a place in subcultural explanations, but the latter does not. In hostile aggression, the goal of the action is simply injury—it is not a secondary goal such as attaining status. In studies of aggression, it has been shown that fights are preceded by arguments that escalated to the point of physical encounter. Secondarily, young males come to the aid of friends in trouble. Whatever the precipitating event, the perpetrators were infuriated and then took action. From interviews with aggressive offenders, Berkowitz concludes, "[t]he men seemed to have very fragile egos, and were quick to define another person's behaviour as an insult or a challenge threatening their self-esteem. This threat tended to infuriate them" (95). Later, when we discuss murder involving friends and acquaintances, a sociological approach that echos this conclusion will be addressed (see Luckenbill 1977).

Psychology deals with the individual propensities of offenders to commit deviant acts. Some psychologists and psychiatrists distinguish between those murderers who exhibit psychiatric disorder and those who do not (Megargee 1982). Terms that have been applied to particular murderers include: sociopath, psychopath, schizophrenic, brain-damaged, paranoid, masochistic, and psychotic (among others). We do not discount these terms and their referents, but we do not think they account for the majority of murders. In fact, they explain only a small number of cases—those that often get much of the public attention. In our discussion of serial and mass murderers in Chapter 5, there are cases in which certain psychological explanations are more compelling than the sociological explanations that we use elsewhere. Throughout our examination of murder, we return to psychological approaches when they fit the precise details of the events being analyzed. There are, of course, virtually always psychological components to face-to-face interactions that often characterize scenarios leading to murder. These play a role in the descriptions of relationships between victims and offenders that follow.

SOCIETAL-LEVEL THEORIES

The major focus of this book rests with the analysis of the micro-level data provided through Statistics Canada. These data provide us with a detailed breakdown of the circumstances surrounding the murder event. But, as we have argued above, individuals do not operate in a vacuum but are subject to the effects of the economy and social conditions in the cities and towns in which they live. We will not review these factors in great detail, but it is important that we present the debates that address the effects of socio-economic conditions on violence.

ECONOMIC INEQUALITY AND CRIME[10]

Krahn et al. (1986), reporting on data drawn from a number of countries around the world, argue that areas with higher levels of income inequality and population change exhibit higher homicide rates. Williams and Flewelling (1988) claim that when people live under conditions of extreme scarcity, the struggle for survival is intensified. These conditions lead to a psychological agitation that may have lethal consequences (Williams and Flewelling 1988:423). Further, in societies where economic disparities predominate, as economic conditions change, there is an impact on the ways in which individuals assess their economic well-being. Those who believe themselves to be relatively disadvantaged can find themselves in conditions that are ripe for homicide. There is strong evidence, according to Blau and Blau (1982), that the conflict of interest over the distribution of resources that economic disparity entails can create a climate of violence. Important in this equation is the effect of relative versus absolute poverty. There may be an intense response to relative deprivation, in which individuals compare their condition to those who are more advantaged. Blau and Blau (1982:126) make the case that aggressive acts of violence seem to result not so much from lack of advantages in an absolute sense but rather from relative deprivation.

The frustration that comes from poverty, unemployment, and poor housing conditions enhances tension in families and raises the level of conflict among family members. This is not to say that poverty or inequality are necessarily causally related to homicide, but they do appear to be highly correlated with the conditions that lead to a fatal outcome. It is the uncertainty of future income and the breaking of routines related to work that provide opportunities for conflict and raise frustrations in interpersonal relations.

Police and other social agencies have expressed a good deal of interest in the role that economic disadvantage plays in homicide among individuals living in inner-city areas. It is not uncommon to hear police officials in Canada talk not only about the problems of dealing with offenders but also about the need to mitigate the poor economic conditions under which people live in inner cities as a way of dealing with the origins of violence. In a recent effort to understand the reasons for high levels of violence in inner-city Edmonton, the mayor appointed a task force led by a police officer. Its report discussed the problems of drugs and alcohol, as well as the problems of family breakup and resulting delinquency. But it also emphasized that many problems are byproducts of the economic destitution faced by people living in the inner city, as measured through high unemployment, poor housing, and inadequate social services. The task force suggested specific steps that should be taken to deal with these problems, including interagency efforts to improve housing.

The change from a responsive mode of law enforcement to a proactive mode of social intervention makes the police accountable for a larger sphere than simply the current behaviour of individual offenders. Thus is introduced a strategy for reducing the chance that individuals in these areas, characterized as poor and frustrated, are likely to be offenders in the first place. Underlying the response is the notion that individuals operate in social environments that are influential in affecting their behaviour.

SOCIAL DISORGANIZATION

It is assumed that social control diminishes with a reduction in the level of social organization in society. The informal structures that manage behaviour exercise less influence over individuals and the formal structures are incapable of handling all of the problems that develop as a consequence of social breakdown. Views about the role of social disorganization in creating disorder can be traced to Durkheim, who argues that more integrated communities have lower rates of crime (Williams and Flewelling 1988:423). The factors that can contribute to a lack of integration relate to the unsettling effects of population change (Wirth 1938); imbalances that occur through overly large age cohorts (Maxim 1985); and tension that occurs in families, identified through the increase in divorce (Gillis 1986).

Blau and Blau (1982) indicate that stresses in society result from the tensions that develop between ethnic groups and ultimately lead to social disorganization. In the United States, they attribute much interpersonal crime to racial tension. In Canada, visible minorities and ethnic groups represent a much smaller proportion of the population. While racial tension has developed in Canada, particularly in the major cities, it has not translated into large numbers of homicides between racially distinct groups. Avakame (1989), in a study of homicides among blacks in Canada, reports that there is a very low incidence of murder occurring in this group and most of the homicides occur within the group and not between blacks and whites. On the other hand, Canadian Indians contribute to homicide in proportions well above their numbers in the population.

Further, Blau and Blau (1982:119) also point out a high correlation between divorce and crime rates. Social disorganization measured through divorce adds an interpersonal dimension to our analysis. The tension created by change in society is reflected in conflict that develops in the family. This may, in time, manifest itself in increased rates of violent crime. Disorganization is clearly at its highest in urban areas, especially those undergoing rapid population change (Wirth 1938; Krohn et al. 1984; Sampson and Groves 1989).

Modern society has witnessed a large-scale migration of people from rural areas into cities, where they enjoy few of the community ties that typified life in the intensely dense social networks of small towns. The break in close-knit ties promotes anonymity through bringing together individuals from diverse backgrounds into highly dense settlements (Wirth 1938). This concentration tends to create tension between people who do not share similar value systems, thereby establishing the potential for misunderstandings and conflict. Urban life has replaced the constant scrutiny of homogeneous communities with the loosely contained "liberated" community (Wellman and Leighton 1979) in which individuals draw support from people who are like them but who may not live nearby or interact with them on a daily basis. This change in community alters the nature of the social support system available to individuals, as the extended family is replaced by the nuclear family, which is supplemented by the school. When these ties become weaker or when the sanctions for offending appear to be less important, the individual may become deviant out of reduced concern about the loss of reputation or the stigmatization that could be applied. This is not to say that there are little or no informal sanctions applied in urban areas, but only that sanctions against deviant behaviour are more evident in small towns where reputations are more clearly on display.

The upheaval brought on by high levels of migration often provokes violent encounters among individuals who reside in the
affected areas, a point reinforced by the work of Williams and
Flewelling (1988).[11]

Analysis has been done to include all of the variables related
to social inequality and social disorganization in one model for
predicting criminal behaviour. Sampson and Groves (1989)
include low socioeconomic status, ethnic heterogeneity, residential mobility, family disruption, and urbanization (Sampson and
Groves 1989:783). They show that structural factors are mediated through community-level forms of social control, including,
for example, the level of involvement in community organiza-
tions.

While the correlations between social disorganization,
income inequality, and homicide is reasonably clear, it is important to note that the effect of these variables on homicide is indirect. The American South and West have much higher homicide
rates than other regions. Researchers variously attribute the differences to the influence of regional cultures (Hackney 1969;
Gastil 1971); tolerance for legitimate violence (Baron and Straus
1988); and racial or economic variations (Blau and Blau 1982).
There seems to be consensus, however, that differences are
impervious to explanations on the basis of a simple model of sub-
cultures-of-violence (Huff-Corzine et al., 1986).

Comparing Canada and the U.S., Straus (1988) points out
notable differences in the proportions of family and stranger
homicides. Between 1961 and 1983, there is a large difference in
domestic homicide, with about 25 percent of U.S. homicides classified as intrafamily compared to about 46 percent of Canadian
homicides (Straus 1988:7). Stranger homicides account for about
one-third of homicides in the U.S. compared to 22 percent of
homicides in Canada, with trends in the proportions of lethal violence among strangers increasing in U.S. urban centres (Williams
and Flewelling 1988) and decreasing in Canadian cities (Silverman and Kennedy 1987). As Hagan (1989) correctly points out,
the best empirical research in the American scene indicates a
strong influence of race on aggregate effects of homicide. This
may be a result of economic deprivation (Sampson 1985; 1987),
inner-city malaise, discrimination, and/or a number of other factors that plague blacks in large cities in the United States. Unfortunately, with the data that are available to homicide researchers, we are unable to test these propositions. Socioeconomic
status of victims or offenders is not routinely tabulated. However,
we can combine our data to form rates and examine trends, as
Sampson has done, providing some substantiation for speculation
about root causes.

Sociological research on differences in Canadian society has emphasized the regional politicization of social and economic concerns. Specifically, higher levels of economic deprivation and social disorganization have placed regions of Canada in positions of relative social disadvantage (Brym 1986). This has consequences for all parts of social life, influencing employment, family relations, and public behaviour. Previous research has shown that violent crime is regionally distributed in Canada, rising from east to west. The east–west phenomenon generally persists over time for personal and property crimes (Hackler and Don 1990).

Lenton (1989), Hagan (1989), and Kennedy et al. (1989) show that structural factors are important in explaining Canadian homicide rates. Kennedy et al. (1991) find that regional variations in homicide rates occur as a result of the social structural distribution of inequality and social disorganization factors in Canada. There is, in fact, a convergence in murder rates between eastern, central, and western Canada in areas with higher levels of inequality and social disorganization. The importance of these structural factors also varies over time. The effect of inequality on the total homicide rate is evident for 1972–76 but not for 1977–81. Family income inequality in 1972–76 is positively associated with homicide. Unemployment in both 1972–76 and 1977–81 is inversely related to homicide, consistent with reports for provincial data (Kennedy et al. 1988). Whereas unemployment has been a perennial problem in Canada, particularly in terms of large regional pockets of disadvantaged workers, it has not necessarily led to an increase in inequality. Unemployment may, however, have led indirectly to population changes in Canada from 1971 to 1981 following linguistic shifts (specifically with movement of large numbers of English-speaking Quebeckers to Ontario) and migrations spurred by economic booms and busts (the most graphic example being the oil boom in Alberta that collapsed in a severe economic downturn).

Conversely, the effect of social disorganization has a stronger effect on homicide in 1981 than in 1976. This does not mean that inequality has no effect in 1981. The additional effects of the percentages of young males within CMAs (Canadian Metropolitan Areas) in 1981 suggests that cohort size may affect relative levels of economic opportunities. These results support the suggestion by Smith (1986) that the relative size of a birth cohort influences the homicide rate. The percentages of young males actually decrease in CMAs in 1981 relative to 1976. The high levels of unemployment and a population shift may lead to a decreased sense of economic well-being and a subsequent increase in homicide rates, even though the absolute measures of economic inequality have shown a clear improvement. An important result of this study is the suggestion that government interventions to remove disparities in income inequality and economic opportunity could coincide with a decrease in homicide rates. Equally, increased resource allocation such as added support for social services may have similar effects (Browne and Williams 1989). We will discuss this in greater detail in Chapter 9.

SUMMARY

The theoretical perspectives examined in this book are primarily focused on the degree of self control exhibited by individuals and the routine lifestyles that challenge this control. We are mindful of the fact, however, that individuals do not live in a vacuum but are strongly influenced by the economic and social conditions under which they live. Changes in these factors can heavily influence the overall direction of behaviour exhibited in a crime such as homicide. While we do not have the data here to relate social and economic factors directly to individual homicides, we are aware that they are a constant that must be considered in any response to this crime. Chapter 8, which focuses on Indians and homicide, deals with some of these issues directly, and we return to them again in Chapter 9.

NOTES

1. The theories deal with the general class of culpable killing. They do not distinguish between homicide and murder. Thus, we refer to murder and homicide interchangeably in this section.

2. "A 2 1/2 year-old Edmonton girl was still in critical condition Monday, one week after she was badly beaten ... The girl's life is in danger from head injuries she received ..." (*Edmonton Journal*, February 19, 1991a:B2). Her babysitter was charged with aggravated assault. If the child dies, he will almost certainly be charged with either second-degree murder or manslaughter.

3. These "hot spots" may not involve the same people because of high transiency in some of their locations.

4. This process is often referred to as internalization of social norms.

5. Power control theory was developed to explain aspects of "common delinquency." Here, it has been adapted to help explain one aspect of adult criminality.

6. Again, this theory was developed to explain delinquency and is adapted here to show how early socialization may affect later behaviour.

7. While not all homicide is conflict-driven, certainly the bulk of it can be attributed to situations in which a lack of self-control leads to con-

flict, assault, and, finally, murder. The major exceptions to this are homicides committed by serial murderers, who have deep and complex motives for this behaviour and murder for hire, which is based on factors related to crime as business. These types of murders are discussed in Chapter 5.

8. See Silverman and Kennedy (1990) for a discussion of the passive routines of the elderly victim of homicide.

9. See the discussion of the battered woman syndrome in Chapter 6.

10. Much of this discussion of macro forces on homicide is drawn from Kennedy, Silverman, and Forde (1991).

11. A strong counterargument concerning the tension encountered in cities is offered in the work of Fischer (1975). However, his arguments address concerns related to absolute size of cities versus rural areas rather than the rapid growth factors, which lead to the loss of social bonds, that we are addressing here.

C H A P T E R   4

Social Relationships
SPOUSES, FAMILY, FRIENDS, AND STRANGERS

Social relationship provides an interesting category with which to begin examining victim/offender interaction. Varying degrees of control exist within the context of social distance and social relationship defines social distance. More generally, social relationship is one of the most important factors influencing the nature of conflict between individuals. Daily routine activities influence the kinds and nature of conflict between intimates. Research on homicide has found relationship categories particularly useful in creating a taxonomy of homicide (see Silverman and Kennedy 1987). It is clear that the conflict that develops between intimates, which sometimes leads to fatal conclusions, has a very different etiology than do the lethal disputes between strangers. The closeness of intimate relationships makes the routine contact between individuals intense and sometimes volatile. The long-term nature of the tie may prevent the conflict from becoming dangerous, or it may actually work to encourage routines that are confrontational and lead to an explosion of anger or revenge.

Contact with strangers presents very different possibilities. At least with intimates we think we can predict their behaviour (good or bad). On the other hand, contact with strangers may make us wary. The frequency with which we interact with strangers will vary according to our routines. Those living risky lifestyles may regularly make these contacts, increasing their chances of becoming victimized in some way. The stranger is feared, although as we will see there is less likelihood that a murder will occur at the hands of someone not known to the victim than at the hands of someone who is intimate. We contact strangers every day but it is rare for strangers to confront or challenge us.

In his homicide research in Philadelphia, Wolfgang (1958) observed that people react differently to the same stimuli depending on relational distance. You are, in fact, much more likely to be killed by someone you love or have loved than by a stranger. However, people fear the stranger more than the intimate. Fear of strangers is fear of the unknown (Riedel 1992). Strangers are a real and persistent part of urban living. The circumstances of city life force us to rely on people with whom we share virtually no intimacy to provide us with a variety of services. Strangers have become a source of apprehension in the city. They are seen as potential threats or potential perpetrators of crime. This sometimes leads to changes in daily routine. We read stories of individuals who become prisoners in their homes due to fear of venturing out of their safe domain; others arm themselves against the "lurking stranger."

Murder perpetrated by strangers is viewed by many as a threat resulting from a general degeneration of society. People perceive a rise in street crime in many urban areas and have, as a result, changed their living habits. Has there been an increase in the proportion of homicides committed by strangers in recent years? Gillis (1986) concludes that murders between individuals with "secondary relationships"[1] and between strangers have increased much more rapidly than murders involving individuals sharing "primary" relationships in Canada between 1961 and 1974.

The results of more recent research in Canada confirm a continued growth in the proportion of stranger homicide. Yet the structural stresses in the environment might seem to impact as much on family as on more distant relationships. Homicide in the context of an emotionally charged atmosphere of an intimate relationship seems easily understood in terms of the interpersonal dynamics of the relationship. The breakdown in communication, the development of angry or hostile interactions, and the onset of interpersonal violence seem to depend greatly on the personality of the individuals, as well as on the stresses that they experience due to family and economic circumstances and their conflict-management skills.

Between the intimacy of spouse and the lack of intimacy of strangers lie intermediate categories of intimacy. Less is written about relationships of family members other than spouses, or of friends and acquaintance relationships, though the latter are involved in a large amount of the homicides that occur in Canada.

The degree of intimacy affects, in part, the offender's reaction to his or her actions. One indirect measure of the emotional response to murder is suicide following murder. While overall in Canada about 10 percent of murders are followed by the suicide of the offender, we will see that this proportion varies greatly according to the relationship of the offender to the victim. We use suicide following murder as an indirect indicator of remorse of the offender. We suggest that, in general, the more intimate the relationship, the more likely suicide will be an outcome.

This chapter is devoted to an examination of social relationships between victims and offenders. We begin with a brief examination of the trends in murder as they relate to social relationship.

SOCIAL RELATIONSHIPS[2]

Figure 4.1 shows relational distance between murder suspects and victims as a proportion of all murder. The proportion of murders in more distant relationships is rising, while proportions of more intimate murders have fallen since the early 1960s. Spousal murder has been considered the leading category for murder for as long as data have been collected in Canada. However, as a proportion of all murder it has been in a continual decline since 1961. In fact, despite popular belief, spousal murder has not represented the highest proportion of murder since the mid-1970s. While murder between spouses has been declining, murders among friends and acquaintances have climbed. It is interesting to note that family murder has remained relatively stable as a proportion of all murder (between 15 and 20 percent), while stranger murder climbs to a peak in 1980 (13 percent) but then falls again, levelling off at around 6 percent in the late 1980s.

Murder during the commission of another crime has shown a gradual climb during the 1961–90 period. It peaks in 1981 and begins to decline as a proportion of all murder, levelling off at about 15 percent throughout the 1980s. Intimate murder, in the form of spousal and other family murder, accounts for about 40 percent of Canadian murder incidents during the 1980s, equalling the proportion of friend/acquaintance events. In the early 1960s, spouse/lover murder alone accounts for 37 percent of the murders. All family murders accounts for 60 percent of Canadian murders in 1961. Of course, it is not possible to compute rates for all of these categories as there is no denominator that makes sense for most. However, it is possible to produce rates for the spousal category, and later in this chapter we will examine those rates.

FIGURE 4.1

SOCIAL RELATIONSHIP BETWEEN VICTIMS AND OFFENDERS, MURDER IN CANADA, 1961–1990*

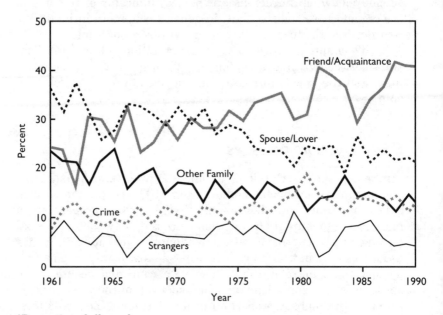

*Proportion of all murder.

The trends in Figure 4.1 confirm the notion that murders among intimates are declining, while murders among friends/acquaintances are rising. However, there has not been any substantial rise in the proportion of stranger- or crime-related murder—the types of murder that generate the most fear in the population.

MURDER IN THE FAMILY: SPOUSES AND CHILDREN

Of all social relationships there is none more intimate than the spousal relationship. In contemporary society, this relationship has come to be defined in a broad way. In earlier times in North America, when one talked of a spouse, one was speaking strictly of a legal marriage. From a sociological point of view, the relevant social arrangement is intimacy and physical proximity. In the intimate relationship, it is assumed that problems are shared.

Those problems that cause most tension in modern relationships include money, other social relationships, and jealousy. Physical proximity makes it possible to strike out, to project problems onto the partner, and to use the partner as a target. Of course, violence is not a requisite of physical proximity. Most intimate relationships do not result in violence. The relationships discussed here involve the worst possibilities of social relationships rather than the best.

In the analysis that follows, "spouse" is used loosely to define intimacy as it is categorized in legal marriages, common-law marriages, separations, divorces, and people living together; these arrangements are combined with a category called "lovers." The categorization is imposed upon us by those who design data-collection techniques. While it may not entirely reflect sociological thinking, it does offer a way of analyzing important social categories and individuals.

The proportion of spousal murder is higher in Canada than it is in the United States. Straus (1987) suggests that the lower the overall homicide rate, the higher the proportion of domestic homicide in a country. His reasoning is that primary groups (particularly the family) have characteristics that engender a certain level of violence while at the same time they restrict serious violence. Family homicide is less subject to sociocultural forces that affect other types of murder. Given the stability of family homicide (compared to the other forms), as the other types of homicide rise, family homicide becomes a lower proportion of the total. Straus says that family homicide creates a "floor-and-ceiling effect" that keeps the rate stable. In effect, he reports that the organization of the family gives us a regularly expected rate for family homicide (1987:21–22). Part of the observed difference in rates between countries may be attributable to high rates of black homicide reported in the United States, where increased numbers of killings in recent years have occurred between nonintimates in black communities (Mercy and Saltzman 1989). Race plays a less important role in affecting homicide in Canada (Silverman et al. 1990).

Wolfgang (1958) finds that arguments between husbands and wives most commonly occur over money matters and jealousy. Killings often take place in the bedroom or the kitchen (Wolfgang 1976). The kitchen, particularly when wives are the perpetrator, has some very handy weapons. Wolfgang reports that one-third of all spousal homicide involve a situation in which the eventual victim is the first to use physical force. "Victim precipitation" is an important part of other forms of homicide as well, but, unfortunately, the Canadian data do not report this aspect of conflict leading to homicide.

The research literature makes it clear that homicide of a spouse is not very often a spontaneous single "blow-up" event. Rather, it is the end of serial violence that takes place in the home. The intimate situation is one in which arguments contribute to heightened tension, which leads to some kind of physical catharsis. This chain of events is often fuelled by the presence of alcohol (and, to a lesser extent in Canada, drugs). Given the intimacy, the lack of problem-solving skills of the participants, the presence of alcohol, and often a history of solving problems through physical violence, homicide within the family is the easiest type of homicide to explain. Violence that emanates from these situations is often the result of longstanding quarrels or antagonisms that have brewed and been tolerated for years. Some event leads to a breaking point or last straw for the offender (Lystad 1980), a scenario similar to the one that Katz (1988) calls "righteous slaughter"—the brewing anger that eventuates in homicide.

It should be noted that, while alcohol is present in a significant number of spousal and other homicide types, some researchers suggest that it is not the cause of the homicide; rather it exacerbates a bad situation, involving, for example, lack of problem-solving skills or financial difficulties (Collins 1989; Gelles and Straus 1988). Drinking also provides a convenient excuse for behaviour that is considered unacceptable by the offender and those around him or her. The claim of drunkenness is supposed to excuse or explain otherwise inexcusable behaviour.

Routine activities theory suggests that the physical proximity itself (coupled with the other problems) should lead us to predict a ripe situation for killing. Goode (1969) suggests that it is probable that intimate emotional links among human beings have their own effects independent of pervasive pressures from the larger culture. The bulk of marriages (legal or otherwise) do not lead to homicide. They are either stable or lead to some other kind of dissolution (e.g., separation or divorce). Parker and Toth (1984) report that "increased domestic and family violence is associated with such factors as low levels of income, experiences of unemployment by male household heads, high levels of marital conflict and labour force participation among female spouses or cohabiters" (4).

SPOUSAL MURDER IN CANADA

Between 1961 and 1990, 2129 wives were killed by their husbands and 782 husbands were killed by their wives.[3] These figures constitute 49 percent of all the female victims of murder incidents but only 10 percent of all the males killed. Spousal murder rarely involves more than one offender or victim. When males kill their spouse they invariably act alone (99 percent), while females sometimes act in concert with another individual to kill their spouse (5 percent). On the other hand, a female spouse killer virtually always kills only one person (99 percent), while 6 percent of their male counterparts kill other people as well (often other members of his family). About 90 percent of females who kill their spouse/lover are married (legal or common-law) at the time of the murder, while the proportion for males is about 75 percent. About 12 percent of males and 5 percent of the female perpetrators are separated—an indirect indication, perhaps, that males are more likely to kill spouse/lovers with whom they are no longer living than are female perpetrators in this category. Sixty-two percent of the female offenders list their occupation as homemaker while 28 percent of the males are labourers and another 11 percent work in manufacturing or mechanical trades.[4]

Males who kill their mates most often do it with a gun (47 percent), while 19 percent each beat or stab their wives to death. On the other hand, 53 percent of wives who kill their husbands stab them to death, while 35 percent shoot the victim.[5] Only 5 percent beat their husbands to death. These findings reflect the usual physical stature differentials between men and women.

Sixty-three percent of female spouse killings are classified as argument-driven, while one-third of male spouse killings are attributed to jealousy[6] and another third to arguments. Only 5 percent of the women and 7 percent of the men are classified as mentally ill when they kill a spouse. Unfortunately, data on drinking and drugs involved in the murders are sketchy, but the literature indicates that most of these crimes involve the use of those substances by the victim and/or offender.

The most common weapon involved in spousal murder is a rifle or shotgun, regardless of sex of the perpetrator. Given the prevalence of handguns in the U.S., it is not surprising that these weapons are used far more often by both males and females in the U.S. than in Canada. In Canada, handguns constitute only 14 percent of the guns involved in female spouse/lover killings and 19 percent of those in which males are the perpetrator. About three-quarters of the spouse/lover incidents take place in the victim's home (no matter whether the offender was male or female). It is unclear from the data what proportion of those homes are also the offender's home.

Most spouse/lover killings involve individuals killing within the same age group. The average age of victim in spouse/lover killings is 37, while the average age for offenders is 39. More wives kill younger husbands than husbands kill younger wives.

PROFILE 4.1a

SPOUSE/ LOVER MURDER

Victim's Gender

Percent

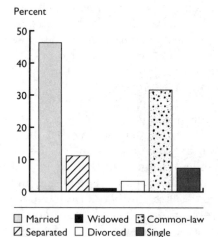

N = 2911.

Victim's Age

Percent

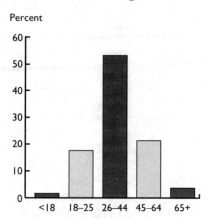

N = 2910 (excludes unknowns).

Victim's Marital Status

Percent

☐ Married ■ Widowed ⊞ Common-law
☒ Separated ☐ Divorced ■ Single

N = 2909 (excludes unknowns).

Victim's Race

Percent

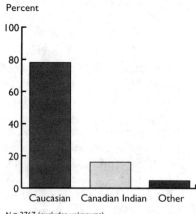

N = 2767 (excludes unknowns).

PROFILE 4.1b

SPOUSE/ LOVER MURDER

Suspect's Gender

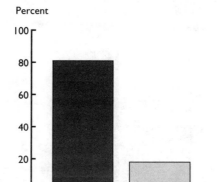

N = 2911.

Suspect's Age

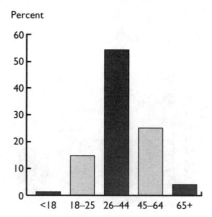

N = 2900 (excludes unknowns).

Suspect's Marital Status

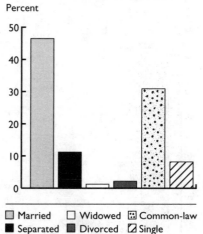

☐ Married ☐ Widowed ⊞ Common-law
■ Separated ■ Divorced ⧄ Single

N = 2900 (excludes unknowns).

Suspect's Race

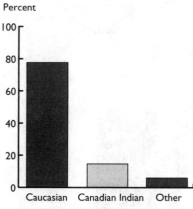

N = 2795 (excludes unknowns).

PROFILE 4.1c

SPOUSE/ LOVER MURDER

Means

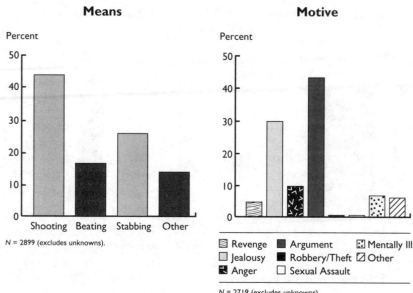

Percent

N = 2899 (excludes unknowns).

Shooting Beating Stabbing Other

Motive

Percent

Revenge ■ Argument ⊞ Mentally Ill
☐ Jealousy ■ Robbery/Theft ⧄ Other
■ Anger ☐ Sexual Assault

N = 2719 (excludes unknowns).

Suicide

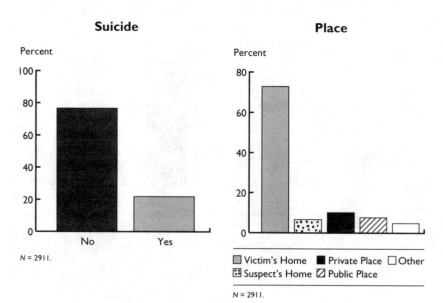

Percent

No   Yes

N = 2911.

Place

Percent

☐ Victim's Home ■ Private Place ☐ Other
⊞ Suspect's Home ⧄ Public Place

N = 2911.

Overall, Canadian Indians kill a spouse or a lover slightly less often than do non-natives (23 percent compared to 28 percent). It should be noted, though, that more of the Canadian Indian relationships are common-law than are the non-native relationships.

About 3 percent of women who kill their husbands follow the act by suicide, compared to 27 percent of men in the same category.[7] We can only assume that many of the cases of a female killing her husband involve abuse by the husband in the first instance; thus, the act is more likely followed by relief rather than remorse. The suicide of males in more than one-quarter of the wife-killing cases implies remorse for this most violent act.

Silverman and Mukherjee (1987) hypothesize that less stable marital relationships are more likely to result in murder. Their study shows that, indeed, murder rates in the "separated" groups are far higher than murder in any other marital group. Those who classify themselves as legally married, as well as those divorced, exhibit more stable relationships than those who have separated. In the case of separated couples, many of the details of the marital dissolution have not been worked out and the combatants are still in conflict about their relationship.[8] Jurik and Gregware (1992) include the following exemplary case in their study of homicides by women.

> The defendant and her ex-husband (the victim) were living together and attempting a reconciliation because the victim had promised to see a psychologist for his problems. During their marriage, the victim had been verbally and sexually abusive to the defendant and her daughter. On the evening of the offense, the defendant and the victim went out drinking at a bar. Afterwards, they began arguing outside the bar in the parking lot. There the victim was seen physically and verbally abusing the defendant .... The defendant shot the victim later that night while he was sleeping. In her ... interview, she stated that he had sworn to kill her when he awoke.

The above event was not the result of a one-time argument or display of anger but rather the culmination of ongoing marital hostilities.

Figure 4.2 shows murder rates for husbands, wives, and married couples. The reader will immediately see that there has not been a great deal of variance over the thirty-year period. There is a decline in recent years in all these categories, which all peak in 1973 and 1976. The rate for wives as victims is as much as four times that of husbands as victims.[9] Nonetheless, the rates are low in general and certainly are not rising. Gillis (1986) attributes at least some of the decline to more liberal divorce laws, which have removed the continued aggravation of a bad marriage. In terms of trends, spousal murder as a *proportion* of all murder is falling, but the *rate* has been relatively stable. This may mean that we can probably expect a spousal murder rate of 0.5 per 100,000 married couples in Canada despite changes in the law or changes in social conditions.

In sum, spousal murders appear to result most often from the problems, tensions, and conflicts endemic in dysfunctional marriages. Attempts to reduce the amount of interpersonal violence in these unions may, therefore, help to reduce the likelihood that they will end in a fatality. The prediction that spousal murder would be the most likely form of murder to be committed by women is supported. The problems women face in handling violence directed at them and in managing their own violence will be reviewed in greater detail in Chapter 6.

FIGURE 4.2

HUSBAND, WIFE, AND SPOUSAL MURDER, CANADA, 1961–1990*

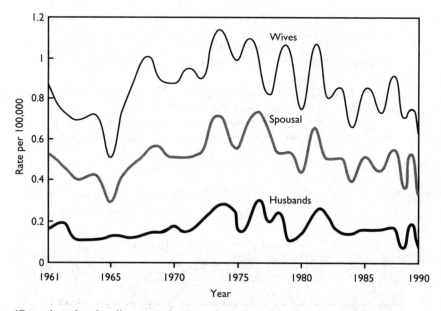

*Rates based on legally married men and women.

PARENTS WHO KILL THEIR CHILDREN

The second kind of homicide within the home involves parents who kill their children, one of the most tragic kinds of homicide. In a later chapter, we deal with children as a general category of victim (defined by age of victim) and describe the theories that best help explain violent actions against them. Here we describe the Canadian data for mothers and fathers who kill their children.

Homicide involving parents and children is often the result of serial violence in which the parent is the offender and the child the victim. The fatal act is likely inadvertent. The offender does not mean to kill the child but in a rage does so.

> ... RL a young father (aged 19), hit and killed his infant son while in an alcohol-fuelled rage. He then dumped the body into the Detroit river and the 15 year old mother and RL concocted a story about the baby being kidnapped. At the trial RL admitted that he had drunk about 22 bottles of beer the day that the seven month old baby died. It was a hot summer day and the baby was crying a lot. RL lost his temper and hit the baby. The autopsy showed that the infant died of beating that left him with head injuries, a punctured heart, bruises and a ruptured liver.
>
> The mother screamed at RL to stop and put the baby in its crib with a bottle. She then noticed that the baby was not breathing, grabbed him and started shaking him and yelled "he's dead"! RL then put the lifeless body in a green garbage bag and deposited it in the nearby river (Ferguson 1991).

This tragic case shows untrained, incompetent parents who are really just children themselves.

Between 1961 and 1990, there were 620 cases of a parent killing a child in Canada. Slightly more of these involve fathers (323) than mothers (298). In 12 percent of the cases in which fathers are perpetrators, and 6 percent of the cases in which mothers are perpetrators, there is more than one victim. Most fathers (96 percent) and mothers (95 percent) act alone.

While mothers kill daughters and sons in almost equal proportions, fathers are more likely to kill their sons (63 percent). Twenty-nine percent of the victims of fathers and 43 percent of the victims of mothers are less than 2 years old. In general, parents are most likely to kill their young children. Seventy-four percent of fathers' victims are under 13 years of age, while 94 percent of mothers' victims fall into that age group. Overall, only 10 percent of the cases involved the killing of an adult child (over 17).

PROFILE 4.2a

PARENTS AS SUSPECTS

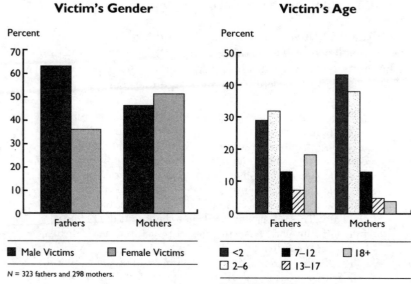

Victim's Gender

Percent

N = 323 fathers and 298 mothers.

Male Victims   Female Victims

Victim's Age

Percent

<2   7–12   18+
2–6   13–17

N = 323 fathers and 298 mothers.

Victim's Race

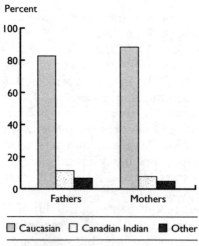

Percent

Caucasian   Canadian Indian   Other

N = 311 fathers and 288 mothers.

PROFILE 4.2b

PARENTS AS SUSPECTS

Suspect's Age

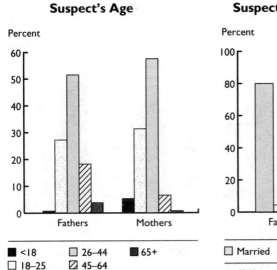

Percent

Suspect's Marital Status

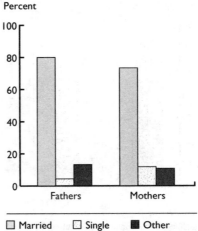

Percent

Suspect's Race

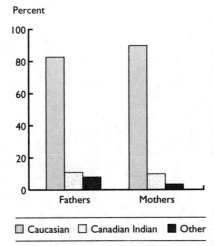

Percent

PROFILE 4.2c

PARENTS AS SUSPECTS

Means

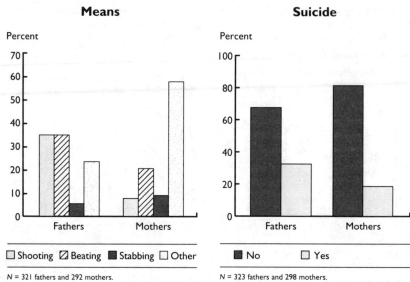

Percent

Fathers   Mothers

☐ Shooting ▨ Beating ■ Stabbing ☐ Other

N = 321 fathers and 292 mothers.

Suicide

Percent

Fathers   Mothers

■ No   ☐ Yes

N = 323 fathers and 298 mothers.

Place

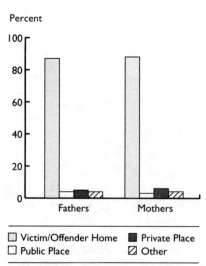

Percent

Fathers   Mothers

☐ Victim/Offender Home   ■ Private Place
☐ Public Place   ▨ Other

N = 318 fathers and 291 mothers.

Most cases of child killing involve Caucasians. Eighty-two percent of the fathers are Caucasian and 11 percent are Canadian Indians. Canadian Indian mothers account for 8 percent of the cases of mothers killing children, while 89 percent are Caucasian women. Offenders tend to be young. Twenty-seven percent of the fathers and 36 percent of the mothers are under 26 years old.

Thirty-five percent of fathers versus 9 percent of mothers kill their children by shooting. When guns are used, most (87 percent) involve long guns. Mothers most often use "other means" (59 percent), which include strangling and suffocating, to kill their children. For both fathers and mothers, use of hands is the most common type of action used to kill their children. Unlike other kinds of confrontations, these almost invariably involve unequal physical stature between the victim and the offender.

When fathers kill their children, the act is attributed[10] to "anger/argument" in about one-half of the cases. Sixty-one percent of mothers who kill their children are considered to be "insane" by those who do the classification. As we discuss in Chapter 6, this finding is an artifact of police coding rather than a reflection of reality.

The most common charge levelled against fathers and mothers following the killing of a child is second-degree murder (formerly noncapital murder). This probably reflects the fact that the primary intention is not killing. Following the homicide event, 32 percent of the fathers and 19 percent of the mothers commit suicide. Obviously, these events engender a good deal of remorse from the offender group.

We take up issues involving children as victims later in the book. Homicide patterns among individuals who are not as closely intertwined interpersonally as husbands and wives or parents and children, but who still maintain a blood tie through family connections, are quite different from those we have just examined.

OTHER FAMILY

Nonspousal family killings account for about 15 percent of all the murders that take place. However, if we deduct from these the cases that involve child-killing by either a natural parent, stepparent, or common-law parent, the "other family" category accounts for only 10 percent of all the murders that take place in Canada. As we have already examined parents killing children and spousal murder, the following analysis refers only to those remaining "other family" events.

PROFILE 4.3a

OTHER FAMILY

Victim's Gender

Percent

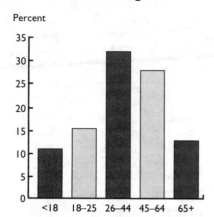

N = 1256 (excludes parent/child).

Victim's Age

Percent

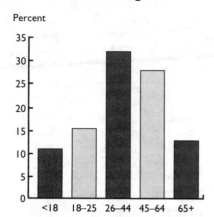

N = 1250   (excludes parent/child).

Victim's Marital Status

Percent

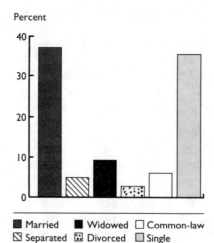

■ Married   ■ Widowed   ☐ Common-law
⧅ Separated   ⊞ Divorced   ▨ Single

N = 1245 (excludes parent/child).

Victim's Race

Percent

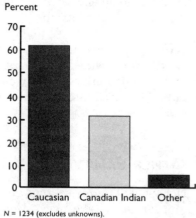

N = 1234 (excludes unknowns).

PROFILE 4.3b

OTHER FAMILY

Suspect's Gender

Percent

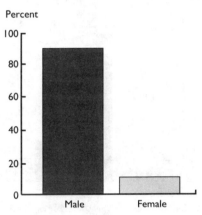

N = 1256 (excludes parent/child).

Suspect's Age

Percent

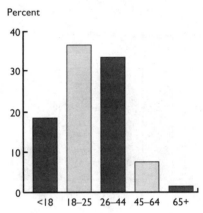

N = 1255 (excludes parent/child).

Suspect's Marital Status

Percent

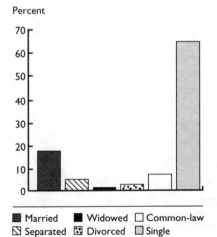

■ Married   ■ Widowed   □ Common-law
◩ Separated   ⊞ Divorced   ▨ Single

N = 1245 (excludes unknowns).

Suspect's Race

Percent

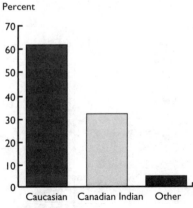

N = 1239 (excludes unknowns).

PROFILE 4.3c

OTHER FAMILY

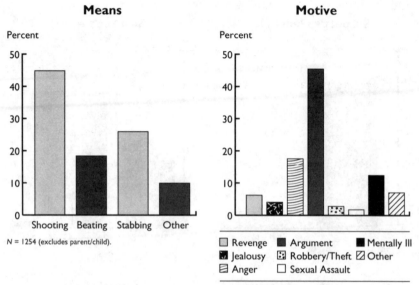

Means

Percent

Shooting   Beating   Stabbing   Other

N = 1254 (excludes parent/child).

Motive

Percent

☐ Revenge   ■ Argument   ■ Mentally Ill
▨ Jealousy   ⊡ Robbery/Theft   ▨ Other
▨ Anger   ☐ Sexual Assault

N = 1170 (excludes parent/child).

Place

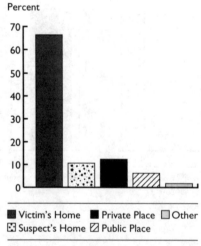

Percent

■ Victim's Home   ■ Private Place   ☐ Other
⊡ Suspect's Home   ▨ Public Place

N = 1180 (excludes parent/child).

We often assume that family should be "closer" than other individuals and that, therefore, grandparents should not be killing their grandchildren, sisters should not be killing brothers, and aunts should not be killing nephews, etc. However, any two people in such a relationship can find themselves in conflict-ridden situations. Certainly, routine activities put them into proximity with one another and social interaction coupled with the social circumstances of the moment may lead to violence. All of the social forces that lead to other kinds of homicide can be active in nonspousal family murders, with alcohol and/or drugs providing a similar spur to violent activities. The "other family" group is especially problematic in terms of intervention or prevention. Who, after all, can one target? We can attempt only to generate conditions in society that are not conducive to violence.

Ninety-one percent of the offenders in nonspousal family murders are male. About one-fifth are under 18 while 70 percent are between 18 and 44 years of age. Almost two-thirds are single and only about 18 percent of the suspects are married. Almost 80 percent of the sample has a Grade 10 or less education and 38 percent[11] indicate that their major occupation is labourer. The most surprising finding when examining family members (exclusive of children and spouses) is that 31 percent of the offenders are Canadian Indian while 61 percent are Caucasian. Canadian Indians perpetrate about 17 percent of total murders, which is the proportion that we would have expected here. The actual proportion is more than twice the involvement of Canadian Indians in murder overall and ten times their expected proportion based on population in Canada (about 2–3 percent of the total population).

Seventy-four percent of the victims are males while 27 percent are female. Victims tend to be somewhat older than offenders. About 60 percent fall between the ages of 26 and 64, while only 27 percent are under the age of 26. Forty-five percent of the victims are married while 36 percent are single. Like the offending group, 32 percent of the victims are Canadian native and 62 percent are Caucasian. Most of these events involve only one victim (92 percent) and one offender (94 percent). There is a slight increase in this kind of murder over the years, but at no point does it form a great proportion of total murders committed.

Most "other family" murders involve shooting (45 percent), followed by stabbing (26 percent) and beating (19 percent). These events occur after arguments (46 percent) or involve anger as a major motivating force (19 percent). About 13 percent are classified as involving mental illness. When shooting is the means, rifles and shotguns are the most common weapon and handguns are rarely used (8 percent). Killings of family members occur in the victim's/offender's home or semi-private places such as the workplace. They rarely occur in public places. It seems that the intimacy in kinship relationships is such that conflict and violence take place in the confines of private places. As would be expected in family or kinship relationships, the vast majority of these cases are intraracial in nature.

We have used suicide following murder as an indirect measure of the amount of remorse involved in murders. We expect that the closer the relationship, the more likely that suicide will follow murder (except in the case of wives killing husbands). While about 10 percent of all murders result in the suicide of the offender, only about 5 percent of the murders of other family members result in suicide—a sharply different picture than what we see in the case of parents killing their children, or even in the case of spousal murder (for men at least).

Canadian Indians kill other family members proportionately more often than do non-Indians (24 percent compared to 16 percent of all murders).[12] Canadian Indians living on reserves and even some in cities often live in close proximity to an extended family. Routine activities theory suggests that proximity and lifestyle would best predict victims of violent crime. Fully two-thirds of the murders in which a female Indian is the perpetrator involve a family member as a victim. Forty-five percent of female Canadian Indians kill their spouse (or lover) and another 19 percent involve other family members (though only 22 of the 357 cases involve a Canadian Indian woman's child). Much of this violence takes place in the victim's or offender's home.

In summary, "other family" murders share with spousal killings a strong focus on interpersonal conflict that occurs in private spaces. The opportunities for escalating tension in these relationships are no doubt less frequent than is the case between spouses, yet "other family" members can also experience an ongoing souring of relations. Killing among Canadian Indians in "other family" circumstances provides a special instance of family murder that should be pursued in future research.

FRIENDS AND ACQUAINTANCES[13]

The fear of homicide is often claimed to be a fear of strangers (Silverman and Kennedy 1987). But statistically you should be more afraid of your friends. The most common relationship between homicide offenders and victims outside of the family is that of friends and acquaintances. One-third of all murder incidents in which there was a known offender (3568) committed in Canada in the 1961–1990 period fall into the friends/acquaintances category.

PROFILE 4.4a

FRIENDS/ACQUAINTANCES

Victim's Gender

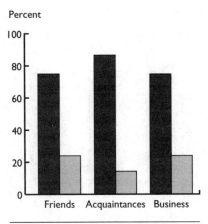

Percent

Male Victims   **Female Victims**

N = 1295 friends, 2022 acquaintances, and 255 business.

Victim's Age

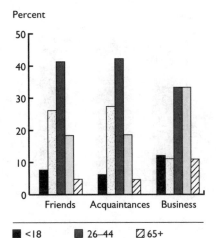

Percent

<18   **26–44**   **65+**
18–25   **45–64**

N = 1294 friends, 2019 acquaintances, and 255 business.

Victim's Marital Status

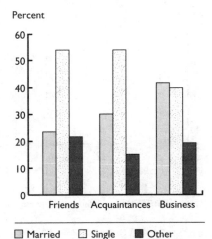

Percent

Married   **Single**   **Other**

N = 1276 friends, 1982 acquaintances, and 251 business.

Victim's Race

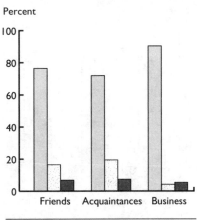

Percent

Caucasian   **Canadian Indian**   **Other**

N = 1244 friends, 1900 acquaintances, and 238 business.

PROFILE 4.4b

FRIENDS/ACQUAINTANCES

Suspect's Gender

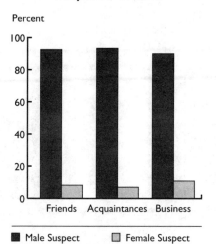

Percent

Male Suspect   Female Suspect

N = 1295 friends, 2022 acquaintances, and 255 business.

Suspect's Age

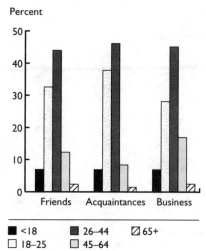

Percent

<18   26–44   65+
18–25   45–64

N = 1294 friends, 2021 acquaintances, and 255 business.

Suspect's Marital Status

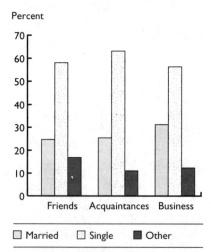

Percent

Married   Single   Other

N = 1271 friends, 1948 acquaintances, and 251 business.

Suspect's Race

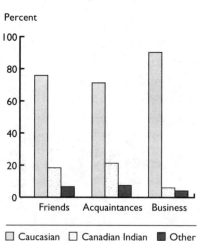

Percent

Caucasian   Canadian Indian   Other

N = 1253 friends, 1946 acquaintances, and 243 business.

PROFILE 4.4c

FRIENDS/ACQUAINTANCES

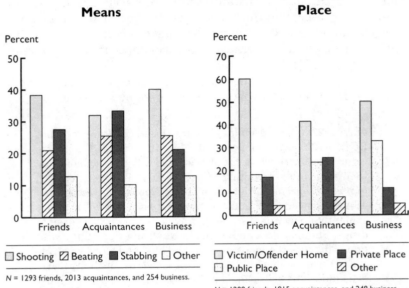

Means

Percent

50 40 30 20 10 0

Friends   Acquaintances   Business

☐ Shooting ▨ Beating ■ Stabbing ☐ Other

N = 1293 friends, 2013 acquaintances, and 254 business.

Place

Percent

70 60 50 40 30 20 10 0

Friends   Acquaintances   Business

☐ Victim/Offender Home   ■ Private Place
☐ Public Place   ▨ Other

N = 1209 friends, 1915 acquaintances, and 248 business.

This category is somewhat tricky to define. We stated earlier that we are interested in the intimacy between offenders and victims. Such relationships can be conceived of in terms of social distance. In terms of intimacy, spouse/lover relationships are certainly more intimate than stranger relationships no matter how stranger is defined. On the other hand, the friends/acquaintances category takes in a very broad spectrum of social relationships, ranging from the intimacy of spouses to the nonintimacy of strangers.

While the level of intimacy is a central component of most analysis of homicide relationships, friends and acquaintances rarely get "special" or separate treatment. There is a large and growing literature on various aspects of spousal homicide, and there is even a literature on the killing of children. Further, homicides that occur during the course of another crime and homicides by people with whom we have no previous relationship (i.e., stranger) have generated a good deal of interest (Riedel 1987). But friends and acquaintances are neglected even though they are the single largest group in Canada, next to family members, involved in homicide. Not only are they a large group but they are growing as a proportion of all homicide involvement.

Our suspicion as to why the friends/acquaintances category has not generated more research attention is that it is not a homogeneous group. Friends and acquaintances represent degrees of intimacy, ranging from feelings of closeness that rival any family intimacy to distance that borders on passing acquaintance. They represent the homicides occurring in and around barrooms and other public venues that make the morning press but attract little attention because of their distance from mainstream lifestyles. They also represent business relationships in which one individual kills another to gain control of the business or to avenge perceived betrayals in the business by a partner.

> JSA, a 21 year old male, is charged with beating to death ECD, a 20 year old acquaintance. ECD decided that she wanted to purchase "a hit of acid" and left the husband and their two children waiting in their van while she attempted to make a purchase. Outside of a local lounge she recognized JSA as someone she and her husband both knew. They also evidently knew that JSA could provide them with the desired drugs. She met JSA and walked away from the lounge with him. This was the last time that the husband saw her alive.
>
> ECD was beaten to death in a local downtown city park. "The multiple bruises and swelling to her head, throat, upper chest and breasts were indicative of 20 to 100 blows from either a foot or a fist." The mother of two had consumed alcohol during the day but was not intoxicated and there were no signs of sexual assault related to the incident.
>
> The motivations for the attack and the specifics of the interaction between the offender and this victim are unclear and illustrate to some extent the limits of attempting to explain this kind of acquaintance killing (Moysa 1991).

Friends and acquaintances would appear to fall into the category of opportunity crime based on situations that enhance conflict and sometimes fatal outcomes. Luckenbill (1977, 1984) examines such homicide as a "situated transaction." In a study of seventy murders, he concludes that such crimes result from "character contests" in which participants attempt to save face at each other's expense. These contests exhibit common patterns of escalation that produce lethal consequences for at least one of the contestants. According to Luckenbill, violent transactions are likely to be characterized by a combination of interactional properties that facilitate their violent conclusions. These properties include: (a) the attack by one party upon some aspect of the character of the other; (b) the attempt by the other to engage in some mildly aggressive identity-saving retaliation; (c) the first party's sustained or hardened attack; and (d) the neutrality or the encouragement of bystanders. Savitz et al. (1991) examine the propositions in Lukenbill's work and show that "of all the homicide cases in Philadelphia that could reasonably be judged (about the presence of a specified character contest immediately prior to the actual killing), over 60% contained the requisite 'contest of will.'"

Luckenbill and Doyle (1989) pursue these ideas with the notion of "disputatiousness." Their model suggests that individuals are distributed along certain structural dimensions and differ in their disputatiousness and aggressiveness. In essence, the worst-case scenario for violence involves a situation in which equals attack one another in a public setting. That is, given different propensities to violence, the situation and interaction will determine the potential of a violent outcome. This type of violence appears to derive from the problems of individuals lacking self-control, who lash out at others in an attempt to harm or gain retribution for loss of face.

Felson and Steadman (1983) report, in their research on cases taken from New York State, a systematic pattern to violent confrontations. The events begin with some kind of character or identity attack that is followed by an attempt to influence the antagonist. Threats are made, evasive action is attempted, and the verbal conflict ends in physical conflict (59). They find that assaults occur when the victim will not comply with the offender's wishes (a finding in concordance with Luckenbill's). Retaliation is important in these events, but it is unclear if retaliation is a face-saving technique or a strategic pose. Further, there is reciprocity in the interactions of victims and offenders. Antagonists respond in kind to aggressive acts. Also, alcohol is present in many of these events.

Felson and Steadman (1983) find that third-party mediation has no effect in reducing the negative outcomes of these conflicts. Third parties attempt to mediate in only about 10 percent of the acts and more often "were likely to engage in aggressive acts or to instigate the conflict" (66). The influence of third parties on the homicide scene is often neglected or forgotten in analysis. Here the problem is simply that if these data are recorded by the police, they rarely get put into a form that is usable for analysis.

Felson and Steadman make some interesting observations about the complexity surrounding victim precipitation in these circumstances. They suggest that they cannot with certainty say who precipitates the event. Certainly, the victim is aggressive and therefore accounts for at least some of the subsequent action.

On the other hand, the offender is more aggressive. There is, of course, also a measurement problem in all this. Not only is the overt expression of aggression important but so are perceptions of the aggressive behaviour. For the moment, it is instructive to know that these events involve interaction and follow a discernible pattern.

Ray and Simons (1987) examine twenty-five homicide offenders. Thirteen of the cases involve friend/acquaintance relationships and only six cases involve a stranger. Six of the offenders justify their actions. They take responsibility for the homicide but say that the victim deserved it. (A couple cite earlier disputes and four cite self-defence as the reason for the killing.) Eighteen respondents provide accounts that they believe excuse or partially excuse their actions. Eight claim debilitating intoxication, four blame stress, three relate a combination of circumstance and intoxication, and three blame scapegoats (1987:64). According to the researchers, some of the offenders may have belonged to a violent subculture but most are members of the lower social strata and manifest many of the problems often seen in that life circumstance—family disputes, alcohol and drug dependence, and periodic unemployment. They are characterized as "living rather dead-end lives." It is interesting to note that the excerpts from transcripts provided in this research contain examples of what others might have classified as "character contests" or "fitting the scenario" as defined by Felson and Steadman. The authors warn that their results should not be generalized to larger urban areas because their setting was a smaller community. It is fair to say that given the 20,000 or so homicides that take place annually in the U.S., these findings should not be generalized at all, but they are nevertheless provocative and worthy of further examination.

The conceptualizations of violent episodes as victim-precipitated or situational transactions all suggest that it is useful to view such episodes as more than a product of the will or motivation of the violent offender. They imply the need to understand violent crime, in general, and homicide, in particular, as an outcome of a dynamic interplay between offenders and victims. The archetype experience of this kind of homicide is the barroom brawl. Young macho single males, likely those with low self-control, interact in a challenging, almost ritualistic, manner that often leads to verbal or physical violence. Given the numbers of young males who go to bars to drink on a regular basis, the total number of violent acts is small.

Machismo as a motivator for murder is well illustrated in the case of "Frank S."[14]

Frank grew up in an abusive home. His mother was a deeply religious woman who beat Frank often. At school he was strapped for defiant behaviour. He was a slow learner and when the kids teased him by calling him stupid, he'd fly into a rage and fight them. He was a good fighter and won—giving him a sense of self-worth. He dropped out of school at 15 and got into crime. He did break and enters and robberies but because of his religious upbringing he often felt guilty about these. At the same time, the life was exciting and he was his own boss. He did some prison time for these crimes. In sum, he was a tough guy, leading a risky lifestyle. The murder occurred when his ex-crime-partner's brother, Ron, came to stay with Frank and his wife. Frank's wife asked Ron to help with some household chore and Ron rudely insulted her. Frank decided that with the insult Ron had signed his own death warrant. He asked Ron to join him in a hunting expedition later that day. By the time they got to the site, Frank's anger had cooled and he really did not want to kill Ron. He "argued with his self" about whether to do it or not and concluded that "it was out of self-esteem that I finally decided to do it. How could a tough guy like me not do it," he pondered. It would not have been manly to walk away from this, so he shot Ron and left him by a stream where they had gone to hunt. Frank was found guilty of first degree murder.

The situational approach can be put into a risky lifestyle framework. Those who value a lifestyle permeated by machismo values, drinking in bars, and violent encounters will more likely engage in the kinds of behaviours and interactions discussed by these researchers. The situational approach would be much improved if the research distinguished the specific social relationships of victims and offenders. It would be interesting to examine differences in victim/offender interactions based on degree of intimacy.

Because of the wide range of relationships involved in the friends/acquaintances category, it may be best to start with a description of which relationships are actually involved. Of those cases in which both the offender and the victim are known and the relationship has been established, only 7 percent of the friend/acquaintance situations are classed as business relationships. Thirty-six percent are "close friends" while 56 percent are described as casual acquaintances. In organizing the profile of offenders, victims, and the offence for these crimes, we think it best to distinguish between the three kinds of relationships. They represent different degrees of intimacy, though it is possible for any of the three to generate intense relationships.

About 93 percent of the offenders in friend/acquaintance-type murder are males. Of the 3572 cases, only 241 involve a female offender. This in itself is interesting as Jurik and Gregware (1992) show that the "situated transaction approach" of Luckenbill (1984) discussed above works much better for male than for female offenders. They argue that other explanations are better suited to instances in which women are offenders. The framework that separates murders into social relationships allows for such an analysis. In the case of friends/acquaintances, we are more likely to be dealing with situations where the impression management explanation works better than in other types of murder.

Whether we are dealing with a close friend, casual acquaintance, or a business relationship, most of the offenders (60 percent) are single. Canadian Indians kill friends and acquaintances in about the same proportion as non-natives. In the case of friendship relationships, Canadian Indians commit 19 percent of homicides involving a close friend and 21 percent involving a casual acquaintance. On the other hand, they are involved in only 6 percent of murder resulting from business quarrels. Conversely, Caucasian offenders commit about 75 percent of close-friend murders and 72 percent of casual-acquaintance murders, while being responsible for 90 percent of business relationship-murders.

In terms of work history, about 46 percent of those who kill close friends and 46 percent of those who kill casual acquaintances list themselves as either in the construction industry or as labourers. The occupation of those killed in a business relationship is spread out through our categories but includes 10 percent in construction, 9 percent managerial, 7 percent manufacturing/mechanical trades, and 23 percent labourers. Most of the killing in these categories is intraracial.

When males kill close friends, 76 percent of their victims are other males; when they kill business associates, 77 percent are male victims; and, when they kill acquaintances, men constitute 87 percent of victims. When women kill in this category, 23 percent of the close friends (N=22), 32 percent of the acquaintances (N=39), and 36 percent of the business associates (N=9) are other women.

Age also differentiates the three kinds of relationships. In the case of close friends, 40 percent of the offenders are under the age of 26 while 34 percent of the victims fall into this category. For casual acquaintances, proportions for the same categories are 45 percent and 33 percent respectively. For business acquaintances, however, both victims and offenders tend to be older; close to 80 percent of the victims are 26 years of age or older, while about 65 percent of the offenders fall into this category.

About half of the victims in close-friend and casual-acquaintance relationships and 39 percent of business associates are single. Most of these killings are intraracial—therefore, it is not surprising that the race of the victim reflects the race of the offender. Ninety-one percent of business-relationship victims and about three-quarters of those in close friendships or casual acquaintances are Caucasian. Conversely, 17 percent of the victims in close friendships and 20 percent in casual acquaintances are Canadian Indians compared to 4 percent of the victims in business relationships. As might be expected, these kinds of events involve suicide only about 3 percent of the time. Less than 2 percent of casual-acquaintance killing, 6 percent of close-friendship killing, and 5 percent of business-relationship killing is followed by the suicide of the offender.

Close to 40 percent of close-friendship killings and business-relationship killings involve shooting. The second most popular method of killing is stabbing, which is followed by beating. However, in casual-acquaintance murder, one-third involve shooting, one-third are stabbings, and 26 percent are beatings. Interestingly, about two-thirds of acquaintance killings are attributed by police to an argument or to anger. But in the case of business relationships, one-third are considered arguments, 17 percent revenge, and 13 percent "mental illness." Casual-acquaintance killing is the most likely to take place in a public place (about 26 percent), while about one-half of business-relationship murder takes place in the victim's or suspect's home, as does close-friendship murder. This makes sense. Close friendship and business relationships imply an intimacy that is not implied by casual acquaintances. All three kinds of events overwhelmingly involve single victims. However, casual-acquaintance murder is slightly more likely to involve more than one offender (11 percent) than the other two kinds.[15]

Another example of drug involvement in a friend-killing illustrates the complexities of circumstances that can lead to murder.

> MW killed a female friend. He went to her house looking for things to steal which he could later sell in order to support his drug habit. He was surprised to find JC, his female friend, at home. He stayed overnight at her place and during the night began to hear voices and hallucinate. Eventually he experienced overwhelming paranoia after he had injected cocaine (the next morning). He claims to have borrowed a rifle to fire shots at imaginary people outside and then to inadvertently point the rifle at JC. He said he kept on firing because he did not know whether he was shooting or being shot.

Psychiatrists, acting as defence witnesses, suggested that it would have been very difficult for MW to form intent given his delusions and hallucinations. The judge was more impressed with evidence from two other forensic psychiatrists who suggested that the killing was intentional. JC was shot eight times at close range. Ultimately, the cocaine addict was sentenced to eight years in prison for manslaughter of his female friend (Barrett 1992).

FIGURE 4.3

TRENDS IN FRIEND/AQUAINTANCES MURDER, CANADA, 1961–1990

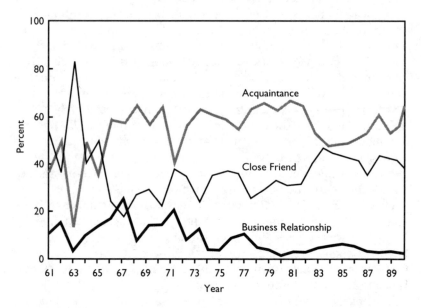

Figure 4.1 showed the growth of friend/acquaintance murders when compared to the other relationships. Figure 4.3 shows trends in the three types of friend/acquaintance murder as they relate to each other. In the early 1960s, friend/acquaintance murder represents only 24 percent of all murders. In the early 1980s, it constitutes 40 percent of all murders (just slightly less than the total amount of all family murder). There is a discernible trend toward growth in the acquaintance category, while the others either fall or remain stable. There are some anomalies in the trends, however. For instance, between 1961 and 1965, close friends are the most likely members of this group to be killed.

After 1965, this proportion drops and then stabilizes toward a slowly rising trend up to 1983 when it again accounts for about 46 percent of these cases. On the other hand, the proportion of business-related murders grows somewhat until the late 1960s but undergoes a slow declining trend through the rest of the period. Since 1965, the casual-acquaintance group has had the highest proportion of friend/acquaintance killing. With the exception of drops in 1971 and in 1982–86, this group has been relatively stable, falling in the 60–65 percent of friend/acquaintance murder range. These trends seem to confirm speculation that the more distant relationships have become dominant in the friend/acquaintance category.

STRANGERS

Riedel (1992) points out that while we fear strangers most, we often find ourselves among strangers. That is, we live in a society in which we depend upon strangers for our goods and services. While most of our time is spent in the intimate environment of our home or the environment of acquaintances and friends at work, in going to or from work (or school) or going out shopping or to an entertainment event we are surrounded by strangers. How can we tell if the stranger approaching us is a threat? We rarely can. We cannot tell until the threat (physical or visual) is made. Under most circumstances, we act as if no one is a threat. We follow the general rules of behaviour and routines we have learned and assume that others will do so also. We expect neither confrontation nor challenge from those we pass on the street or encounter in a bank or bar. In fact, of the countless encounters between strangers each day "a small fraction results in violence for a few people" and even fewer result in death (Riedel 1992).

Still, fear of strangers is an entrenched part of our public psyche. Strangers represent the unknown. We do have routine ways of avoiding interactions with strangers or formal methods of dealing with them. There are certain kinds of small talk that is appropriate when dealing with checkout persons at grocery stores, and there are actually quite rigid rituals and normative behaviour involved in riding on an elevator with strangers. These routines allow us to move through public space in ways that allow us to avoid conflict and maintain orderly relations with others.

Breaking routines is what makes individuals feel vulnerable to the stranger. At these times, it is difficult to assess the reactions of people that one does not know or with whom one has had

PROFILE 4.5a

STRANGER MURDER

Victim's Gender

Percent

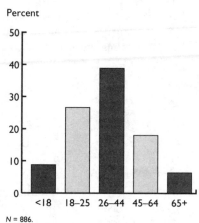

N = 886.

Victim's Age

Percent

N = 886.

Victim's Marital Status

Percent

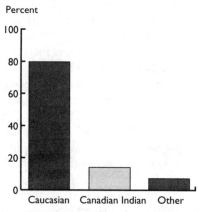

■ Married ■ Widowed □ Common-law
▨ Separated ⊡ Divorced □ Single

N = 865 (excludes unknowns).

Victim's Race

Percent

N = 825 (excludes unknowns).

PROFILE 4.5b

STRANGER MURDER

Suspect's Gender

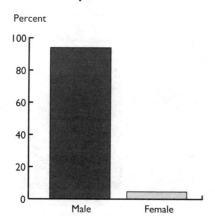

Percent

N = 886.

Suspect's Age

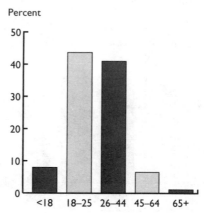

Percent

N = 882 (excludes unknowns).

Suspect's Marital Status

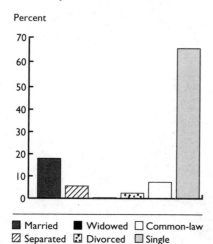

Percent

■ Married   ■ Widowed   ☐ Common-law
▨ Separated ▣ Divorced ☐ Single

N = 836 (excludes unknowns).

Suspect's Race

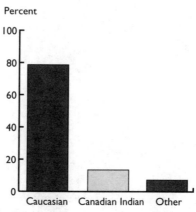

Percent

N = 826 (excludes unknowns).

PROFILE 4.5c

STRANGER MURDER

Means

Motive

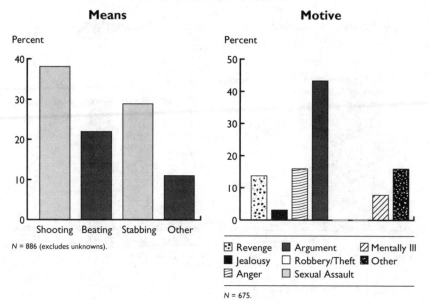

Percent

N = 886 (excludes unknowns).

⊡ Revenge   ■ Argument   ▨ Mentally Ill
■ Jealousy   ☐ Robbery/Theft   ▩ Other
▨ Anger   ☐ Sexual Assault

N = 675.

Place

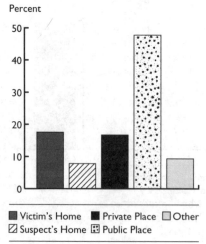

Percent

■ Victim's Home   ■ Private Place   ☐ Other
▨ Suspect's Home   ⊡ Public Place

N = 827 (excludes unknowns).

no previous contact. Any act of violence by strangers toward others seems illogical as it does not appear to be motivated by the factors that generate conflict in intimate relations. The apparent unpredictability and randomness of certain stranger homicides contribute to the view that this type of homicide is difficult to avoid and protect against.

In reality, 60 percent of the murders perpetrated by strangers in Canada occur during or after the commission of another crime. Where there is no previous crime, the fact that people are classified as "strangers" is more likely an error in the reporting process than the reality in many instances (Polk 1990). Often there is also some kind of interaction between victim and offender in crimes in which murder is a byproduct of the offence. For instance, the eventual victim enters a bar and talks with a stranger over drinks for the period of time. They may exchange first names or no names at all. The victim slights the offender in some way. A fight that results in a fatal outcome ensues. Is this a stranger murder? In the police report, it would likely be classified as "no known previous relationship"—a stranger murder. This is a troublesome classification as it was the victim/offender interaction that led to the assault/murder. Similarly, the victim who is kidnapped by a serial killer, even though she or he may be a stranger at first, interacts with the offender for a fair amount of time before the actual killing takes place. The interaction itself may trigger the ultimate outcome.[16]

MA, 25, was charged with second degree murder after an argument between himself and another motorist at a suburban Toronto intersection. SL, the victim, 34, was shot because of a dispute over the victim's driving habits. One of the cars was driven by a security guard from an automatic teller machine service. His car and that of the assailant were involved in a "cat and mouse" chase which erupted into an argument between the occupants of the cars after the cars had stopped. MA approached the other car and got into an argument. The security guard was hit in the face with a bottle. Another man then shot SL at point blank range. "His chest was all smashed up and he was bleeding from the mouth and his eyelids were fluttering," reported a witness.

Details of this Scarborough, Ontario case are rather confusing but the case involves individuals who did not know each other but were involved in an interaction before the event which resulted in one individual being shot to death (*Edmonton Journal* 1991b).

Both Riedel (1992) and Polk (1990) point out that there are different kinds of strangers. The unknown person walking down a street is qualitatively different from the stranger who enters your office. There are tacit assumptions made about the latter that cannot be made about the former. Simply indicating that the stranger is unknown does not help much (Riedel 1992). Gillis (1986:135) points out "that injuries or insults that could be considered minor if inflicted by a stranger may elicit outrage if perpetrated by a loved one. In the latter case there has been a violation of trust and the gap between expected and actual behaviour is wider."

We have divided stranger murders into those that occur during or after the commission of a crime and those in which there is no known relationship between victim and offender. Those that occur in conjunction with another crime account for 12 percent of all Canadian murder (averaged over the 1961–90 period) and are discussed in the next chapter. Those in which there is no known motive account for about 7 percent (N=886) of murder incidents but have never accounted for more than 13 percent (in 1980).

While seemingly motiveless, stranger murders account for only 7 percent of all murder, these generate the most fear in the general population because any one of us or a loved one might become a victim.

> In August 1988, a 29 year old mother of two was beaten and strangled in a downtown Edmonton Light Rail Transit (subway) washroom. When her body was discovered at 2:30 p.m. (by a woman who was going to use the washroom) clothing and personal items were missing (*Edmonton Sun* 1988).

The case of Cathy Greeve became almost daily news in Edmonton until the perpetrator, subject of a massive search effort, was apprehended. The story of this "stranger" killing emerged gradually.

> Ronald Nienhuis told police he panicked and killed Cathy Greeve accidentally. He saw her outside of the washroom in the Light Rail Transit station. He was attracted to her. After an attempt at conversation he thought she liked him and he acted on that assumption—"I reached over and gave her ass a feel." She screamed. He grabbed her by the throat and pushed her into the washroom. She fought all the way. He pushed her against the wall. According to Nienhuis she went down and did not come up again. He claims that he tried to revive her but when she did not respond, he decided that she was dead. To make the event look like a robbery and a sex crime he took her skirt and panties. He disposed of these articles nearby. He tried to prop her up but she kept falling so he

tied her pantyhose around her neck with the other end attached to the toilet hand hold. She had received two blows to the head but she died of strangulation as a result of the "noose" around her neck. Nienhuis claims to have been "stone-drunk" throughout the event (Barrett 1990).

Although charged with first-degree murder, ultimately Nienhuis was found guilty of manslaughter because there was not enough evidence to prove intent. Needless to say, this neither pleased the family of Cathy Greeve nor a public that wants these strangers who generate so much fear punished with the full force of the law.

Stranger murder in Canada is a male domain (96 percent). Perpetrators are young (about half are under 26 years of age), single (62 percent), and Caucasian (79 percent). They tend to kill in public places (48 percent) and rarely in a victim's home (17 percent). This clearly distinguishes them from other subgroups of murder offenders. Most often they shoot their victims to death (40 percent), but stabbing (29 percent) and beating (22 percent) are also common. As one would expect, few of these crimes are followed by suicide of the offender (3 percent). About one-quarter of stranger murders result in no motive being classified. Of the rest, 42 percent are classified by police as arguments. This lends some credence to Polk's (1990) argument that these are not really "strangers" in the sense of never having had any interaction at all.

Victim demographics are somewhat different from offenders. While most are male (80 percent), they tend to be older than or come from the same age group as offenders. Thirty-six percent of victims are under 26 years of age and 39 percent fall into the 26–44 age category. Like offenders, most are single (54 percent) and Caucasian (80 percent).

The fact that the majority of stranger murders take place in public places and are often the result of what the police have called "arguments" confirms our earlier discussion about the role that public lifestyles can play in creating risk and is one of the distinguishing features of this kind of crime. Ninety-four percent of stranger murders involve only one victim, but 16 percent have more than one offender. The latter proportion is substantially less than occurs in "crime-based murder" but greater than is found in the more intimate family categories.

The categorization of murders by social relationship provides an important basis by which we can discern differences in routines and in the nature of the social conflict that develops between individuals. The risky lifestyle that entails being in public places exposed to strangers provides a different type of threat from the lifestyle of living in a domestic relationship that is violent and abusive. The outcome may be fatal in either situation, but the precautions that one can take and the predictability of the outcome are clearly quite different. The avoidance of dangerous public places may be an easy strategy to follow, but the avoidance of violence in domestic relationships is often complicated by dependency, the presence of children, and fear of reprisal.

Issues of lifestyle are confronted again in later chapters. A final example points out the difficulty of classifying stranger murders.

> EJF stabbed to death DJC at a notorious Edmonton hotel. They had been drinking. They argued over a glass of beer. They pushed one another prior to the fatal attack. Bouncers separated the two but as EJF was being pulled away from DJC he reached around a corner with his knife and stabbed DJC in the heart. He could not see DJC but knew where he was. It was a fatal stab in the dark. As intent to kill could not be proved, EJC was convicted of manslaughter (Plischke 1992).

The newspaper article classifies them as "strangers," but can we really be satisfied that the protagonists were strangers and not acquaintances by the time of the event? And if the assault had not been fatal, who would be the victim and who would be the offender? These questions are not easily resolved but they are important when we think about the relationships involved and the peculiarities of internecine assaultive behaviour.

SUMMARY

This chapter has provided a great deal of evidence that the social relationship of victims and offenders can be very influential in defining the circumstances of the homicide event. The level of intimacy can promote strong emotional reactions that culminate in out-of-control conflict or can be so distant as to diminish the impact of the murder on the offender. The domestic murder that evolves from sustained conflict obviously differs greatly from the barroom murder that emerges from a short but heated exchange. The application of the theories of social control and routine activities to these relationships illustrates how common elements of risky lifestyles can lead to fatal outcomes. Let us turn now to events in which relationship is not as useful a tool in explaining homicides, namely those cases based on crime or sex, which sometimes culminate in serial or mass murders.

NOTES

1. Nonintimate.

2. Victim/offender relationship is divided into five categories. The most intimate group is labelled *spouse/lover* and includes husbands, wives (legal and common-law), estranged lovers, and those identified as involved in a love triangle. It represents those relationships in which there was likely "romantic involvement" and a good deal of intimate interaction. The second group consists of *family members* (legal and common-law) such as parents, grandparents, nieces, nephews, uncles, aunts, and siblings. The third (more socially distant) category of *friends/acquaintances* comprises victims and offenders involved in business relationships, friendships, casual acquaintances, and other nonkinship relationships. *Strangers* include those who shared no known domestic or other relationship.

3. This section describes intergender spousal homicide. The term "spouse" is used to encompass intimate relationships between males and females. In some of the analysis, only legal marriage is considered, but that is a narrow category. For all intents and purposes, the offenders and victims in the group to be described are males who have killed females or females who have killed males in situations in which the police report described their relationship as a spouse, ex-spouse, or lover. Same-sex homicides (14 female and 200 male) are omitted from the analysis because, while certain aspects of their relationship are the same as intersexual relationships, other aspects are different enough to eliminate them. In the case of spouse/lover homicide, we are dealing with a dyad. It makes sense to compare and contrast males who kill their mate with females who kill their mate.

4. Four hundred and ninety-one out of 2357 cases were "unknown" occupation.

5. The finding that wives most often stab and husbands most often shoot is a persistent one in the literature (Wolfgang 1976; Howard 1986).

6. By the police.

7. Wolfgang (1976), using Philadelphia data, found that 19 percent of the husbands and 2 percent of the wives followed the homicide by suicide.

8. As pointed out earlier, the proportion of homicide involving spousal relationships has declined. But, of course, that decline is in relationship to a homicide rate that has been generally climbing. In order to see the homicide trend for intimate unions, the best we could do was calculate homicide rates for legally married couples. It is almost impossible to find a population base for common-law couples.

9. There are more or less equal numbers of married males and females, but there were 1302 incidents involving female victims of husbands and only 271 incidents of male victims of wives. (Again, legally defined marriage is the only type of union included in these data.)

10. By the police in coding the event.

11. Of the cases in which occupation is reported.
12. Includes killing of children.
13. At the time of the killing, "friend" is obviously a misnomer, but "former friend" is too awkward to make a useful label.
14. From Ray Enright's interview files. Names have been changed.
15. This likely reflects the nature of internecine conflict among acquaintances (e.g., in bars).
16. The term used in the statistical coding of this information is "no known previous relationship," which really means no relationship before the events that lead up to the homicide.

C H A P T E R 5

Crimes
SEXUAL, THEFT, SERIAL, AND MASS MURDER

The homicide data gathered by police and compiled by Statistics Canada provide a categorization of events based on the fact that the killing occurs during or after another crime has taken place. While many of these murders could probably be coded as stranger-based, the fact that they accompany another crime makes them interesting in and of themselves.

We will probe the different types of crime-based murder in this chapter, emphasizing the opportunity factors associated with the initial crime, as well as the subsequent murder. In addition, we include a discussion of serial and mass murders. Serial killing is often closely tied to sex crimes, while mass murder may or may not involve close relationships.

CRIME-BASED MURDER

GUNS FOR HIRE

Television and other media have popularized the concept of the hit man so well that it is a part of general knowledge and conversation. The life and times of the hit man have been glamorized in films such as *Prizzi's Honor*. If robbery is the ultimate form of street crime, then contract-killing is the ultimate form of premeditated murder. The criminal law defines first-degree murder as "planned and deliberate"—this is a keynote of contract-killing.

Planned and deliberate murder that involves a hired killer, is execution. The motivation from the point of view of the killer is simply the payment for doing the crime (money or perhaps drugs). There may be other motivations if one is part of an organization that kills as a matter of course. That is, in the classic mob-style killing the killer is also doing the job as a sign of loyalty to the organization. One means of mob killing is arson, which is used as a technique of revenge against rivals. We do not really differentiate these kinds of killings from those in which there is an individual contract on a single person. The motive in both cases is likely revenge.

In Canada, when we learn of a contract-killing it is because it has gone wrong. At least some of the unsolved homicides in Canada likely involve either a contract-killing (e.g., murdering a spouse for insurance money or infidelities) or a killing linked to organized crime. A prime location for contract-killings is the large city. Montreal in particular has a history of this kind of crime in Canada. The headline of the *Gazette* on July 15, 1981 reads "Police have solutions to only one-third of Montreal Murders." Of the forty-four murders in the area, seven were believed to involve "the underworld settling accounts."

Donald Lavoie took part in at least twenty-seven killings while he acted as an "enforcer" for organized crime in the Montreal area in the 1970s. Lavoie pulled the trigger in fifteen of these hits. He is "soft-spoken, articulate and introspective." (*Gazette*, May 11, 1983). For some reason, he fell out of favour with the organization and was slated for termination. When he learned of this, Lavoie turned informer and testified in several murder trials in Montreal. His testimony alone resulted in convictions in many cases that were formerly "unsolved." As an informer, Lavoie was questioned about the circumstances of seventy-six murders and "shed light on all of them" (*Maclean's* 1982). He received immunity from the murders in which he was involved (but not from some of the other crimes) and was placed under police protection.

A 1985 newspaper interview with Lavoie lends some insight into the mind of a contract killer:

Alain Stanke: How old are you?

Donald Lavoie: I am 42 years old. My life can be split into three stages: my childhood, my 12 years as a criminal and killer and now my new life.

Q: What do you remember from your childhood?

A: The only thing I remember from my early years is the fact that I was a child, like all the other ones. I lived in a normal family. A father, a mother, brother and a sister. Then, when I was 6, my parents split and I was sent into an orphanage. This is what I remember best: the separation of my parents and the orphanage. I have never accepted it. I don't wish to say that one is predestined for crime because of an unhappy childhood. But I think it was a factor. I considered it unjust to be put in an orphanage while having parents. I didn't accept that situation. I reacted by refusing authority, by being unruly and undisciplined. I would be punished—often too severely. I was given a cold bath lasting two, and sometimes three hours. I was forced to sleep in my underwear during the winter nights on ice-cold tile floors. Not all my teachers were like that, some were more humane.

Q: Were you ever an altar boy?

A: Yes. I liked helping out at the altar and being in the presence of priests. I knew mass by heart. I liked to dress as a priest, and to play reading mass.

Q: Did you wish to become a priest?

A: Yes, I would have liked it.

Q: You then believed in God?

A: Yes, I believed in God and I still do. I'll believe in God forever.

Q: As a child did you make any plans for the future?

A: My only dream was to get out of the orphanage and go back home. Unfortunately this never happened.

Q: And your first love affair, do you remember?

A: I must have been 17 or 18, I don't think it made a deep impression on me.

Q: How about the first time you had sexual intercourse?

A: That goes back to the day when I got my first paycheck of $35. I offered myself to a prostitute.

Q: Do you remember the first time you saw a dead person as a child?

A: I must have been 6 years old then. I remember indeed. It was my grandfather. I was asleep in the orphanage. It was probably 10 o'clock at night. They woke me up. My father took me home. There was violet drapery and beautiful candlesticks. Everybody was weeping. It was my first contact with death.

Q: Do you remember your first robbery?

A: It happened in my hometown. I managed to get into a grocer's shop after removing a window. I stole cigarettes, watches and I emptied some cash registers. The next day, it was a front-page story in the newspaper. It was the first time that I saw my offence in the press. The paper called it a "professional robbery." I was flattered.

Q: Do you have any children?

A: Yes, four. Two with one woman and two with another woman.

Q: Do you remember the day your first child was born?

A: I remember the birth of all my children. I was present during their births. I prefer not to talk about my children.

Q: What is the most beautiful thing you remember in your life?

A: Good Lord. I don't have many nice memories. I have none. I spent my childhood in an orphanage. There is nothing nice that can happen to you there. Still, once, when I was about 12 years old, one of my professors took me to his home in Montreal during a holiday and there I saw television for the first time in my life ... That's all in the way of nice memories. As to my adult life, there is nothing nice in it.

Q: You have participated in some 30 murders. How many people did you kill with your own hands?

A: I would say about ... 15. When I decided to change my life in 1980, I provided the police with very precise information about 76 murders.

Q: For how many years did you work as a hired killer?

A: Twelve years.

Q: What did you do to join the underworld?

A: It was the result of a spell of despondency. After losing my job, I wound up in a bar located in an ill-famed area of Montreal. There, I ran into a man named Claude Dubreau and a bunch of criminals. We rapidly became friends and that's how it all started. I needed money, so I borrowed some from a man named Claude Dubois and immediately I entered the world of the "untouchables." They were all murderers, all killers. To be part of the team, one had to prove his worth. One had to be a killer. Otherwise, he could not belong.

Q: What was your reaction the first time they asked you to kill somebody?

A: It's a chain reaction. When the "big boss" told me to do it, it seemed to me to be logical. There was no way out. "The man to kill," he said, "is very dangerous and if you don't kill him, it's he who will kill you or send you to jail" … which is not a more pleasant alternative. I don't think there was a choice for us.

Q: And you "bought" it without any discussion?

A: First, I was convinced that sparing the life of the man in question would have been unwise because of the risks it entailed and then, I had no choice in the face of the big boss and his henchmen. In a world of this sort, you don't try to be different and play your own part. If you do it, you may be sure you won't do it very long. Your own friends will take care of you and put two bullets through your head …

Q: As to your first murder, did you do it alone or were you a mere "assistant"?

A: I didn't do the first one all by myself. I was just helping. It was brutal. It was done with a shovel.

Q: What impression do you still have today?

A: I found they went about it in the most difficult way there is to kill a person. I admit I didn't feel at ease that night.

Q: But it wasn't enough to make you drop that profession?

A: After that murder, once it was done with I tried to forget … but since I stayed with the group I just carried on. It's easy to kill. Anyone can do it.

Q: Before killing a person, did you pause and ask why were you going to do it?

A: No, never. I didn't have to think about it. As I have said, there was no choice. I did most of the murders simply because I had orders to do it. And then, once you have killed a person, it's easy to do it a second, a third time …

Q: Did you commit your murders with a weapon?

A: Yes, a pistol. Much of the time with a .375 magnum, sometimes in another way …

[Once, when he was under the influence of cocaine, Lavoie shot a man to death and then fatally stabbed his woman companion. It was the first woman Lavoie had ever killed. He had never acted with greater sadism. The blows were so brutal that the blade of his knife broke in three parts. He was arrested after this slaughter and charged with the double murder. But a jury acquitted him.]

Q: What did you do before the killings? Did you get drunk or did you take drugs?

A: Alcohol and drugs are a daily habit in this milieu. It's not only something for festive occasions. There's no way of knowing whether you are "tight" or real drunk. One is in a state of intoxication all the time.

Q: What were the precautions you would take before?

A: First, it was absolutely necessary to be disguised. I was an accomplished master of disguise. We had wigs, false mustaches, glasses, hats … Afterward, one had to make sure not to leave traces behind, fingerprints or convincing evidence.

Q: How did you feel before opening fire?

A: I was always nervous. But you get things under control. It's not very difficult because the whole thing lasts a few seconds.

Q: How many seconds?

A: It depends. Let's suppose that you walk into a place and that you have to stay there a few minutes, the time you need to find your victim. Then it may take a bit longer. But normally there are always "spotters" and "scouts" to get in first and detect the victim for us, the "hit men," and who inform us about everybody's exact position. In a case like that, one walks in, one opens fire … and gets away.

Q: How do you aim your shots best?

A: My boss always taught me to shoot first into the body "to slow down" the victim, and then in the head, to finish it off.

Q: Can you tell me what your thoughts were at the very moment of opening fire, when you press the trigger?

A: When I start shooting, there is only one thing on my mind—to make a safe escape.

Q: What are the thoughts of the man who is about to die, the one who is facing your gun?

A: Oh Lord. The ones who saw me coming saw me at the last moment. I don't think they had any time to think ...

Q: What were your own thoughts just after a killing?

A: Immediately afterward, I used to recollect all my moves to make sure I had made no error—to be sure there were no witnesses, that I hadn't left anything behind. When I saw somebody stalking through the neighborhood, the job didn't end with the murder. It was necessary to track down the witness to eliminate him, too.

Q: Did you have any misses?

A: None whatsoever. I think that if you miss once, the other ones do not miss you. If you ever make the slightest mistake, it's your turn to be eliminated.

Q: Do you read the paper on the following day?

A: Yes, to see how the police go about the investigation, what news reporters have to say and also to see if there have been any tips or witnesses.

Q: Were you earning big money?

A: Yes, I earned lots of money, and I spent lots of it.

Q: Were you paid for each assignment, or did you draw a regular wage?

A: We all had a cut on the sale of drugs in our territory. I have always had enough money. When I was short of it, all I had to do was ask.

Q: How much money did you have on you most of the time?

A: Five or six thousand dollars. In those days, all I used to do to figure out how rich I was consisted of putting my hand on the pocket and feeling the size of the wad of banknotes. If the bulge was shrinking, I knew it was time to go and ask for more.

Q: Did you ever think of leaving the underworld?

A: I had always planned to pull out one day. I kept waiting for a big coup ... like all criminals. You spend your time waiting for a big coup, such as putting $1 million in your pocket.

Q: You never grew tired of such a life?

A: It's a very exacting kind of life. You are always tense. You must always be on your guard. If you are not afraid of the police, you are afraid of the rival gang ... The life expectancy in this milieu is not very long.

Q: While working as a killer for hire did anybody advise you to quit the underworld?

A: No ... when you belong to the underworld, you meet only underworld characters.

Q: Killing a person in cold blood apparently calls for a special bent of character.

A: I believe one must be completely desperate and this can happen to anyone .... Anybody can do what I have done. In my case, I would have never thought when I was 26 or 27 that I would become a killer.

Q: If you had been asked to kill a good friend while you worked as killer for hire, would you have refused?

A: Yes, it did happen once and I refused. It was precisely why they decided to kill me (Stanke 1985a, 1985b).

Contract killers are an interesting group to speculate about in terms of self-control. They do not seem to be low self-control people but rather individuals who have learned a set of norms that are very different from those of conventional society. Certainly, they live risky lifestyles. Levi (1989) suggests that contract killers have to be socialized into the work of killing. They learn "techniques of neutralization" to be able to carry out the job. In effect, these techniques distance the killer from his prey and allow him to kill another person without feeling remorse. The professional killer is not interested in the "motive" for having an individual hit—that reduces the distance from the subject. The hit man develops a coldness toward his acts and his targets. In effect, it's just a job.

The data from Statistics Canada cannot identify contract killers or contract-killings. It is fair to say, though, that these crimes account for only a small proportion of killing in Canada. Our data set shows that 3.3 percent of all of the murders are attributed to a general category called "gangland." The offender is a "craftsman" who does not expect to be caught, or considers the probability of being caught a cost of the job. In either case, these kinds of homicides are virtually impossible to deter.

ROBBERIES[1]

Robbery is both a crime of violence[2] and a property crime. Victims of robberies are faced with injury, threat of injury, and, in the cases we examine, death. At the same time, the goal of the robber is material gain and he or she is willing to pursue this goal in a face-to-face confrontation with a victim who is either pre-chosen or who happens to be in the wrong place at the wrong time. We can examine homicides in the course of robbery in a variety of ways. From a legal point of view, various kinds of murder are distinguished on the basis of the intent involved in the crime. For the law, intent is distinct from motive and motive is irrelevant to intent. If a robber intends to take material goods and uses a gun to do so, can intent to kill be implied? Not according to a recent Supreme Court decision. Hence (under the 1991 Criminal Code), if the robber intends to commit a theft crime but for one reason or another the victim is killed, at most he or she will be charged with second-degree murder.

Deaths during robberies assume a number of forms. Those most often portrayed on television involve assassination of the victim in order to eliminate witnesses to the event. The robber enters a store or a gas station when no other clients are present, takes the money, then shoots and kills the victim. This kind of event appears to be relatively rare in Canada. A second kind of killing during robbery happens when the offender panics or the victim resists. The media phrase "your money or your life" may, in fact, be meaningful to some robbers. When resistance takes place, some victims are more vulnerable than others. Cook (1987), Fox and Levin (1991), and Kennedy and Silverman (1990) point out the vulnerability of elderly victims confronted by robbers who may use unnecessary force in restraining their victims, leading to a fatal injury.

Some robberies are planned. Many, though, use targets of opportunity rather than preplanned targets. In either case, there are several steps involved in the robbery including, at times, finding a target. According to Gottfredson and Hirschi (1990:30):

> In the ordinary robbery, a young male in his late teens or a group of young males in their middle teens approaches a solitary person on the street and, either through stealth (purse-snatching) or intimidation gained by size or numerical advantage (but sometimes with a weapon), demands valuables. Once the transaction is completed the offender runs from the scene and the victim begins to search for means of calling the police.

PROFILE 5.1a

ROBBERY/THEFT MURDER

Victim's Gender

Percent

Male   Female

N = 1398.

Victim's Age

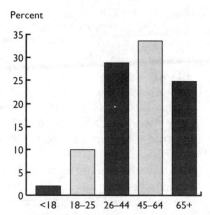

Percent

<18 18–25 26–44 45–64 65+

N = 1397 (excludes unknowns).

Victim's Marital Status

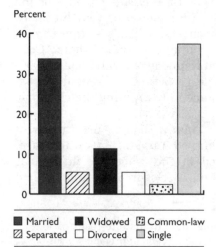

Percent

■ Married   ■ Widowed   ⊞ Common-law
▨ Separated □ Divorced   ▢ Single

N = 1380 (excludes unknowns).

Victim's Race

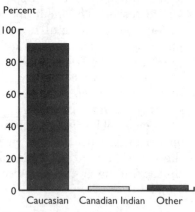

Percent

Caucasian   Canadian Indian   Other

N = 1337 (excludes unknowns).

PROFILE 5.1b

ROBBERY/THEFT MURDER

Suspect's Gender

Percent

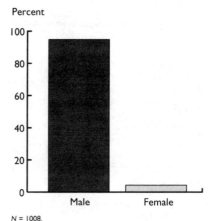

N = 1008.

Suspect's Age

Percent

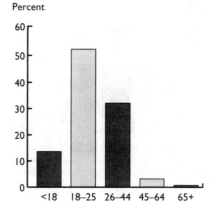

N = 1007 (excludes unknowns).

Suspect's Marital Status

Percent

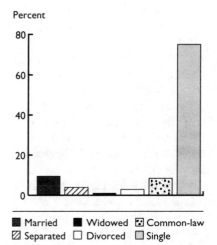

- ■ Married ■ Widowed ▣ Common-law
- ▨ Separated ☐ Divorced ▥ Single

N = 972 (excludes unknowns).

Suspect's Race

Percent

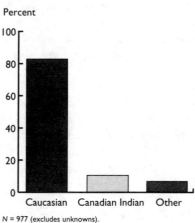

N = 977 (excludes unknowns).

PROFILE 5.1c

ROBBERY/THEFT MURDER

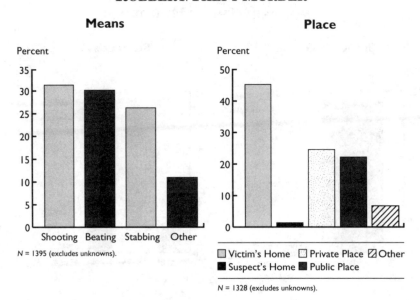

Means

Percent

35 30 25 20 15 10 5 0

Shooting Beating Stabbing Other

N = 1395 (excludes unknowns).

Place

Percent

50 40 30 20 10 0

☐ Victim's Home ☐ Private Place ☒ Other
■ Suspect's Home ■ Public Place

N = 1328 (excludes unknowns).

If that is indeed the typical robbery, then it does not represent the typical robbery/homicide, which is more likely to occur off the street and typically involves some type of weapon (though, again, the elderly victim is most likely beaten to death).

According to findings in the United States, both robbery and robbery/murder are typically committed by offenders who do not know their victims. In the United States, many robberies and robbery/homicides are drug-related incidents in which the offender is "ripping-off" a fellow dealer or a user. A minority of robberies involve some element of revenge against rival drug units. This kind of robbery does take place in Canada's largest cities, but it rarely results in anyone's death. Hence, the decision to kill may be preplanned in some robberies (Dietz 1982), but, in most cases, killing is a consequence of accident or bad luck. Cook (1987) argues that robbery rates and robbery/murder rates follow similar patterns, which is an indication that the assailant's primary motive is robbery rather than murder.

The data set we have been using throughout the book does not distinguish between robbery and other kinds of theft leading to murder. Hence, we combine them for purposes of analysis. There were a total of 1398 robbery/theft murder incidents (about 11 percent of all murders) in the 1961–90 period under examination.

Most offenders in robbery/theft murders are young (two-thirds under 26), single (76 percent) males (96 percent). In thirty years, only forty females have been implicated as offenders for robbery/theft murder. About 11 percent of the offenders are Canadian Indian while 83 percent are Caucasian. Of those for whom education is known (567 cases), close to 60 percent have less than a Grade 10 education. Further, of those for whom the information is available (524 cases), 46 percent listed their occupation as labourer.

Robbery/theft murders are generally intraracial. Victims tend to be older Caucasian males. Eighty-two percent of the victims are male, and almost 60 percent of them fall into age categories above 44. This age group is evidently a reasonable target group for theft given that it is likely to have possessions and money and may be perceived to be vulnerable. Offenders tend to be younger than the victims. In most other types of murder, victims and offenders are more demographically similar.

Almost equal proportions of robbery/theft involve shooting (31 percent), beating (30 percent), or stabbing (27 percent) of the victim. In shootings (398 cases), 47 percent involve a handgun, a very high proportion compared to other Canadian murder events.

About 43 percent of the thefts take place in the victim's home, while 24 percent occur in other private places and 22 percent occur in public places. Most of the thefts involve a single victim (95 percent), but about half of the thefts involve more than one offender.

SEX CRIMES AND MURDER

There are two major kinds of sexual offenses[3] that result in homicide. The first is a singular type of rape that results in death of the victim for reasons similar to those itemized in the robbery case. Death in these instances results from resistance by the victim, panic on the part of the offender, or by design to eliminate the only witness. The second kind of rape resulting in murder is serial rape, in which the offender chooses victims on the basis of their sexual attractiveness to him but with the purpose of both sex and killing. "Sexual homicide results from one person killing another in the context of power, control, sexuality, and aggressive behaviour" (Burgess et al. 1986:252).

In Canada, between 1961 and 1990, 525 sex-related murder incidents were tallied (about 4 percent of all murders). The vast majority (94 percent) of sex/murders in which there is a relationship listed for victim/offender are attributed to strangers.[4] We suspect that the proportion is actually smaller than this, but the classification scheme is not precise enough to pick up all of the

PROFILE 5.2a

SEXUAL MURDER

Victim's Gender

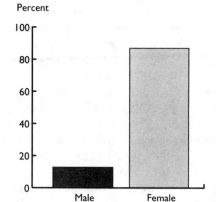

N = 525.

Victim's Age

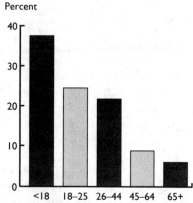

N = 525.

Victim's Marital Status

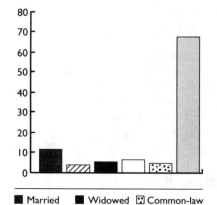

■ Married　■ Widowed　⊡ Common-law
▨ Separated　□ Divorced　□ Single

N = 520 (excludes unknowns).

Victim's Race

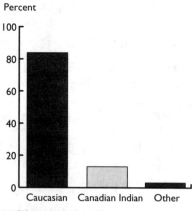

N = 512 (excludes unknowns).

PROFILE 5.2b

SEXUAL MURDER

Suspect's Gender

Percent

N = 392.

Suspect's Age

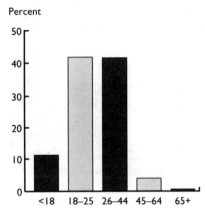

Percent

N = 392.

Suspect's Marital Status

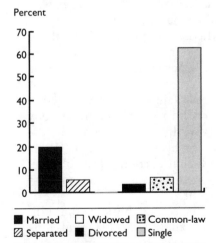

Percent

■ Married □ Widowed ⊞ Common-law
▨ Separated ■ Divorced □ Single

N = 388 (excludes unknowns).

Suspect's Race

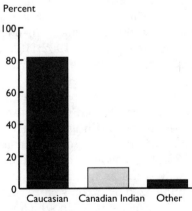

Percent

N = 383 (excludes unknowns).

PROFILE 5.2c

SEXUAL MURDER

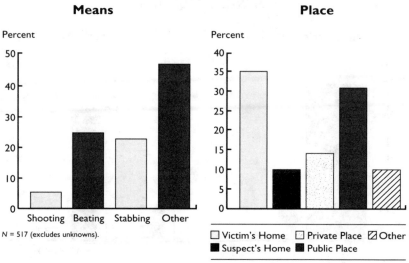

Means

Percent

Shooting	Beating	Stabbing	Other

N = 517 (excludes unknowns).

Place

Percent

☐ Victim's Home   ☐ Private Place   ☑ Other
■ Suspect's Home   ■ Public Place

N = 457 (excludes unknowns).

relationships that might be involved.[5] Killing as a part of a sex crime is seen as "impersonal, predatory and self-seeking behaviour ... The victim in most sex killings, as is so often the case in robbery killings, is just someone who is in the wrong place at the wrong time" (Dietz 1982:113). For example, Warr (1988) documents cases where a burglar enters a house, finds a lone female asleep, and rapes her.

Most sexual assault does not result in death of the victim. Lack of cooperation or resistance on the part of the victim may instigate the killing. Offenders typically exhibit some inadequacy in the masculine role and are hostile to women (Dietz 1982:115). The view of sexual assault that currently prevails is of a power-dominant relationship, with the assault component emphasized over the sexual component.

One of the ways in which we can be reasonably sure that killing is rarely the primary motive in a sexual homicide is that guns are rarely used in this kind of homicide. The Canadian data confirm earlier findings in U.S. studies (Dietz 1982). In an extensive study of thirty-six convicted sex murderers, Ressler et al. (1988) find that the offenders come from relatively decent socioeconomic backgrounds and have average or above-average intelligence. However, the researchers find several aberrations in these offenders' family backgrounds. Nearly 70 percent of their families have histories of alcohol abuse and over half have some history of psychiatric disorders. About half of the offenders have families with criminal histories and in half of these cases there is a history of sexual problems among family members. The study details other family problems, including abuse and neglect (even when the neglect is very subtle). About two-thirds of the cases contain examples of psychological and physical abuse in the childhood histories. "The individual development characteristics of the thirty-six murderers showed the presence of sexual problems and violent experiences in childhood and adolescence, and a dominant sexual fantasy life" (Ressler et al. 1987:24; see also Burgess et al. 1986).

The authors, using a psychological approach, report that "analysis of twenty-four checklist items indicates that over 50 percent of the murderers reported the following present in childhood: daydreaming (82 percent), compulsive masturbation (82 percent), isolation (71 percent), chronic lying (71 percent), enuresis (68 percent), bed-wetting (68 percent), rebelliousness (67 percent), nightmares (67 percent), destroying property (58 percent), fire-setting (56 percent), stealing (56 percent), cruelty to children (54 percent), and poor body image (52 percent)" (1987:29).

The above list was characteristic of the thirty-six subjects through childhood and adolescence and even into adulthood. Of course, there is no control group in the Ressler et al. study, and the sample itself is hardly random. Nonetheless, the chronicling of such behaviours is an interesting starting point for the examination of sex murderers and does represent one of the most comprehensive interview studies on the subject.

Other distinguishing characteristics of the sex murderer include early sexualization/fantasy and early expressions of sexually aggressive fantasies.

A notorious Ottawa case illustrates the most bizarre type of this case. Robert Poulin had sexual fantasies, often perverse, often fuelled by magazines which he collected. He also had thoughts of suicide (which he committed to paper). In 1975 the 18 year old, quiet, normal, intelligent "boy" was able to purchase a shotgun at a local Ottawa store. In his room at his middle-class home he kept a large number of pornographic magazines, sex aids and the gun which he purchased. On Monday, October 27, 1975 he lured Kim Rabot to his house, handcuffed her to a bed, raped her and stabbed her multiple times. He then used his pornographic magazines to attempt to burn down his parent's home with the dead body of Kim in it.

Following the rape and arson, Robert Poulin entered St. Pius X High School, pushed open the door to room 71 and fired his shotgun into the room. Several students were injured but no one died. This is clearly not the normal or typical rape/murder. It is the case of a very disturbed young man whose psycho-sexual maladjustment and extreme depression was not recognized by his parents, his classmates, his teachers, his neighbours or anyone else who knew him. It is the kind of event which, fortunately, happens rarely in Canada and is horrifying and frightening when it does happen (Cobb and Avery 1977).

Psychological approaches probably better explain these kinds of behaviours than do sociological theories. Nonetheless, for the single sexual killing in which sex is the motivation and killing is not intended, the sociological theories that have been espoused in this book so far should have equal validity, with low self-control, opportunity, and low self-esteem likely the most relevant explanatory factors in these fatalities.

Offenders in Canadian sex/murder offences tend to be young males.[6] Fifty-three percent are under 26 years of age, and forty-two percent are between 26 and 44. Most of the offenders (63 percent) are single, while 27 percent are married or living common-law. About 83 percent of the offenders are Caucasian and 11 percent are Canadian Indian. The bulk of sexually oriented murder is intraracial. Of those for whom we have information, 54 percent have less than a Grade 10 education and 40 percent list their occupation as labourer.

About half of sex murders involve older offenders and younger victims—a trend opposite to the age distribution for theft/murder. Almost two-thirds (66 percent) of the victims of sex crimes leading to murder are under 26 years of age and 87 percent are female. Most victims (69 percent) are single while about 16 percent are married (legal or common-law). Eighty-two percent of the victims are Caucasian and 12 percent are Canadian Indians. Over one-third of killings during a sex crime involve strangulation. The more usual means of committing murder are less likely to occur in this kind of crime (stabbing, 23 percent; beating, 25 percent; shooting, 5 percent).

Most of these crimes take place in either the victim's or suspect's home (45 percent), while 31 percent take place in public places. Most sex-based murders involve only one victim (96 percent) and one offender (92 percent)—the latter is another difference between robbery/theft murder and sex/murder events.

One kind of rape that is included in the data are "single" rapes that start out as something far more innocent. Because we cannot distinguish circumstances for each case, we cannot tell the extent of "date rape" that results in death. A case from an earlier time in New Brunswick history illustrates the point.

One Sunday in 1942 the body of Bernice Connors was found
under a pile of moss in a field by Harbour Road. Bernice, 19,
had gone to a dance at the Community Hall of Black's Harbour. She never returned. An investigation resulted in the
arrest of Tom Hutchings, an RAF officer stationed at the air-
force base at Pennfield, New Brunswick. The Crown's case
was entirely circumstantial but revealed so many links
between Hutchings and the event that he was eventually
found guilty. Bernice Connors came to her death as a result of
injuries to her head and neck and haemorrhaging. She had
consumed alcohol and she had been raped. There was evidence of lacerations that were eventually connected to the
kind of pen knives issued to RAF service men (Grant 1983).

This rape murder in war-time New Brunswick is more common but no less horrifying than the Poulin description given earlier.[7]

As pointed out earlier, traditional sociological theories have
been less than effective in explaining the crime of rape. Rape is
tied to aggression, feelings of inadequacy, and certainly one could
add low self-control on the part of the offender. Sometimes death

FIGURE 5.1

PROPORTION OF ALL MURDER INVOLVING
SEXUAL OR THEFT/ROBBERY OFFENCES AS A
CONCOMITANT CRIME, CANADA, 1961–1990

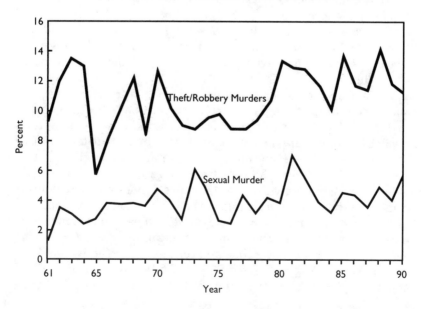

results from factors discussed earlier. The crime of rape murder is rare but generates great fear. It is also a crime that is very difficult to deter, often finding its victims (sometimes unavoidably) in the wrong place at the wrong time.

Trends in Robbery and Sexual Murder

Figure 5.1 shows that both theft/robbery and sexual murders have been gradually rising as a proportion of all murders. Theft/robbery murder offences contribute between 6 percent (1965) and 14 percent (1988) of all murders. While the proportion is generally low, it is notable that it is in an upward direction. Similarly, sex-crime based murders have ranged between 1 percent (1961) of all murders to 7 percent (1981), and while the line is flatter than that for theft/robbery, it is still in an upward direction.

Crime-based murders are the ones that the public fears most—they conjure up images of lurking strangers waiting to pounce on and kill unsuspecting victims. Given their currently low proportions, there is no reason for immediate alarm. On the other hand, a continuation of the trends shown in Figure 5.1 should be considered an unhealthy sign for Canadian society.

SERIAL AND MASS MURDERS

Serial and mass murders have both become topics of great interest in criminology. Since 1985, at least ten books have appeared on bookshelves and libraries with titles like *Serial Murder: An Illusive Phenomenon* (Egger 1990); *Mass Murder: America's Growing Menace* (Levin and Fox 1985); *Serial Murderers and Their Victims* (Hickey 1991); *Serial Murder* (Holmes and De Burger 1988); and *Hunting Humans* (Leyton 1986). If mass murder and serial killers have not become an epidemic, at least books about them have.

The books about serial killing and mass murder do not agree on the definition of the phenomena. It might be best at this point to differentiate the two in the easiest possible way. Mass murder involves killing many people at the same time, or at least in the same incident. It is sometimes called "simultaneous killing." For instance, a murderer who goes from house to house killing individuals in each place would be classed as a mass murderer in the same way that someone sitting on the top of a tower and shooting into a crowd, killing many people, is classed as a mass murderer. Serial killing, on the other hand, is the killing of one (and occasionally more) people at a time and continuing the activity of killing individuals over a longer period of time. Most books on the general topic treat the two kinds of killing within the same covers. It seems to us, however, that there is a fundamental difference between the two types of killing. The problem really boils down to the kinds of components or variables taken into account in the definition of a phenomenon. Some definitions focus only on the numbers of victims while others define the crime by generating a profile of the "typical" offender.

Mass murder in the family is explained in a different way than mass murder involving strangers or other intimates. In effect, mass murder involving intimates has readily available explanations. The event is no less horrifying for the fact that we can explain it. There is not much to differentiate the father who kills a family of three from a father who kills a family of four. From an analytic point of view, those kinds of events should be grouped together. They are not the same as the individual in the tower who, having reached some last straw in a series of frustrations, shoots people he does not know. The conception of mass murderer held by the public is not that of the father who kills his entire family and then commits suicide; in the public's mind, it is the stranger/mass murderer who is feared.

For the purposes of our analysis, we would add to the definition of the mass murderer the spontaneity of the attack and the relationship to those who are killed. Levin and Fox (1985) acknowledge this extended definition in their chapter on James Rupert, a 41-year-old resident of Hamilton, Ohio, who on Easter Sunday 1975 killed (without warning) his 65-year-old mother, his brother, his brother's wife, and their eight children. James Rupert was a mass murderer who killed his entire family.

Serial killers are most likely to kill strangers, or those with whom they have brief acquaintances, rather than intimates. Their relationship to their victims revolves around their motive (e.g., sex, power, or some perverse conception of reality). The specific definition used by researchers determines the number of murderers one classifies in this group, and the kinds of analysis one is likely to use. The following are examples of definitions that are currently being used:

> Based on our study of forty-two mass killers and the FBI data on simultaneous homicides, we have developed a composite profile of a mass murderer ... he is typically a white male in his late twenties or thirties. In the case of simultaneous mass murder, he kills people he knows with a handgun or a rifle; and [in the case of] serial crimes, he murders strangers by beating or strangulation (Fox and Levin 1985).

> Repetitive homicide continuing if not prevented; primarily one on one; the victim is usually a stranger or a slight acquaintance; the motive is not the conventional passion

crime or victim-precipitation; there is likely an unclear intrinsic motive and the act is rarely for personal gain or profit (Holmes and De Burger 1988: 18–19).

A serial murder occurs when one or more individuals (males in most known cases) commit a second murder and/or subsequent murder; is relationshipless (no prior relationship between victim and attacker); is at a different time and has no apparent connection to the initial murders; and is usually committed in a different geographical location. Further, the motive is not for material gain and is believed to be for the murderer's desire to have power over his victims. Victims may have symbolic value and are perceived to be prestigeless and in most instances are unable to defend themselves or alert others to their plight or are perceived as powerless given their situation in time, place or status within their immediate surroundings (such as vagrants, prostitutes, migrant workers, homosexuals, missing children, and single and often elderly women) (Egger 1990:4).

Hickey (1991) provides the broadest definition: "To include all types of serial killers, the definition of serial murder must clearly be as broad as possible." By including the notion that any offender who through premeditation killed three or more victims over a period of days, weeks, months, or years, Hickey was able to identify several women as serial killers. He is one of the few authors who includes cases of women serial or mass murderers.

In essence serial murders should include any offenders, male or female, who kill over time … Usually there is a pattern in their killing that may be associated with types of victims selected or the method or motives of the killing. This includes murderers who, on repeated basis, kill within the confines of their own home … In addition, serial murders include those men and women who operate within the confines of a city or state or even travel through several states as they seek out victims. Consequently, some victims have a personal relationship with their killers and others do not, and some victims are killed for pleasure and some merely for gain. Of greatest importance from a research perspective is the linkage of common factors among the victims … Commonality among those murdered may include several factors, any of which can prove heuristic in better understanding victimization (Hickey: 8).

Before reading the above "scientific" definitions, the reader probably thought that he or she knew what serial or mass murder was. These definitions may confuse more than they help. To sort out this problem, we can start by referring again to the simplest distinction between mass murderers and serial murderers. As noted above, that distinction simply refers to the number of people killed and whether they are killed simultaneously or one after the other with some time separation. Rather than attempt to build on this distinction as a definition, we shall analyze the data in terms of a variety of significant variables that have been identified in the research literature to date, including relationship to the victim, profiles of victims and offenders, and, certainly, the psychological state of the offender and the apparent (or not so apparent) motive.

When a serial killer is stalking the streets of a city or town those living in the area are under his spell. Headlines and stories in the press reveal the details of each victim's demise in the goriest detail permissible. Fear in the community is heightened. The fallout from the publicity will range much farther than the local environs, particularly if the killings persist over a long period of time. A notable recent example involves the so-called Green-River slayings, which have been taking place at least since 1982 in the Seattle–Washington area. A task force was set up to investigate the killings and finally a suspect was arrested; however, he was released for lack of evidence. On a semi-regular basis, media reignite anxiety generated by the Green River killer. In the northwest U.S. and even in the southwest of Canada, interest in the case is so intense that a book has been written about the investigation, even though there has been no resolution to the killings.

Several books about serial killing attempt to estimate the number of serial killers in the United States on an annual basis. Suffice it to say that information upon which one could accurately estimate the number of victims of serial killers is lacking. Indeed, the most accurate statement on the subject is "[t]he incidence of serial murder in the United States in currently unknown, as is the prevalence of active offenders" (Kiger 1990). We do not know how many serial killers are operating at any given point in time. We can, of course, estimate through newspaper sources the amount of mass murder that has taken place in a particular period—a technique successfully utilized by Levin and Fox in identifying forty-two mass murderers (which include serial killers) in the Boston area between 1978 and 1982. Others have tried to estimate the numbers of serial killers by using FBI data and the numbers of missing children and stranger-type homicides known in the United States (see, for instance, Holmes and De Burger 1988), but these attempts are, at best, guesses.

Hickey (1991:18–19) provides the most interesting estimate of serial killers as he names many of the killers and indicates the kind of killers and the number of victims in each case. "Spanning the time-frame between 1795 and 1988 the findings from these data represent the victims of thirty-four women and one hundred and sixty-nine men in the United States. They are responsible for a minimum of fourteen hundred and eighty-three homicides and a maximum of two thousand, one hundred and sixty-one homicides." A few serial killers killed so many people that the best Hickey can do is approximate a range. He lists nineteen mass murders (simultaneous killings) that occurred in the United States between 1949 and 1990. As is indicated in virtually all of the literature, about half of the mass murderers killed people they knew and the other half murdered randomly (or otherwise killed people they did not know). These mass murderers include the notorious Richard Speck, who strangled eight nurses, and Charles Whitman, who shot sixteen people (mostly students) from a tower in Texas. Hickey indicates that between 1795 and 1988, there were 203 serial offenders in the United States.

While it is not an unknown phenomenon in Canada, serial and mass murder does not come close to approximating U.S. levels. In a chapter titled "Interviews, Foreign Offenders[8] and Unsolved Cases," Hickey reviews mass and serial murder back to the year 1430 and identifies three Canadian cases between 1958 and 1988 among the non-U.S. group. In 1958, Peter Manuel killed nine victims; in 1980 to 1981, Clifford Olson[9] killed eleven or more victims; and, between 1974 and 1981, James Odo killed three or more victims. In fact, there have been few documented cases of either type of crime in Canada. It seems, however, that some American mass murderers have spent time in Canada. It is reasonably clear that some of these (e.g., Charles Ng) did not kill anyone while in Canada, whereas a mass murderer such as Henry Lee Lucas claims Canada as one of the three countries in which he killed, though positive proof of his activity is lacking.

Most research has simply described the nature and extent of mass/serial killing, but inevitably reasons for the behaviour are sought. Some general characteristics of mass murderers can be gleaned from the literature. It seems that most if not all of these cases involve an individual reaching a breaking point. Something snaps—at which point the individual picks up the weapon of choice and marches off to right the perceived wrongs of society. Here, indeed, are echoes of Katz's (1988) description of righteous slaughter. This may involve entering a McDonald's restaurant as James Huberty did in California in 1984 and shooting twenty-one people, or it may involve picking up one of your collectible weapons and killing your family as James Rupert did. The perceived motives of the offender are often not understandable but sometimes they are made clear, even if they do not make sense to the average observer. A case in point, which is discussed in more detail later, is that of Marc Lepine of Montreal.

The serial killer is a very different kind of individual. The serial killer may plan his killings long in advance and may "case" surroundings, or he may take advantage of opportunities that are presented to him at random. He may use deception to lure a victim or he may use force. A few characteristics of serial killers stand out. First, they often have charismatic or at least "pleasant" personalities. Second, they are almost without exception sociopaths or psychopaths; that is, they do not feel remorse for their behaviours.

These two characteristics aside, profiles of modern serial killers exhibit enormous diversity. In fact, while many researchers have tried to create typologies for serial killers, their own data usually undermine the typology, so mind-boggling is the variety of motive and background characteristics. In fact, Levin and Fox (1985) wisely point out that the serial killer is extraordinary in his ordinariness. Virtually all of the books on the subject point out that the serial killer is not someone you can pick out of a crowd.

Often the typologies revolve around the motive for the murder. This is probably the most fruitful way of classifying the murders but does not always work. For instance, the killing of females by Edmund Kemper III involved mutilation of the bodies, necrophilia, both family and nonfamily victims, and a variety of methods. Ultimately, though, the explanation from Kemper himself was that "he was killing his mother all along, and once she was dead he could stop the murder spree" (Hickey 1991:142). The point to be made here is that many serial murders exhibit a variety of apparent motives. The apparent motive often involves sex, but deeper psychological motives are found to be the driving force.

Probably the most frightening aspect of certain serial/mass murderers is both their ordinariness and their intelligence. Of course, some fit a stereotype of a not-too-bright person with a horrid social background that can (perhaps) explain their behaviours. For instance, Henry Lee Lucas came from a poverty-stricken background in which he was regularly beaten and was forced to watch his mother (who was a prostitute) have sex with her clients. Reading transcripts of the Lucas case leads one to see an individual disadvantaged in every possible sense.[10] On the other hand, there are the cases of serial killers like Ted Bundy and Kenneth Bianchi. These individuals were "smart" and could act normally. Both were students at institutions of higher education. Both achieved social success and were highly regarded by those who knew them.

Bianchi, as depicted in *Frontline*,[11] was a charming, somewhat charismatic individual with high verbal facility, who managed to con his way through life. In fact, his case became notorious in the academic community because he conned experts in "multiple personality syndrome" into believing that he had multiple personalities that caused him to commit (with his cousin Angelo Buono) the gruesome, violent sexual murders that he perpetrated. Bianchi convinced a psychologist and a psychiatrist with impeccable credentials that he was a classic multiple personality, and that it was his alter ego, Steve Wallace, who committed the crimes.

The prosecution hired Martin Orne, a psychiatrist from the University of Pennsylvania, to attempt to debunk the multiple personality issue. To their credit, it was the detectives involved in the case who first thought that Bianchi was a con artist rather than a "sick person." Had Bianchi been able to get away with the multiple personality defence, he would have been declared not guilty by reason of insanity and sent to a mental institution until he was "cured," at which time he could have been released.

However, Orne and the detectives involved in the case were able to show that Bianchi was a fake. Orne suggested to Bianchi that it was odd that he had only two personalities given that most multiple personality cases involve more than two. Virtually immediately, under "hypnosis" Bianchi revealed a third personality named "Billy." Further, Bianchi overacted in some of the situations that Orne created for him while he was supposedly under hypnosis. For instance, he shook hands with a nonexistent third person, which is not a normal reaction under hypnosis. The detectives uncovered the fakery by finding an actual person whose identity Bianchi had "assumed" as one of his personalities.

Bianchi and his cousin perpetrated a series of sexual murders that involved kidnapping and torture. Martin Orne's conclusion was that Bianchi was a sexual psychopath—not a terribly satisfying term when the nature of the acts is considered. Could Bianchi really not stop himself or is it possible (as stated by an interviewee on the *Frontline* film) that Bianchi is simply "evil"? If the latter is the case, then social scientists are wasting their time attempting to analyze these cases. Evil is not a useful social scientific construct, though sometimes it is the only word strong enough to define our revulsion with the offenders and their crimes.

With our data on Canadian homicide, we can identify mass murderers (four or more victims) but we cannot identify victims of serial killers. There is no way within the data coding to link murders to offenders. Cases may remain unsolved for some time; that is, a serial murderer could kill individuals over a number of years and never be linked to these murders. On the other hand, we can easily determine how many cases involve four or more victims. Between 1961 and 1990, there were seventy-two cases (out of the approximately 12,000 incidents we examined) that involved four or more victims in one incident. The seventy-two cases resulted in 359 victims, an average of almost five people per case. Several cases involved between thirteen and forty-eight victims, and at least some included multiple killings by arson, a technique commonly employed by members of the organized crime community to wreak havoc and revenge.

Table 5.1 shows the perpetrator's relationship to the primary[12] victim in the multiple murder cases.

T A B L E   5 . I

Murders in Which there were Four or More Victims by Social Relationship, Canada, 1961–1991

RELATIONSHIP	NUMBER	PERCENT
Spouse/Lover	18	27
Other Family	23	35
Friend/Acquaintance	9	14
Stranger	4	6
Crime	12	18
Total	**66**	**100**

Fifteen cases involve a husband killing his wife and (most likely) other family members and three involve "lovers."

> WR, a 55 year old chartered accountant, killed three of his stepsons and his second wife. He then went to the grave of his first wife and shot and killed himself. He used a .303 calibre rifle in all of the killings. Some neighbours felt that the family appeared to be happy while others thought the family had some problems. WR was characterized as a gentleman and a loving husband. Most people felt that they were pretty well financially set, that they took an active interest in their kids and their lives and careers as well as in sporting activities. Accounts of the family characterize them as stalwart citizens active in community affairs, hard-working and "comfortable" in economic terms. Some friends thought that WR might have been depressed over his father's recent death and his failure to sell his $400,000 home, one of the two houses he owned.
>
> In this case, we simply do not know what was going on in WR's mind that would lead him to this end. It is likely that no one will be able to find out (Lavigne and Tenszen 1991).

No wives killed husbands (and others) in mass murder incidents. Fathers and mothers killing their children account for another fourteen cases. Other kinds of family relationships account for seven of the cases and friend/acquaintance killing produces nine cases. This leaves us with six unsolved cases and sixteen cases that took place in the context of a crime or involved a stranger (about one-tenth of 1 percent of the murder incidents in Canada). Two of the cases in which strangers killed four or more people are attributed to mental illness by the police.

Males are the perpetrators in 90 percent of these cases. The six cases involving female perpetrators all had family members as victims. Fifty-six percent of the cases involve shooting as the method and 35 percent involve "other" means, including strangling and suffocation. The number of cases on a yearly basis shows no indication of an increase with time. The yearly range in numbers is between one and six over the thirty years. The peak period is between 1975 and 1977 in which a total of sixteen cases took place. Most recently, between 1986 and 1990, there were one or two cases of mass murder per year.

Sexual crime is identified as a concomitant crime in only one case, while four involve theft/robbery. Most of the crimes take place in the victims' home (74 percent) and only 7 percent occur in a public place. Of the known offenders, 92 percent are Caucasian and 5 percent are Canadian Indians. All of the killings are intraracial. The vast majority of mass murder cases (81 percent) involve some type of intimacy between the offender and victims. Only 15 percent of the killings occur during the course of some other kind of crime.

The above cases are certainly an interesting subgroup of murder cases occurring in Canada and deserve further study. There is, however, no trend toward an increase in the number of mass murders, occurring yearly, nor is there any sense that what currently exists is "epidemic" in proportion. (Because these murders involve mainly family relationships, there is probably little that can be done to prevent their occurrence.) The Canadian situation thus differs from that portrayed by U.S. based media, in which mass or serial killings seem to have become a regular event.

CANADA'S SERIAL MURDERER: CLIFFORD OLSON [13]

Clifford Olson is a serial killer. In a nine-month period ending in August 1981, he killed eleven children in British Columbia. In fact, he was only apprehended for the killing of the eleventh child, and there is some uncertainty about the number that he actually killed. Though eleven are attributed to him, he may have actually killed more both in British Columbia and in neighbouring provinces. He has been evasive at best about his full involvement.

Two things make Olson special—he is a Canadian serial killer who did his deeds in Canada, and he struck a monetary deal with the government. Olson, 41, married with a small child when arrested, killed three boys and eight girls ranging in age from 9 to 18 between November 1980 and August 1981. The children were variously sexually abused, beaten, strangled, and stabbed. The female victim for whom the murder charge was laid was found naked with multiple stab wounds about 80 kilometres up the Fraser Valley from Chilliwack on July 25, 1981. On July 17, 1981, Olson had been put under surveillance, but between that time and his arrest about a month later he killed four times. While under surveillance, he picked up two female hitchhikers. Police feared for the safety of the girls so Olson was arrested and charged with impaired driving. In Olson's rented van, they found an address book with the address of one of the murder victims.

Olson had a long history of relatively minor offences ranging from fraud to burglary. "As a child [he] was a bully and con artist to his teachers" (*Maclean's* 1982a). He liked to be the centre of attention and some thought he was a promising boxer. He also acted as an informer in at least one criminal trial. Like other serial killers, he is diagnosed as a psychopath or sociopath but is not legally insane. He knew what he was doing.

Olson's case makes it into the pages of American books on serial killings not for the uniqueness of his killings but rather for the uniqueness of their aftermath. While Olson was initially apprehended for only one of the killings, he was a suspect in many more. But the police did not know where the bodies of the victims were buried. Olson asked for $10,000 in exchange for each body to which he directed the police. The prosecutors reluctantly agreed to pay but felt it would set a dangerous new precedent. Eventually, $90,000 was paid to Olson's wife. The prosecutors felt that by retrieving the bodies they would solidify their case against Olson for first-degree murder (they were concerned that, without the bodies, he may have been convicted only of second-degree murder.) Further, many of the parents wanted, first, to be certain that it was their children who were the victims and, second, to give them an appropriate burial.

Other parents and citizens were outraged at the deal made with Olson. Police and prosecutors regularly make deals with killers and other criminals, but what distinguishes this case is the horrible nature of the crimes and the publicity given to "the deal." Olson had failed in his attempts to negotiate an earlier deal whereby in exchange for the bodies he would have been guaranteed time in a mental institution rather than in a prison, where he felt he would be a target.[14]

Olson is currently serving life in prison for first-degree murder (not parolable before twenty-five years) in the Kingston Penitentiary. He shows no remorse for his crimes. His wife has since divorced him and, with her son, changed residences.

CANADA'S MASS MURDERER: MARC LEPINE[15]

On December 13, 1989, at around 5 p.m., Marc Lepine, a 25-year-old male from a Montreal working-class area, walked into the University of Montreal's Ecole Polytechnique and began a shooting rampage that ended with fourteen women killed, as well as his own suicide and notoriety as Canada's worst mass murderer in modern times. In fact, Lepine had perpetrated the worst mass murder in North America since 1984 (James Huberty in the McDonald's massacre, San Ysidro, California). Lepine entered a classroom of about sixty engineering students and demanded that the women move to one side of the room. When no one moved, he fired two shots into the ceiling. He shouted "You're all a bunch of feminists, and I hate feminists." He told the male students to leave the room, which they did. He then opened fire and shot and killed six of the women. Over the next twenty minutes, he stalked various areas of the school, shooting female victims as he found them. Ultimately twenty-seven were shot and of these fourteen died. Finally, he turned the weapon on himself. Despite his calm and cool demeanor during the killings, it is evident that Lepine harboured a seething rage against women.

He grew up in Montreal's working-class east end. He neither smoked nor used drugs and he had no criminal record. He was remembered after the fact as someone who was "strange and far away." His self-perception was that of a failure. He failed to achieve his ambitions both in work and with women. In a letter found on his body, Lepine blamed his own unhappiness on women. He was a failure at most of his academic endeavours despite signs that he was quite intelligent. He received high grades in some academic subjects but dropped out of several of the courses he began. Lepine's approach to women was equally unsuccessful. Those who remember him more positively indicate that he was withdrawn but always polite.

One interpretation of the scanty data available about Lepine is that something brought all of his unhappiness to a peak and provoked his quest for revenge. Since he blamed women for many of his failures, women would be the target. Because Lepine killed himself, we will never learn directly what this final outrage was and what his perceived motivation might have been.

The aftermath of the Lepine massacre was quite extraordinary. Lepine used a Ruger mini-14 semiautomatic rifle found in many sporting shops across Canada. It uses a .223 calibre bullet and can hold up to fifty rounds of ammunition in its magazine. It is American-made and in 1989 cost between $560 and $650 Canadian dollars. It is lightweight and accurate. About 2000 of these rifles are sold in Canada annually and it has become a popular weapon with SWAT teams. Immediately after the Lepine massacre, outraged citizens and government officials called for tighter controls on the sale of all weapons and a ban on this weapon in particular. The solicitor general introduced legislation to tighten some of the gun laws. However, it is our opinion that such laws are symbolic and have little effect on deterring the kind of crime perpetrated by Marc Lepine. Someone without a criminal record can buy a rifle after a required waiting period. Once he or she has the weapon, the precipitating event can still happen and the weapon will be readily available. If the weapon is not semiautomatic, the killing will take longer or there will be slightly fewer victims. But the legislation will not stop the event itself. We should keep in mind that the Lepine massacre is the only event of its type in recent memory; it does not predict a trend.

The second major aftermath of the massacre was a political reaction of a different sort. One issue that distinguishes this event from other mass killings that have taken place in Canada and elsewhere is the fact that the target group was a single gender. Had Lepine lined up the men in the classroom and shot them instead of the women, there would have been no less outrage in the country but the specifics of the reaction would have been quite different. Activists in the Canadian women's movement used the Lepine case as a metaphor for all kinds of oppression of women. They used the specific incident to raise levels of awareness about women and violence against women.

In the context of all mass murderers, Lepine is not unique. He was a loner who would have had a relatively normal profile had it not been for the severe mental anguish he suffered, brought on by perceived failure linked to women. Something (undefined) snapped and he went on a rampage killing fourteen young women. This is the scenario promoted by Helen Morrison, a Chicago-based psychiatrist who has studied serial and mass murderers for twenty years (*Maclean's* 1991).

A third and little noticed aftermath of mass murders is their effect on the families of the victims and witnesses to the event. Feelings of guilt have overwhelmed some of the Lepine massacre witnesses, and, in at least one case, there was a suicide. Similarly, for the families of Lepine's victims, the scars of the massacre are likely permanent. Marc Lepine represents the very worst case of a mass murder that has occurred in Canada in recent history. It places us in the unfortunate and undesirable position of having our very own Richard Speck or James Huberty.

SUMMARY

Crime-based murders are readily distinguished from murders that are identified as based on relationship. Theft-related murders are not generally motivated by anger or social conflict but rather appear to result from bad luck or circumstances that go wrong during the commission of the robbery. Sex murder can be similarly unpremeditated—sexual attacks that did not go as planned (e.g., meeting unforeseen resistance); other sex murders are deliberately planned. The aspects of opportunity are relevant here, as are elements of poor social control, although it should be pointed out that, in sex and theft-related murders, we are dealing with individuals who are already committed to performing a criminal act rather than those who allow violence to escalate out of control. The routine activities of some of the victims of these murders may place them in the wrong place at the wrong time, while other victims are stalked.

Serial and mass murderers constitute a somewhat different group when we consider that it is clearly their intention to kill, and that the psychological breakdown accompanying this impulse is much stronger (particularly in the case of serial killers) than that found in other murderers. The explanations offered by Katz (see Chapter 3) about the seductions of crime and murder as thrill add a further dimension to the profile of serial and mass murderers. Psychological insights into the sources of low self-control and breakdown in these killers may be of some use, but the fact remains that the nature of serial and mass murders makes them difficult, if not impossible, to predict or to deter.

NOTES

1. Besides the homicide itself, there are two types of crime "coded" by Statistics Canada when a homicide has taken place. Crimes are either theft-oriented (mainly robbery and some burglary) or sexually oriented. Here, we briefly examine characteristics of offenders, victims, and the offence for each type of crime-related homicide. It should be noted that the following examination includes only crime-related homicides that were solved (that is, we know about both the offender and the vic-

tim). Hence, the total number of cases is 988. Seven hundred and ten of these were theft while 278 involved sexual crimes.

2. Robbery may involve only threat (rather than physical injury), but from a technical/legal point of view, this is enough to qualify it as a violent crime.

3. Rape is no longer a crime in Canada. In 1982 the law that defined rape was replaced by the crime of sexual assault. Sexual assault includes a much broader spectrum of criminal behaviours. In the text that follows, we use the term "rape" to apply to all aggravated sexual assaults, generally defined by "penetration."

4. The Canadian homicide data set does not lend itself to analysis of both kinds of rape. In fact, all the data tell us is that one of the motivations in the offence was sex; we cannot tell what the specific sex act was.

5. See our discussion of strangers in Chapter 4.

6. As would be expected, of the 278 cases only two involved a female offender. Unfortunately, we do not have data that illuminate the nature of these two events.

7. Because this example is a 1942 event, it does not appear in our data set. However, it is likely a typical example of this kind of crime.

8. The chapter is mistitled. It incorrectly identifies serial killers from other countries as "foreign." They would only be foreign if they had been operating in the United States. A French serial killer killing in France is not "foreign."

9. The years for Olson are identified as 1973–81 but in fact the eleven killings took place in the nine months leading up to August 1981.

10. For a fascinating description of Lucas, see Egger (1990).

11. A documentary television show produced for the Public Broadcasting System in the U.S.

12. The victim with the closest social relationship. Six cases involve an unknown relationship or were unsolved.

13. Most of the description of Olson is adapted from Levin and Fox 1985; Hickey 1991; *Maclean's* 1981, 1982a, 1982b, 1982c.

14. Child killers, especially those whose offences involve sex with children are often targets for assault and even murder by other inmates who abhor those kinds of crimes as much as the rest of the population.

15. Much of the discussion of Lepine is derived from *Maclean's* 1989, *Newsweek* 1989, *Time Magazine* 1989.

Special Offenders
WOMEN, CHILDREN, AND
THE ELDERLY

Homicide is predominantly committed by young adult males. Of interest to us in this chapter are homicides perpetrated by members of other groups, specifically women, children, and the elderly. The conditions and circumstances under which these individuals kill are quite different than is the case for young adult males. Much of the variation in behaviour of men and women can be attributed to socialization deriving from different styles of upbringing in the home. The risk-aversion of women, and their more restricted lifestyles, make them less likely to participate in certain types of behaviour in public places. However, the tensions in families that derive from struggles between partners in intimate relations make them more likely offenders in family situations. We would expect to find similar types of trends for younger children (though not necessarily for teenagers, particularly young males) and for the elderly.

The crimes committed by women, the elderly, and children often elicit different responses—e.g., in terms of sentencing—from the criminal justice system than do those committed by adult males. We will examine murder by these groups of offenders in some detail to further understand the circumstances in and means by which it occurs.

WOMEN MURDERERS[1]

Adler (1975) suggests that female criminality is increasing as females become more equal to men and experience various types of freedoms not available to them in the past. Homicide researchers have taken up the call to determine whether female homicide

PROFILE 6.1a

FEMALE AND MALE SUSPECTS

Victim's Gender

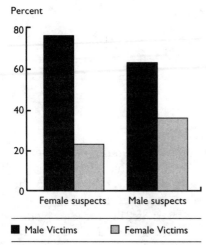

Percent

Female suspects   Male suspects

■ Male Victims   ▨ Female Victims

N = 1314 female suspects and 11,514 male suspects.

Victim's Age

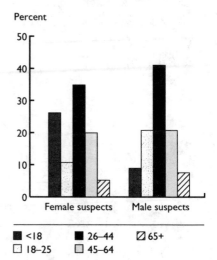

Percent

Female suspects   Male suspects

■ <18   ■ 26–44   ▨ 65+
□ 18–25   □ 45–64

N = 1312 female suspects and 11,502 male suspects.

Victim's Marital Status

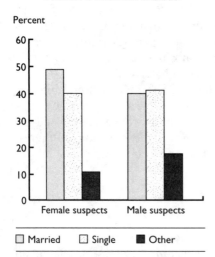

Percent

Female suspects   Male suspects

□ Married   □ Single   ■ Other

N = 1303 female suspects and 11,363 male suspects.
Married includes common-law.

Victim's Race

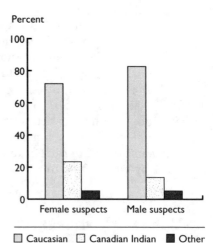

Percent

Female suspects   Male suspects

□ Caucasian   □ Canadian Indian   ■ Other

N = 1255 female suspects and 10,966 male suspects.

PROFILE 6.1b

FEMALE AND MALE SUSPECTS

Suspect's Age

Percent

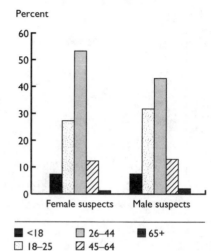

■ <18   ▣ 26–44   ■ 65+
□ 18–25   ▨ 45–64

N = 1310 female suspects and 9423 male suspects.

Suspect's Marital Status

Percent

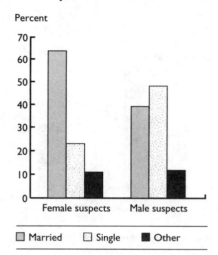

▣ Married   ▢ Single   ■ Other

N = 1297 female suspects and 9225 male suspects.
Married includes common-law.

Suspect's Race

Percent

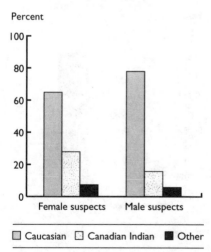

▣ Caucasian   □ Canadian Indian   ■ Other

N = 1261 female suspects and 9102 male suspects.

PROFILE 6.1c

FEMALE AND MALE SUSPECTS

Means

Place

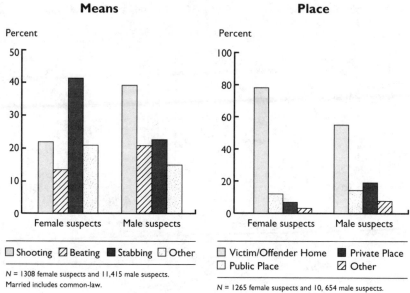

Shooting Beating Stabbing Other

N = 1308 female suspects and 11,415 male suspects.
Married includes common-law.

Victim/Offender Home Private Place
Public Place Other

N = 1265 female suspects and 10, 654 male suspects.

Concurrent Crime

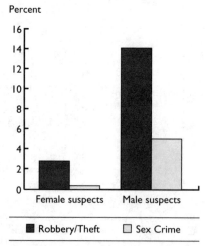

Robbery/Theft Sex Crime

N = 1230 female suspects and 9903 male suspects (total).

PROFILE 6.1d

FEMALE AND MALE SUSPECTS

Social Relationship Between Victims and Suspects

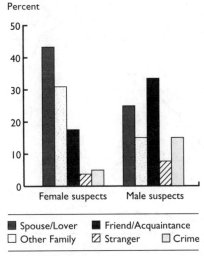

Percent

Female suspects   Male suspects

■ Spouse/Lover   ■ Friend/Acquaintance
□ Other Family   ▨ Stranger   □ Crime

N = 1314 female suspects and 9442 male suspects.

rises in tandem with advances in female equality. The rarely stated assumption in this research is that females commit more homicide because they become more like men as social equality rises. The argument follows that as women gain equality with men (for example, rising to executive positions in business), they will experience the same stresses as men. In terms of crime, as women become more equal with men they will begin to commit white-collar crimes. Liberated from the routines of home life and child care, they will be free to take up arms and commit robbery, following risky lifestyles that parallel those of young men. None of the research to date, however, has been able to show that there have been vast increases in the amounts of robbery or assault perpetrated by women.

Do the same arguments apply to homicide? In fact, some of the progress women have made (in Canada) should result in lowered homicide rates. For instance, as divorce laws change and make it easier to get out of marriages, stress should be dissipated and circumstances that would otherwise lead to violent or fatal behaviours should be circumvented (Gillis 1986).

FIGURE 6.1

GENDER SPECIFIC RATES FOR MURDER OFFENDERS, CANADA, 1961–1990*

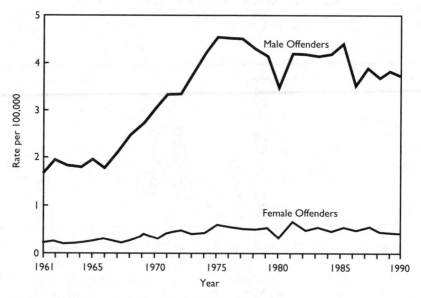

*Rates calculated on the basis of male and female populations.

Between 1961 and 1990, there were 1314 cases of female offenders in our data set, about 12 percent of all of the murders we analyze. The trend in rates of killing by women, as shown in Figure 6.1, has been very stable since the early 1970s, with an average offender rate of about 0.45 per 100,000 women.[2] Figure 6.1 raises a fascinating question about the male offender rate. Why does the male rate rise while the female rate remains stable? This variation could be an indication that the larger societal forces related to violence affect men more than women.

Overwhelmingly, female offenders kill members of their own family (75 percent). Of those, 40 percent kill their husband or common-law husband, while 22 percent kill one of their children. The women who commit these crimes are relatively young. Thirty-four percent are under the age of 26. Most are white (65 percent), but a large proportion (28 percent) are Canadian Indians. Sixty-five percent of the female offenders are married (legal or common-law), while 24 percent are single. About 55 percent of female offenders have less than a Grade 10 education.[3] Following the murder event, only 6 percent of these offenders commit suicide, indicating a low level of remorse.

Seventy-six percent of the victims of female offenders are males. Forty-two percent of the victims are listed as married (legal or common-law), while 40 percent are single. Seventy-two percent of the victims are Caucasian, and 23 percent are Canadian Indians. The victims are often very young. Twenty-six percent are under 18 but another 36 percent are between 26 and 44. The age distribution should not be surprising given that the victims are usually either the husbands or the children of offenders.

Females most often kill alone (89 percent) and kill only a single victim (95 percent). They usually stab their victims (41 percent), although almost one-quarter use a gun (23 percent). Police classify the motive in these cases as anger or an argument 64 percent of the time, and as mental illness-related 21 percent of the time. The event most often occurs in the victim's home (68 percent); rarely in public places (7 percent). Seventeen percent of murders by females are classified as first-degree murder (compared to 24 percent of the male-perpetrated murders).

SPOUSE KILLING[4]

One explanation for the prevalence of females who kill in domestic situations is the battered wife syndrome, as first espoused by Lenore Walker (1979), which generally involves women who are considered to be "trapped" in a battering relationship that makes them victims of serial physical and psychological abuse. Walker argues that women acquire learned helplessness in these situations.

According to Brodsky (1987), "Learned helplessness portrays a psychological condition which is based upon the finding that when an individual is subjected to repeated experiences over which she perceives she has no control or escape that may result in impairment in motivation and control of future outcome even after the uncontrollable situation disappears." In one way or another, the woman feels dependent on her current situation. She may be dependent on the male for economic support or for other types of support, or she may be dependent because she has children and sees no way of protecting the children if she leaves. She may feel or in fact be threatened by the male if she expresses a wish to leave; she may fear that the male will hunt her down after her departure. The point to emphasize about learned helplessness is that the woman *perceives* that she cannot leave the situation. This becomes a critical factor when juries need to be convinced that the woman could not simply have walked away from a bad situation.

Walker and others distinguish the battered wife on a variety of criteria, including low self-esteem; traditional views about the home and female sex roles; acceptance of the guilt and blame for the batterer's action; severe stress reactions with psychophysiological complaints; feeling that no one can help them unless they improve themselves (Cipparone 1987:427; Thompson 1986:75).

Walker describes three phases that occur during the cycle of violence. In the first phase, the male raises the level of conflict and tension between himself and his partner. This is sometimes done by name-calling, by demeaning, and by physical abuse. Dissatisfaction is expressed by the batterer with the woman. The woman tries to placate the male. When she can no longer control his violence, she attempts to withdraw from him and from the situation. In the second phase, the batterer unleashes uncontrolled rage that manifests itself in severe physical abuse. The final phase is the batterer's attempt to apologize and promise that he will not engage in the behaviour again. In the first few instances of the cycle, both the victim and the offender may believe that this is the end of the cycle. The offender may continue to believe that the cycle ends with the apologies and the showering of gifts, but after several instances the victim is unlikely to share the belief (Walker 1984).

At some point, the victim in the battering may attack the offender in self-defence. Issues arise in the courts as to the imminence of danger to the victim when she has attacked a sleeping offender or one who has his back turned toward her. Brodsky (1987) argues that juries need to be educated concerning the nature of the syndrome so that they will understand that the threat need not be immediate, but the victim's feeling that she is protecting herself from imminent danger (death) is real.

Interest in the battered woman syndrome from the perspective of this monograph is specific to cases in which serial violence culminates in murder—that is, while most serial beatings do not result in death,[5] some do.[6] It should be noted that in terms of murder, the battered woman syndrome creates both offenders and victims of women. On the one hand, the syndrome is involved when serial assault crosses the line between injury and fatality, and, on the other hand, it may be involved when a victim turns on her offender and kills him. In the latter case, empirical studies in the United States have shown that a great deal of female homicide offences are a reaction to the battered woman syndrome. Again, we lack Canadian data that would confirm the U.S. finding, but it is nonetheless safe to assume that a large amount of spouse killing by females in Canada is a direct result of serial attacks by their cohabitants. When women do kill in Canada, they kill a spouse or lover 44 percent of the time.

As pointed out earlier, one of the problems with the self-defence argument in these cases is that the ordinary citizen believes that the battered woman can simply walk out of an abusive relationship. There are several reasons why this does not happen. These include: a strong belief in the institution of marriage; a desire not to harm the husband's career; a desire to avoid the embarrassment of admitting to physical and sexual abuse; a feeling of helplessness and inability to make decisions; a well-justified fear of reprisal if she tries to leave, coupled with a financial inability to do so; the presence of children; a desire not to admit failure in the case of a second marriage; the hope that things will improve in the long run; a feeling that she is his property and is responsible for the abuse; the need to believe in the husband when he apologizes and swears that the battering will never happen again; and her contentment with the relationship between battering incidents, especially as she remembers his tenderness just following each attack (Thompson 1986).

To the average citizen, some of the above reasons may seem trivial in the face of being beaten. However, to the victim they are compelling enough to control her behaviour. Victims of the battered wife syndrome tend to exhibit low self-esteem and an inability to assess rationally their situation and their own strengths. They are often fearful and suspicious of others and develop fatalistic attitudes toward people and life in general. This is a part of the learned helplessness discussed above.

The court, when it accepts the battered wife defence, in effect modifies the doctrine of self-defence. Normally in a self-defence situation, the threat to the individual is immediate, but when a battered wife reaches a breaking point, there may be no immediate threat and therefore no defence of self-defence. In accepting the battered wife defence, the court is concluding that the woman had reason to fear for her life, if not immediately then in the near future, based on past behaviour of the homicide victim. In terms of Wolfgang's (1958) analysis, this constitutes a form of victim precipitation—i.e., the victim (husband) was the first to use physical force and he continued to do so.

Cipparone (1987) indicates that the traditional legal standard justifying the use of deadly force against another person is that the other person must have had a reasonable belief that (1) the victim was faced with an imminent threat of death or serious bodily harm; (2) deadly force was necessary in order to avoid or prevent such harm; (3) the victim has effectively withdrawn from the encounter and communicated the withdrawal to another person.[7] In Canada, the parts of the Criminal Code that are most relevant are section 34(2) and section 37.

Section 34(2) states that

everyone who is unlawfully assaulted and who causes death or grievous bodily harm in repelling the assault is justified if

(a) he causes it under reasonable apprehension of death or grievous bodily harm from the violence with which the assault was originally made or which the assailant pursues his purposes; and

(b) he believes, on reasonable grounds that he can not otherwise preserve himself from death or grievous bodily harm."

Section 37 states that if attacked one should use no more force than is necessary to prevent the assault or the repetition of it.

The battered woman's claim is most likely to be successful if she killed the batterer during an acute battering incident. A case of this type will usually produce grounds for a good self-defence argument that meets the required legal standards. It is more difficult, however, to show proof of imminent threat of death or serious bodily harm in those cases in which the killing occurred during a period of relative calm. The average jury member may, again, question the woman's inability to leave the undesired environment and in so doing fail to understand that the female's perceptions and values were such that she could not walk out on her untenable situation.

THE SUPREME COURT OF CANADA: LAVALLEE V. R.

The decision that will determine Canadian legal attitudes toward the battered woman syndrome defence was handed down by the Supreme Court on May 3, 1990. The case had gone to the Supreme Court on appeal. The appeal involved the adequacy of the trial judge's instructions to the jury regarding expert evidence, but the broader issue was the utility of expert evidence in assisting a jury confronted with a plea of self-defence to a murder charge by a (common-law) wife who had been battered by the deceased.

The case of Lavallee v. R. is paradigmatic of the battered wife syndrome as it has been elucidated above, and the implications of the Supreme Court decision will be far-reaching indeed. In describing the decision and its likely aftermath, we begin with a portion of the police transcripts that describe, in Lyn Lavallee's word, the actual murder event.

Me and Wendy argued as usual and I ran in the house after Kevin pushed me. I was scared. I was really scared. I locked the door. Herb was downstairs with Joanne and I called for her but I was crying and when I called him I said, "Herb, come up here please." Herb came up to the top of the stairs and I told him that Kevin was going to hit me, actually beat me again. Herb said he knew and that if I was his old lady things would be different; he gave me a hug. Okay, we are friends, there's nothing between us. He said, "Yeah, I know" and he went outside to talk to Kevin leaving, the door unlocked. I went upstairs and hid in my closet from Kevin I was so scared … My window was open and I could hear Kevin asking questions about what I was doing and what I was saying. Next thing I know he was coming up the stairs for me. He came into my bedroom and said, "Wench, where are you?" and he turned on my light and he said, "Your purse is on the floor" and he kicked it. Okay, then he turned and he saw me in the closet. He wanted me to come out but I didn't want to come out because I was scared. I was so scared. [The officer who took the statement then testified that the appellant started to cry at this point and stopped after a minute or two.] He grabbed me by the arm right there. There's a bruise on my face also where he slapped me. He didn't slap me right then, first he yelled at me then he pushed me and I pushed him back and he hit me twice on the right hand side of my head. I was scared. All I thought about was all the other times he used to beat me. I was scared, I was shaking as usual. The rest is a blank, all I remember is he gave me the gun and a shot was fired through my screen. This is all so fast. And then the guns were in another room and he loaded it, the second shot, and gave it to me. And I was going to shoot myself. I pointed it to myself, I was so upset. Okay, and then he went and I was sitting on the bed and he started going like this with his finger [the appellant made a shaking motion with an index finger] and said something like "You're my old lady and you do as you're told" or something like that. He said, "Wait till everybody leaves, you'll get it then" and he said something to the effect of, "Either you kill me or I'll get you." That was what it was. He kind of smiled and then he turned around. I shot him but I aimed out. I thought I aimed above him and a piece of his head went that way (R. v. Lavallee 1990: 337–38).

It is clear that the relationship between Lyn Lavallee and the victim, Kevin Rust, was volatile and punctuated by frequent arguments and violence. They would go through periods of fighting in which the defendant would receive bruises and even fractures. She explained to her family physician that she received these injuries from falling from a horse. (It is fairly typical of battered women to attempt to hide the real source of their injuries.) Further, after many of the fights, Rust would shower her with flowers and other gifts to try and make up. After a period of calm, the beatings would begin again. The violence was severe.

In the original Manitoba case, the expert testimony was provided by psychiatrist Dr. Fred Shane. Shane's opinion was that the appellant had been terrorized by Rust to the point of feeling trapped, vulnerable, worthless, and unable to escape the relationship despite the violence. The continuing pattern of abuse put her life in danger. Shane felt that Lyn Lavallee sincerely believed she would be killed that night if she did not kill Kevin Rust first (339). The doctor's opinion was based on four hours of formal interviews with the appellant, a police report of the incident (including the appellant's statement), hospital reports documenting eight of her visits to the emergency departments between 1983 and 1985, and an interview with the appellant's mother.

The appeal against the use of Shane's testimony as evidence was based on two grounds. First, it was argued that because none of the information that Shane used to form his opinion was "proved in evidence," his expert opinion should not be allowed to be placed in evidence. Neither Lyn Lavallee nor her mother testified, which led the prosecution to argue that the interviews with both she and her mother constituted hearsay and were therefore inadmissible. Second, the prosecution argued that the jury should be able to make up its own mind about issues of admissible evidence, and that the expert testimony was unnecessary and superfluous. The judge in the lower court had admitted Shane's evidence.

In writing for the Supreme Court, Justice Wilson says,

> Expert evidence on the psychological effect of battering on wives and common-law partners must, it seems to me, be both relevant and necessary in the context of the present case. How can the mental state of the appellant be appreciated without it? The average member of the public (or of the jury) can be forgiven for asking: Why would a woman put up with this kind of treatment? Why would she continue to live with such a man? How could she love a partner who beat her to the point of requiring hospitalization? We would expect the woman to pack her bags and go. Where is her self-respect? Why does she not cut loose and make a new life for herself? Such is the reaction of the average person confronted with the so-called "battered wife syndrome." We need help to understand it and help is available from trained professionals (R. v. Lavallee 1990: 349).

Justice Wilson, in this opinion, also confronts the issue of the "reasonable man." Claims made by the feminist movement that the law reflects maleness and a male orientation are substantiated by this case (see Comack 1991). What would a reasonable man do in Lyn Lavallee's circumstances? It is hard to say because a reasonable man virtually never has to confront such an issue. We can instead ask what a reasonable person would do when we take into account the variables of gender, physical stature, and psychological state.

Does the defendant have a reasonable apprehension of death? The Supreme Court decision refers to an earlier Canadian case that used the battered wife syndrome as a defence against murder. This case, known as R. v. Whynot (1983), involved a defendant who shot her husband while he was passed out in his truck. The deceased had administered regular beatings to his wife and others in the family. On the night in question the deceased had threatened to kill the offender's son. The Nova Scotia Court of Appeal held, in essence, that it is inherently unreasonable to apprehend death or grievous bodily harm unless and until the physical assault is actually in progress (R. v. Whynot 1983: 353). According to the Justice Wilson decision, "expert testimony can cast doubt on these assumptions as they are applied in the context of a battered wife's efforts to repel an assault." It is likely that both sections 34 and 37 of the Criminal Code will have to be reinterpreted as a result of this decision.

Justice Wilson explains the behaviours involved in this case in terms of the stages predicted in the Walker Cycle Theory of Violence (Walker 1979). We have in Lyn Lavallee an individual who was beaten, who felt she could not leave the relationship, who genuinely loved the person beating her, and who, finally, felt she would be killed if she did not immediately take action. This is the interpretation of the defence psychologist, which, if admissible, suggests that Lavallee had reasonable grounds to believe that her life was in imminent danger, even though the assault was not in progress. She felt incapable of escape. On the subject of admissibility, Justice Wilson says,

> I think the question the jury must ask itself is whether, given the history, circumstances and perceptions of the appellant, her belief that she could not preserve herself from being killed by Rust that night except by killing him first was reasonable. To the extent that expert evidence can assist the jury in making that determination, I would find such testimony to be both relevant and necessary. (R. v. Lavallee 1990: 362)

By way of summary, Justice Wilson offers six principles upon which expert testimony is properly admitted in cases of the battered wife syndrome.

1. Expert testimony is admissible to assist the fact-finder in drawing in for instances in areas where the expert has relevant knowledge or experience beyond that of the lay person.

2. It is difficult for the lay person to comprehend the battered wife syndrome. It is commonly thought that the battered women are not really beaten as badly as they claim, otherwise they would have left the relationship. Alternatively, some believe that women enjoy being beaten, that they have a masochistic strain in them. Each of these stereotypes may adversely affect consideration of a battered woman's claim to have acted in self-defence in killing her mate.

3. Expert evidence can assist the jury in dispelling these myths.

4. Expert testimony relating to the ability of an accused to perceive danger from her mate may go to the issue of whether she "reasonably apprehended" death or grievous bodily harm on a particular occasion.

5. Expert testimony pertaining to why an accused remained in the battering relationship may be relevant in assessing the nature and extent of the alleged abuse.

6. By providing an explanation as to why an accused did not flee when she perceived her life to be in danger, expert testimony may also assist the jury in assessing the reasonableness of her belief that killing her batterer was the only way to save her own life (R. v. Lavallee 1990: 362–63).

Justice Wilson cautions, however, that battered women may kill their partners for reasons other than self-defence. The mere fact that the appellant is a battered woman does not necessarily entitle her to an acquittal. The focus must be not on the woman but on what she did and whether it was justifiable. Thus the interpretation by the Supreme Court, while it expands the defences to homicide offered under the Criminal Code, does not give carte blanche to women to kill their battering husbands. It does, however, create a defence that was not previously possible by including the notion that relevant expert opinion is admissible even if it is based on second-hand evidence.

The Supreme Court has held that the battered wife defence is a legal defence in Canada. A defence can be based on the facts of the case combined with expert testimony concerning the psychological state of the victim. Expert testimony can be based on interviews that, prior to the Supreme Court decision, would have been considered hearsay. While we do not know the frequency with which battered wives kill their husbands, we can expect and predict that the number of such cases utilizing the battered woman syndrome as a defence will increase dramatically in the near future.

WOMEN WHO KILL THEIR CHILDREN[8]

While husbands or other cohabitants are the prime target of female killers, the second most frequent target is other family members, including children (Silverman and Kennedy 1988). In examining child victims of female parents, we divide the group into those who are charged with infanticide versus those who kill children but are charged with some other type of homicide.

The crime of infanticide is a strange and little used statute in the Canadian Criminal Code (see Chapter 2). That is not to say that the crime does not happen, but only that people are rarely charged under it. Between 1974 and 1990, only sixty-nine charges of infanticide were laid by police across Canada. According to Osborne (1987), the crime originated in England where courts did not like to give the ultimate penalty (whether death or life imprisonment) to mothers who had killed their children. The law encompassed what were then contemporary notions of the medical situation merely as a convenient way of avoiding the maximum penalties for this offence. Prior to the legislation, English common-law stipulated that mothers guilty of infanticide be treated in the same way as any other murderer.

The medical notions reflected in the current Canadian law have been regarded with scepticism by medical practitioners for quite some time. In effect, the law suggests that having a baby can cause a woman to be "a little bit crazy."[9] The Law Reform Commission of Canada suggests that the law of homicide be revised to exclude infanticide. If this happens, women who kill their infants will be subject to the same first- and second-murder laws as anyone else who kills another human being. It is probable that no matter what happens to the law, the courts will continue their longstanding practice of showing lenience toward mothers who kill their children.

In our discussion of infanticide, we have chosen to use a very narrow definition of the act by illustrating our points with the data about women who have been charged with infanticide in order to compare with data for noninfanticide killing. It is important for the reader to remember that many more women kill children or infants than are charged with the act. Our discussion divides women who kill their children into those who have been charged with infanticide and those who have not. We do not place age restrictions on the children for the second category. In the infanticide category, by definition, the children are classified as infants (under the age of one year). As will be seen, our argument is that different explanations are required for the different types of categories.

In the case of noninfanticide child-killing, violence against children can be addressed by using two somewhat different hypotheses. First, mothers who physically abuse their children occasionally do so to the point of killing them. Explanation for the beating is found in the violent family situation. Second, some mothers who beat their children to the point of death are transferring anger from the actual source of their distress and using the child as an available target. In either case, the source of difficulty lies in the family interaction. While we cannot directly measure these family interaction variables, we can examine the differences in the means of commission and motive in order to glean clues about the viability of these two explanations in accounting for this form of murder.

Mothers who are charged with infanticide are most likely drawn from a different population than the noninfanticide child-killing mothers. The infanticide mothers are likely to be younger and less mature. Our categories include mothers who kill their children, mothers who kill very young children and are charged with infanticide, wives who kill husbands, and women who kill people not in the first three categories. When comparing mothers who kill their children with other types of female-perpetrated homicide, differences appear between these perpetrators and others, and between those committing infanticide and noninfanticide mothers.

Women who violate the maternal role and kill their children are declared mentally ill in 67 percent of police reports (36 percent for those committing infanticide).[10] While U.S. researchers report similar findings (Weisheit 1986; Wilbanks 1982), there is little evidence to support a "mentally ill" hypothesis. Straus (1980a, 1980b), whose family violence data for the U.S. are probably the best currently available, believes that only about 10 percent of intrafamily violence can be accounted for by psychological factors. Police who support a mental-illness hypothesis likely view women who kill children as inconsistent with gender stereotypes and with socially understandable behaviour. "If they kill their kids, they must be crazy."

Straus suggests that the marriage licence is a hitting licence. The ability to have (or get) children is also a hitting licence. Noninfanticide mothers may hit their children simply because they cannot control their anger and frustration. They may hit, as well, because they cannot cope with children or because violence is directed against them. They may be untrained in child care, not knowing what to do with, or expect from, an infant or toddler.

Overwhelmed by the situation, they may strike out at the object of their frustration.

Noninfanticide mothers are younger than other female perpetrators, while infanticide mothers are barely more than children themselves. Mothers (infanticide and noninfanticide) use their hands to kill their offspring (see Totman 1978; Weisheit 1986; Wright and Leroux 1991). Noninfanticide mothers tend to beat their children, while those committing infanticide suffocate or strangle their offspring 40 percent of the time. The finding that noninfanticide mothers beat their children to death offers some indication that their child-killing is an extension of child abuse.

The factor that differentiates infanticide mothers from the noninfanticide group is (legally defined) intention to kill the child. Infanticide suggests that there is a mental condition that mediates the event. In fact, it seems that the social-psychological factor that governs infanticide is immaturity. As our data indicate, offenders are very young and unmarried. They do not commit suicide out of remorse for their crime, and they use a variety of means to kill their offspring. Those who have kept their pregnancies a secret probably see no option except to kill the child—to avoid discovery, and to avoid shame and stigma for themselves and their family. They seem in no way equipped to mother a child. Perhaps unsurprisingly, the most common occupation of those committing infanticide is "student." Unwanted pregnancies were undoubtedly widespread in this group.

Several researchers do, in fact, point out that a high proportion of out-of-wedlock pregnancies are unwanted (Smith et al. 1974).

> A recent example of a 16 year old who hid her pregnancy serves to illustrate the point. She gave birth to the child alone, was afraid of the consequences of discovery, and strangled or suffocated the infant (she was too confused to remember what she did). The body was left in a garbage bag in a truck full of garbage. The mother's charge was reduced from first-degree murder (carrying a life sentence, not parolable for twenty-five years) to infanticide (for which she received two years probation) (*Edmonton Journal*, 1987).

Most killing by females involves close family members and is relatively easy to explain. (There has been no observed increase in killing by females in the time period encompassed in our data.) Both entrapment in an abusive relationship and an inability to cope with children are typical of routines that place some women in situations that lead to child-killing. Strategies to diminish these acts must focus on getting women out of abusive situations, and on targeting those behaviours that are compatible with child abuse.

CHILDREN WHO KILL[11]

There has been a great deal of publicity recently in Canada given to cases of individuals charged with murder under the Young Offenders Act. The sensationalist tone adopted by the media in their treatment of these cases tends to create the impression that youths are committing inordinately high numbers of murders, and, moreover, that these offenders are receiving inordinately light sentences for crimes that, in the adult world, would be treated much more severely. The inference is that the youths who kill are incorrigible criminals who murder during the commission of other crimes, and that there is little or no deterrent value to the sentences under the Young Offenders Act.

With few exceptions (see Cormier et al. 1978; Markus and Cormier 1978; McNight et al. 1966; Toupin 1988), sociological/ criminological studies of youth murder that have been done are from the United States and for the most part draw their data from single geographical areas.[12] In using the American studies as a basis for comparison, two problems emerge. First, each employs a different definition of "youth." Goetting (1989) uses 15 as a cutoff age; Zimring (1984) compares those under 16 with those between 16 and 19; Rowley et al. (1987) categorize youth as those under 18 years of age. Second, American discussions of homicide are inevitably confounded by the racial issues intrinsic to that country where the focus has been on the black and, increasingly, the Hispanic offender. Race as an issue in Canada tends to focus on Canadian natives, since it has been this minority that has been disproportionately visible in terms of crime statistics (see Chapter 8 for a full discussion of homicide among Canadian Indians). In spite of these concerns, the American research provides both a point for comparison and a set of research questions that can be pursued using Canadian data.

Zimring (1984), in a study of age-specific rates in New York City, shows that homicide for those under 16 is substantially lower than rates for the general population. He also finds that there has been a decline in juvenile homicide[13] since 1973, and that as age of offender increases, the homicide rate increases. For those 13 years old the rate is 2.5, while for those 19 it is 34 per 100,000. Zimring (1981) argues that children commit crimes as they live—in groups. He finds that there is a decline in group-

PROFILE 6.2a

YOUNG SUSPECTS

Victim's Gender

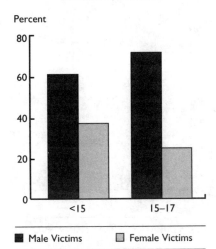

Male Victims   Female Victims

N = 146 suspects <15 and 648 suspects 15–17 years of age.

Victim's Age

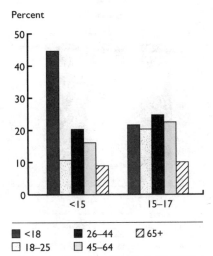

■ <18   ■ 26–44   ▨ 65+
□ 18–25   □ 45–64

N = 146 suspects <15 and 645 suspects 15–17 years of age.

Victim's Marital Status

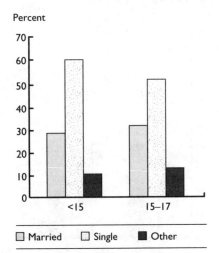

□ Married   □ Single   ■ Other

N = 144 suspects <15 and 642 suspects 15–17.
Married includes common-law.

Victim's Race

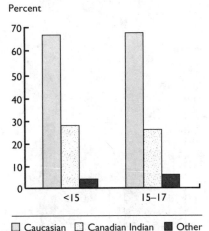

□ Caucasian   □ Canadian Indian   ■ Other

N = 139 suspects <15 and 618 suspects 15–17.

PROFILE 6.2b

YOUNG SUSPECTS

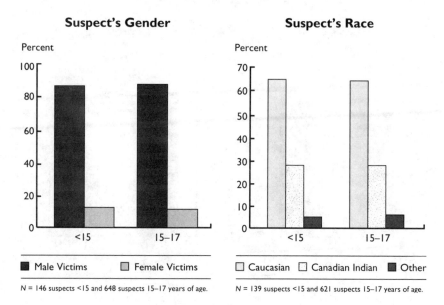

Suspect's Gender

Percent

■ Male Victims ▨ Female Victims

N = 146 suspects <15 and 648 suspects 15–17 years of age.

Suspect's Race

Percent

□ Caucasian □ Canadian Indian ■ Other

N = 139 suspects <15 and 621 suspects 15–17 years of age.

PROFILE 6.2c

YOUNG SUSPECTS

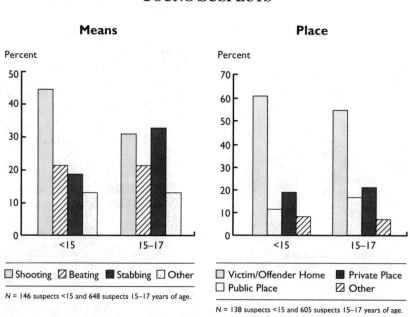

Means

Percent

□ Shooting ▨ Beating ■ Stabbing □ Other

N = 146 suspects <15 and 648 suspects 15–17 years of age.

Place

Percent

□ Victim/Offender Home ■ Private Place
□ Public Place ▨ Other

N = 138 suspects <15 and 605 suspects 15–17 years of age.

PROFILE 6.2d

YOUNG SUSPECTS

**Social Relationship Between
Victims and Suspects**

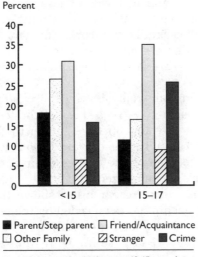

Percent

■ Parent/Step parent □ Friend/Acquaintance
□ Other Family ☒ Stranger ■ Crime

N = 146 suspects <15 and 648 suspects 15–17 years of age.

perpetrated homicides and in felonies as the age of the offender increases. Regarding weapons, he reports that the order of means of commission is shooting, stabbing, beating, and other.

Goetting's (1989) study of youth homicide in Detroit from 1977 to 1984 is hampered by the fact that the population of arrestees consists of only fifty-five juvenile cases—a surprisingly low statistic in a city that is plagued by drugs and has one of the highest homicide rates in the United States (54.6 per 100,000 in 1987). She defines homicide by children as homicide by those under 15 years of age. She finds that most of her offenders and victims are black and male. About 28 percent kill strangers, 27 percent kill acquaintances or friends, 17 percent kill close relatives; these proportions, Goetting claims, are similar to the general homicide findings. She also finds that youth homicide almost always involves same-sex and same-race killing, while 67 percent involve victims older than the offender. About 22 percent of these homicides take place during a crime (in addition to the homicide). Fifty-eight percent involve guns, and 19 percent involve stabbings or beatings.

Rowley et al. (1987) find that 7 percent of the homicide offenders in the U.S. in 1984 are under 18. In their study of 787 offenders for whom data were available, the age range of offenders is 10–17; 73 percent are white, and 13 percent are female. Eight percent of the offenders kill their parents, 9 percent kill other family members, 49 percent murder acquaintances, and 33 percent kill strangers. There is a clear relationship between theft and social relationship. The closer the relationship, the less likely theft is involved in the homicide. There is also a relationship between age and social relationship. Younger children are more likely to have killed family members. Further, the more socially distant relationships are more likely to involve multiple offenders. Finally, males are more likely to kill strangers than are females.

For purposes of our analysis, youth are defined as any individual under the age of 18, regardless of the legal prerequisites for qualification as a "young offender" under the Young Offenders Act. The bulk of the analysis is concerned with individuals under the age of 18 who commit the crimes of first- or second-degree murder. Youth are dichotomized into those under 15 and those between 15–17 as earlier research has shown these to be useful categories. Relationship has been coded by the police as the most intimate relationship between an offender and a victim, which reflects the fact that we are dealing with children and not adult perpetrators.

To a limited extent, we are able to replicate Zimring's (1984, 1981) studies using Canadian data. Direct comparisons are probably not appropriate given that Zimring uses data from New York city for a five-year period, while we use nationwide data for a thirty-year period. Nonetheless, the age pattern in which murder rates rise with age of offender were duplicated. The New York data reveal rates ten times that of Canada. This dramatic finding might lead to further research with more comparable data sets. Given the drug situation in the United States compared to that in Canada, it might be reasonable to predict a nationwide rate of juvenile murder in the United States that far exceeds that in Canada.

Figure 6.2 shows that the Canadian age-specific murder rate for juvenile offenders rises with age. Figure 6.3 compares the homicide rates for New York City youth from 1975 through 1980 with the homicide rates for Canadian youth between 1961 and 1990. In both cases, the homicide rate[14] rises dramatically with the age of the offender. In the case of New York City, the rate rose from approximately 2.5 per 100,000 for those 13 years of age to approximately 30 per 100,000 for those 17 years of age (Zimring 1984). The Canadian rates range from .23 per 100,000[15] for those

FIGURE 6.2

YOUNG OFFENDER HOMICIDE RATES, CANADA, 1961–1990*

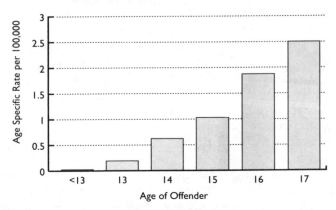

*Juvenile populations and juvenile homicide averaged over thirty years.

FIGURE 6.3

AVERAGE YOUNG HOMICIDE OFFENDER RATES, CANADA, 1961–1990; NEW YORK CITY, 1975–1980*

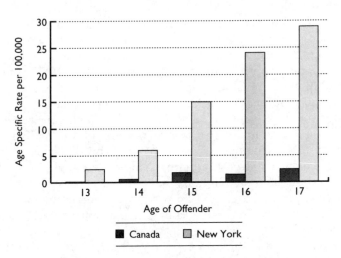

*New York City data adapted from Zimring (1984).

13 years of age to 2.5 per 100,000 for those 17 years of age. The proportionate increase, then, is essentially the same for both populations. In the thirty-year period between 1961 and 1990, Canadian juveniles between 13 and 15 committed 237 murders (averaging eight per year for the entire country). In the five-year period from 1975 to 1980, New York City juveniles between the ages of 13 and 15 committed 217 murders (averaging forty-three per year for one city). A comparison of general crime statistics between the United States and Canada indicates an expected difference of a magnitude of three or four times in this regard. Even taking into consideration the fact that New York City's crime rate is well above the national average, the magnitude of differences noted are much higher than expected.

Similar to the proportions reported by Rowley et al. (1987) for the United States, 7 percent of the homicides in Canada are committed by persons under the age of 18. As relational distance between offender and victim increases, so too does the probability of victimization by more than one offender in both the United States and in Canada. Crime-based homicide is the most likely of all murders to have multiple offenders as perpetrators. While the Canadian data confirm the general U.S. finding that most homicide involves single offenders and victims, there are some interesting differences between the United States and Canadian data. For every category of social relationship, there is substantially more multiple-offender perpetration in the United States than in Canada; other than the possibility of drug-related events, there is no immediately forthcoming explanation for this phenomenon.[16]

Between 1961 and 1990 in Canada, there were 794 incidents of murder involving offenders under the age of 18. Eighteen percent of these (146) involved children under 15 years of age. Close to 30 percent of both perpetrators under 15 and those 15–17 were Canadian Indian youth, a finding replicating Moyer (1987) that is examined in detail in Chapter 8.

When Canadian youth kill, 62 percent of victims of the younger children (under 15) and 73 percent of victims of older youth (15–17) are males. Forty-five percent of the victims of younger children are under 18 years of age, while the ages of victims of the older children are more evenly distributed across the age categories. Canadian Indians make up 28 percent of the victims of younger offenders and 26 percent of the victims of older offenders. There does not seem to be a rise in murder committed by younger children over the thirty years. In fact, there are between only one and thirteen cases a year over that time period, with the peak occurring in 1977. Similarly, murder by those 15–17 rises through the mid-1970s but has stabilized since that time.

Very few of these events are followed by the suicide of the perpetrator. Shooting is the most common means of murder commission for younger offenders (45 percent), while stabbing is slightly more frequent (33 percent) than shooting (31 percent) for older youth. This is the same pattern observed in the American studies.

As might be expected, 45 percent of the victims of younger offenders are family members and another 31 percent are friends/acquaintances. The Canadian proportion for the killing of family members is almost twice as high as the percentages reported in American studies (Goetting 1989; Rowley et al. 1987). Of all the cases involving offenders under 15, 18 percent involve children killing parents[17] and another 14 percent involve brothers and sisters killing each other.[18] In the case of older offenders (15–17), 12 percent kill parents.[19] For the older group, thirteen cases involve a young mother killing her infant.

What is surprising in the Canadian data is the extent to which criminal acts (besides the murder) are involved in murders committed by youth. In this case, the proportions between American and Canadian youth are similar. For the older group, 22 percent involve theft/robbery, while 7 percent involve a sexually related crime. For the younger offenders, the proportions are 14 percent theft/robbery and 3 percent sexually related.[20]

It is not easy to decide on the basis of these data why kids kill. For the older youth, internecine conflict is almost certainly involved in many of the events. Some of the crimes they perpetrate lead to death (planned or inadvertent). Some youths are living risky lifestyles in which drugs and alcohol play a major role. For others, conflict with their parents coupled with the availability of weapons leads to killing. Still others seem to be motivated by greed alone.

> Darren Huenemann was an upper middle class student at a Victoria high school. He was considered to be a nice kid and a "good boy." He was doted on by his mother and grandmother, who instilled in him a sense of middle class and materialistic values. Darren talked to friends about killing his grandmother and mother to get a very large inheritance. They thought he was joking. He was not. Eventually he convinced two friends, who were dazzled by his lifestyle, to kill the two women in return for money and status as his "special friends." He told the boys when and where the women would be together at his grandmother's home and how to get into the house. On Oct. 5, 1990, the boys entered the grandmother's Vancouver home, beat and stabbed the women to death and took money from the house. They disposed of the weapons on the ferry ride back to Victoria. The trail leading to Darren's conviction is complex but resulted mainly from his

early boasting about the plan to a female friend. Darren was found guilty of first degree murder (Birnie 1992).

THE ELDERLY OFFENDER

Gottfredson and Hirschi (1990) suggest that as age rises, crime declines. Hence, it is expected that the elderly offender will contribute less to crime than members of any other age group except the very young. Be that as it may, the elderly offender has generated a good deal of interest in criminological literature since the early 1980s. For most bureaucratic purposes, 65 years of age constitutes "aged," but there are other definitions in many circumstances. Studies of the aged and aging criminal have used cutoffs that include ages 35, 40, 55, and 65.[21] There are few theoretical rationales for using one age instead of another. The reason is that chronological age provides a convenient marker but does not really tap the theoretical concepts that are concomitant to aging. The cutoff age implies (either tacitly or openly) certain things about the subjects who fall into the age group. It implies a change in lifestyle, a diminishing social circle, a disassociation with the work environment, social isolation, and diminishing physical capacity and stamina.

The reader will note two important things about the list of concomitants to age and crime. First, the description does not fit everyone. We all know individuals past any of those age categories who are physically fit and highly active. Further, we know people who have continued in the work environment and have exactly the same social circle that they have had all their working life. Second, the age cutoff does not really inform the life change that is theoretically relevant—retirement. Retirement by its very nature implies a change of lifestyle, a withdrawal from the work environment, and often a change in social circle. Some theorists connect major changes in life to the death of a spouse, which is also not directly age-related. Much of the American literature uses 55 as the cutoff age, but rarely is it justified theoretically. In our research, we use 65 partly to be consistent with work that has been done on elderly *victims* and partly because it is the age that is probably closest in terms of the theoretical concerns to which we have alluded.

One thing that studying elderly offenders reveals is that most criminological theories were developed to explain the behaviour of delinquents and young adults, and those theories have to be modified to help explain elderly criminality. For instance, Akers et al. (1988) try to utilize social learning theories to explain

PROFILE 6.3a

SUSPECTS 65+ YEARS OLD

Victim's Gender

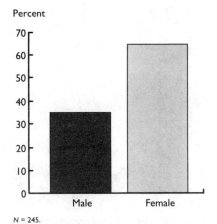

N = 245.

Victim's Age

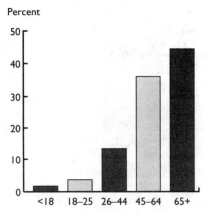

N = 244 (excludes unknowns).

Victim's Marital Status

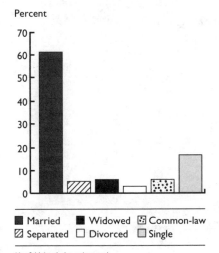

■ Married   ■ Widowed   ⊡ Common-law
▨ Separated ☐ Divorced   ☐ Single

N = 244 (excludes unknowns).

Victim's Race

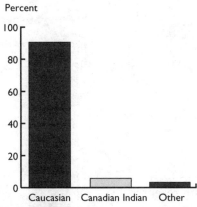

N = 232 (excludes unknowns).

PROFILE 6.3b

SUSPECTS 65+ YEARS OLD

Suspect's Gender

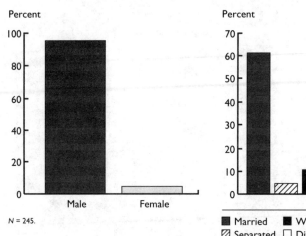

N = 245.

Suspect's Marital Status

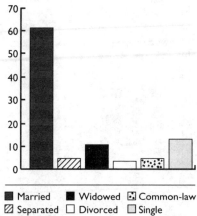

Legend:
■ Married ■ Widowed ⊡ Common-law
▨ Separated ☐ Divorced ☐ Single

N = 238 (excludes unknowns).

Suspect's Race

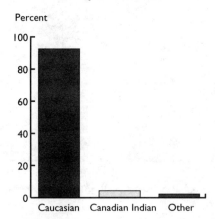

N = 234 (excludes unknowns).

PROFILE 6.3c

SUSPECTS 65+ YEARS OLD

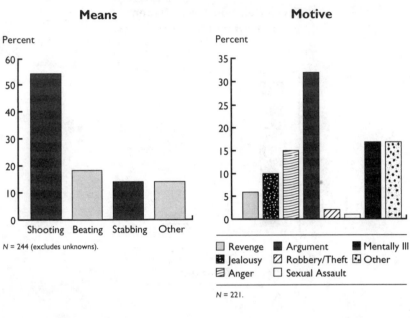

Means

Percent

Shooting   Beating   Stabbing   Other

N = 244 (excludes unknowns).

Motive

Percent

☐ Revenge   ■ Argument   ■ Mentally Ill
▨ Jealousy   ▨ Robbery/Theft   ⊡ Other
▨ Anger   ☐ Sexual Assault

N = 221.

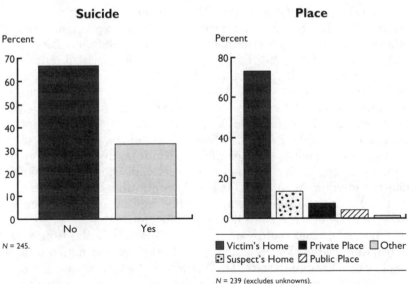

Suicide

Percent

No   Yes

N = 245.

Place

Percent

■ Victim's Home   ■ Private Place   ☐ Other
⊡ Suspect's Home   ▨ Public Place

N = 239 (excludes unknowns).

PROFILE 6.3d

SUSPECTS 65+ YEARS OLD

Social Relationship Between Victims and Suspects

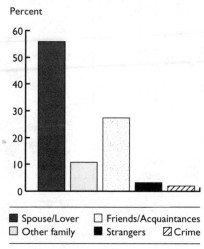

Percent

Spouse/Lover □ Friends/Acquaintances
□ Other family ■ Strangers ☒ Crime

N = 245 (excludes unknowns).

elderly criminality. Others (e.g., Fishman and Sordo 1984) use theories involving the aging process itself to explain deviant behaviour among aging criminals. Malinchak (1980), employing Miller's (1983) focal concerns, suggests that the elderly also have focal concerns that lead them to crime.

Subcultural theory was designed initially in a delinquent environment and later utilized to describe adult communities (Wolfgang and Ferracuti 1967). It is theoretically feasible that the elderly individual who has been a part of the subculture of violence throughout his or her life will continue in that environment to be aggressive or otherwise antisocial. This view of the elderly individual as one who is simply continuing a life of crime is at odds with the general empirical finding that a high proportion of elderly offenders are first-time offenders.

Similarly, one could ponder how Hirschi's social control theory might apply to the elderly. While the general notion of a weak or strong bond to society may work in attempting to explain elderly crime, one would again be suggesting that the change in behaviour with age is simply an extension of one's behaviour throughout life. Alternatively, one might link a change of behaviour to the loss of a significant other, but, of course, the age cutoff at 65 is not likely, in itself, to accompany such an event.

Some kinds of elderly criminality, particularly elderly violence, have been interpreted as a symptom of a mental disorder or "organic brain disease" such as senility (Gewerth 1988). However, in their examination of the elderly, Kratcoski and Walker (1988) eschew this theory of criminality and deal instead with elderly crime through the use of routine activities theory. The advantage of this approach in studying the elderly is that it is behaviourally rather than motivationally based. While it may not satisfy the quest to learn why these crimes occur, it can help predict certain aspects of the behaviour that provokes them. Following Kratcoski and Walker, we outline how routine activities theory explains elderly involvement in murder.

Elderly homicide offender/victim relationships will be significantly higher within the same age category than will nonelderly offender/victim relationships. As one ages, one's social circle ages as well. As physical stature declines with age, the theory suggests that there would be a lower proportion of firearms in elderly rather than nonelderly homicides.

Routine activities theory suggests that the elderly individual will spend more time at home than younger persons, due in part, to withdrawal from the work environment. Based on the notion of a convergence of time and space of offender and victim, one would predict that the elderly offender would commit homicide against those who are in the home (e.g., spouse, family members). Kratcoski and Walker expect to find "the ratio of elderly male to elderly female offenders to be less than the ratio of younger male to younger female offenders." This would be consistent with the notion that most elderly homicides would involve spouses. It is also consistent with a finding in earlier research on the elderly (Shichor 1985).

Given the domestic nature of the homicides, it is likely that elderly offenders will act alone when they commit the homicide. Suicide following homicide will be higher than in other types of homicide. A significantly greater proportion of elderly homicides than nonelderly homicides will occur in the home. Canadian Indian involvement in elderly murder will be significantly lower than Indian involvement in other types of murder. The rationale here is that, while Canadian Indians kill within their families, Canadian Indian cultures generally revere age and it is less likely that elders will have the motivation to kill.

We utilize the entire population of Canada for the thirty-year period, a cutoff age of 65, and the comparison group of the rest of the offenders in our sample. An examination of the data shows that the elderly are rarely involved as murder offenders. Only 2.3

FIGURE 6.4

VICTIM/OFFENDER RELATIONSHIP BY AGE OF OFFENDER, CANADA, 1961–1990

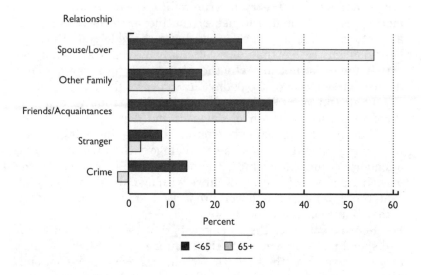

Relationship

Percent

■ <65   □ 65+

percent (245) of the total number of murders involve offenders aged 65 and over. Given that about 8 percent of the population in Canada is 65 or older, the proportion involved in murder is lower than might be expected.

Most murder by those 65 and older is perpetrated against a spouse or lover (56 percent). Another 11 percent involve other family members. It is extremely rare for someone over 65 to be involved with either a concomitant crime or stranger murder (a total of thirteen cases in thirty years). The remaining 27 percent of the murders committed by the elderly are perpetrated against their friends and acquaintances. Ninety-six percent of the elderly murder is committed by males, which compares to 88 percent for those under 65. In effect, this means that in a thirty-year period only nine females 65 and older committed murder.

Only 5 percent of murders by the elderly are committed by Canadian Indians (versus 17 percent for the under 65 group.) Ninety-three percent are committed by Caucasians. When elderly males kill, 35 percent of their victims are male and 65 percent are female—a reversal of the findings for those under 65, where 37 percent of the victims are female and 63 percent are male. Of the nine elderly female offenders, all but one killed a male (compared to 76 percent of those under 65). All of the 245 elderly suspects acted alone in committing their murder (compared to 86 percent of those under 65).

Kratcoski and Walker (1988) find that their prediction that most offenders would kill people in the same age range as themselves does not hold. However, they compared those over 65 with those 15 to 59. There is nothing magical about the age cutoffs, and it is very likely that those who are 65 (or 60) kill those just on the other side of that line, for instance people in their mid-50s. In the case of our group, 45 percent kill people 65 and older and 36 percent kill people between the ages of 45 and 65. Hence, by modifying the hypothesis slightly to include those in the concomitant age categories we confirm the hypothesis.

More than 73 percent of murders by the elderly occur in the victim's home, compared to about half of the nonelderly murders. A further 14 percent occur in the suspect's home. Very few (only 4 percent) occur in public places. Following murder, fully one-third of the elderly offender group commit suicide (compared to about 9 percent of those under 65), confirming Kratcoski and Walker's hypothesis.

Fifty-four percent of the elderly murders (compared to 36 percent of the rest) involve shooting (see Figure 6.5). Eighteen percent beat their victims, 14 percent stab them, and 14 percent use other means. In interpreting these findings, we suspect that there may be a factor of "frailty" in which a gun becomes a great

FIGURE 6.5

MEANS OF MURDER COMMISSION BY AGE OF OFFENDER, CANADA, 1961–1990

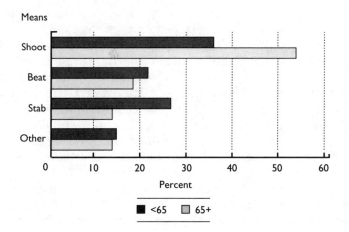

equalizer. More probably, though, the simple availability of guns is what determines whether or not they will be used.

The distribution of motivations as determined by police coding is very similar for those over 65 and under 65. There is a higher amount of "mental illness" listed for the older group, which more likely reflects police sensibilities than it does any real understanding of motive. There is, of course, a suspicion that at least some of the murders that are followed by suicide are motivated by a desire to end mutual suffering rather than by arguments or anger.

There does not seem to be a trend toward an increase in elderly murder. The peak years for elderly murder are 1977 and 1987 (eighteen cases each), with declines following each of those years. However, there are only about ten or fifteen of these events per year in Canada, and only eight cases in 1990, the most recent year in our study.

SUMMARY

Because most murder is perpetrated by adult males, other groups that commit murder are interesting in their own right. When women kill, the target is most likely a member of their own family. Most often their victims are males. A woman often kills her spouse after a series of incidents in which she was a victim of assault. In 1990, the Supreme Court of Canada modified the doctrine of self-defence to include the "battered woman syndrome" (Lavallee v. R.). While a significant step for women, the defence is likely to generate controversial court action.

Next to spouses, women most often kill their children. There are two major circumstances in which such killing takes place. Noninfanticide child-killing likely represents child abuse gone awry. In a fit of rage or frustration, the mother strikes out at the child in a way that inadvertently causes death. In cases of infanticide, young females, ill-equipped to have children and unable to care for them, kill them as a means of coping. Over one-quarter of the women who kill in Canada are Canadian Indians. Their murder rate is alarming and may reflect circumstances peculiar to their living conditions. Female murder, as indicated by social relationship with the victim, is quite different from male murder. Overall, females account for only about 12 percent of all murder offenders, and that proportion does not seem to be rising.

In examining children who kill, we offered a comparison with U.S. data. About 7 percent of U.S. and Canadian murders are perpetrated by those under 18 years of age. However, the rate of youth murder in Canada is only a fraction of that in the U.S. Male youths are the most likely perpetrators of murder in both countries.

Canadian youth homicide is about twice as likely to involve a family member as U.S. youth homicide. However, about equal proportions of Canadian and U.S. youth perpetrators are involved in crime-related homicide. Younger children are more likely to kill family members, while older children are involved in less intimate homicide.

While we are able to describe the population and the distribution of youth homicide in the two countries, explanations for the events are not easily obtained. The conflict of a child with a parent is understandable, but the degree of animosity necessary for such a relationship to result in homicide is more difficult to comprehend; the perpetrators are likely low self-control individuals who find themselves in difficult living arrangements.

The elderly constitute less than 3 percent of murder offenders. The vast majority of perpetrators are male. More than one-half of their murders are perpetrated against a spouse. In total, about two-thirds of their victims are family members. Following the murders, close to one-third of the elderly offenders commit suicide, an indirect measure of remorse. Our examination of the elderly offender was placed in the context of routine activities.

N O T E S

1. For purposes of comparison, the profile charts include both genders.

2. The average rate of homicide by females over the period 1961–90 is about 0.4 per 100,000 women in the population. The average male offender homicide rate for the same period is about eight and a half times higher than the female rate, at 3.33 per 100,000 males in the population.

3. Education information is available for only 44 percent of the offenders.

4. While the discussion below is concerned with the battered woman syndrome, women kill their spouses under other conditions as well. We cannot, however, differentiate one type from the other with these data. We concentrate on battering in the spousal relationship because of societal concern and because of the importance of the court decision discussed.

5. The estimates of the incidence of wife assault (700 per 100,000) with half of those being victims of multiple assaults is quite astounding (Juristat 1990.) Estimates of the proportion of couples in which the male engages in wife assault range from 11 percent to 18 percent (see Lupri 1989; Smith 1987; Kennedy and Dutton 1989).

6. Unfortunately, our homicide data do not include information that illuminates this issue. Police do not generally record information concerning serial assault or calls to a particular address (on a cumulative basis), and, even when they do, it does not find its way into the national data set. If this data element were to be collected by the Canadian Centre for Justice Statistics, we would have national data that could point to the extent of battered woman problem.

7. For a substantial minority of jurisdictions, there is a need to provide proof that there were no safe avenues for retreat available to the person who had resorted to the use of deadly force (these are conditions necessary in U.S. jurisdictions).

8. Much of the literature review and orientation in this section is drawn from Silverman and Kennedy (1988), reproduced by permission. While data in this section cover 1961–83, the proportions indicated have not changed between 1983 and 1990.

9. There is evidence that at least some women suffer from a neurochemical imbalance following birth that manifests itself in emotions varying from deep depression to rage—emotional states could be used to explain violence against infants.

10. Interestingly, only 6 percent of women who kill their spouses are declared mentally ill, versus 9 percent of those who kill acquaintances or family members.

11. Much of the material in the first part of this section is taken from W. Meloff and R. Silverman (1992), reprinted by permission. Between 1961 and 1990, there were a total of 146 homicide incidents attributed to children under 15 years of age and 648 incidents of homicide attributed to those between 15 and 17.

12. For instance, Goetting, (1989) uses 55 cases from a seven-year period in Detroit; Zimring (1984) uses 286 cases of children under 16 and 1111 cases of youth between 16 and 19 from New York City between 1975 and 1980. The only recent national American study that encompasses all types of juvenile homicide was done by Rowley et al. (1987).

13. Various authors refer to "youth," "juveniles," and "children" in discussing this kind of crime. Even though these terms have specific meanings in the adolescence literature, they will be used interchangeably here.

14. In order to calculate age-specific rates, it was necessary to use data provided by the "relative trends" database compiled by the Canadian Centre for Justice Statistics. This was combined with a definition of youth that was essentially chronological (i.e., under 18 years of age). Unfortunately, this combination introduces some errors into the equation but was the only way in which it was possible to generate both a numerator and a denominator for the calculation. Because the information is averaged over thirty years, we are convinced that the error level is minimal and that the overall pattern that appears in Figure 6.2 is an accurate portrayal of the age/homicide relationship.

15. The average rate for those under 13 is .023 per 100,000.

16. In fact, using a chronological definition of youth, the rate of youth homicide has been stable or decreasing recently (Silverman 1990).

17. Only two of these cases involve daughters killing parents; the rest are all male offenders.

18. Four of these offenders are sisters; the rest are brothers.

19. Eight cases involve daughters killing parents, while the rest (sixty-nine) involve sons.

20. These percentages are different than those in the profile table because they were generated in a separate run and based on a lower total number of youth (due to unknown cases). It should be noted that over the thirty years there were seventeen theft/robbery and four sex-related homicides for younger offenders.

21. Gartner and Piliavin (1988) suggest that the cutoff age that probably makes most sense is the mid-30s. Their reasoning is that the highest crime-committing age group is between the years of 15 and 30; therefore, crime declines after the age of 35. The Gartner and Piliavin argument is absolutely logical as long as one is doing some kind of time series analysis of aging and crime. For most of the studies that use a cross-sectional methodology (i.e., one point in time), 35 is not really a very useful basis for dividing up the population for analysis.

C H A P T E R   7

Special Victims
CHILDREN, THE ELDERLY,
AND WOMEN

Contemporary interest in child abuse, elder abuse, and violence against women leads us to the study of these groups of victims. In this chapter, we present findings from some of our earlier studies of child and elderly victims, but we update the data to reflect the most current information available. In the final section, we examine female victims of murder.

CHILDREN AS VICTIMS[1]

In Chapter 4 we focused on relationships and were concerned with parents who kill their children. Here we are interested not only in the victims of parents but in all child homicide victims. While all homicide is disturbing, the killing of children somehow seems more tragic. In many cases, children are killed by parents who abuse them. In Canada, little has been written about children who die through homicide. Even the U.S. child-homicide literature often suffers from limited samples and constrained jurisdictions. Frequently, the research dwells on psychiatric causes or clinical samples (Resnick 1969, 1970; Browne and Palmer 1975; Cole et al., 1968).

In one of the earliest nonclinical studies, Adelson (1961) examines forty-six childhood homicides taking place over a seventeen-year period in Cuyahoga County. The children are identified as "preadolescent." Adelson's sample was generated by coroner's office records, and no single racial group dominates his data as victims or offenders. Thirty-six of the forty-six children are killed by a parent or someone standing *in loco parentis*. Beatings are a common mode of child killing and many of the assailants are classified as "mentally ill" by Adelson.

Resnick (1969), in reviewing "the world literature on child murder from 1951 to 1967," finds 155 reported cases of which 131 are filicides. While the eclectic sample makes generalizations difficult, a few of the findings are worth noting. There are twice as many maternal filicides reported (eighty-eight mothers compared to forty-three fathers). Thirteen percent of the maternal filicide and 28 percent of the paternal filicide involve "head trauma" or beating.

Kaplun and Reich (1976) study 112 homicides of children under 15 occurring in New York City in 1968 and 1969. They find that in over two-thirds of the cases the assailants are the parents or their common-law partners. The older the victim, the less likely the offender is a parent. Mothers are most often the assailants, while fathers are assailants in about 10 percent of the cases. "There was a pattern of long-term familial child maltreatment extending to siblings and continuing after the murders" (1976:809). Homicide assaults, Kaplun and Reich argue, are generally unpremeditated and impulsive. The studies by Kaplun and Reich (1976), Resnick (1969), and Adelson (1961) are oriented to the mental state of the assailant and other precipitating factors in the homicide of children. Of the three studies, only Kaplun and Reich obtained a sample from which some generalizations can be drawn.

Goetting (1986) establishes a profile of victims and offenders using thirty-six parents or parent figures arrested in Detroit between 1982 and 1986 for killing their children under 6 years of age. She finds that offenders are overwhelmingly black, young, undereducated, unemployed, and likely to have an arrest record. The relationship with the child "is severed in a rage of impatience and anger at a private residence as a result of beating or shaking" (10). This underlines the importance of family abuse as a precursor to homicide among children. In an earlier study (Silverman and Kennedy 1988), and in Chapter 6, we speculate that children killed by women mainly fall into one of two categories—"child abuse gone awry" or infanticide by very young mothers. Goetting's findings lend credence to that speculation.

In Illinois between 1973 and 1982, Miller (1983) finds a decreasing number of killings between ages "under 1" and 11 years (but she does not calculate age-specific rates). She also finds that, while adult males are more often victims than adult females, murdered children are almost as likely to be female as male. Children who are under 14 and victims of homicide are overwhelmingly black in Chicago and white outside the city. Finally, child homicide victims are most often the victims of beatings as opposed to stabbings or shootings. Family members are the perpetrators in 49 percent of the Chicago child killings and 71 percent of those outside of Chicago.

The most recent research on child homicide uses a social structural approach to the issue and deals with age-based rather than relationship-based analysis. Fiala and LaFree (1988) analyze cross-national homicide rates and find that "high levels of female labour-force participation, coupled with low levels of female status and welfare spending, result in high child homicide rates" (432). They relate high levels of economic stress to a societal-level model of child abuse as measured by the child-homicide rates.

In her research, Gartner (1990) finds differences in the correlates of homicide for younger and older children and for adults. For instance, family dissolution predicts higher child-homicide rates for older children, while low welfare spending predicts higher child-homicide rates for younger children (as was suggested by Fiala and LaFree 1988).

In other research using World Health Organization data, Christoffel and Liu (1983) find that the child-homicide rate in the U.S. is "atypically high." An examination of the data indicates that the median U.S. child-homicide rate for very young children (<1) is about 1.5 times that of Canada, while for older children (1–4) the rates in the U.S. and Canada are very similar. Earlier work (Christoffel and Stamler 1981) showed that homicide rates for children in developing countries are independent of homicide rates for all ages, while in developed countries the relationship comes closer to a significant correlation. They argue, therefore, that in developing countries there is a unique infantile pattern of homicide, while in developed countries there is an increased risk for children based on a societal pattern of homicide.

Daly and Wilson (1988a), using a sociobiological approach, show that younger children are killed at a higher rate than older children. They link this finding to increased bonding by parents to older children (particularly females) as they approach reproductive age. They further suggest that mothers rarely kill older children and predict similar patterns for fathers.

Silverman et al. (1990) examine racial differences in child homicide in Illinois versus Ontario. Illinois white children have more in common with their neighbours to the east in Ontario than they do with the black children who are killed in their own state. The black victim is distinct in the method of crime commission, the relationship to the suspect, and the age of the perpetrator. The data provide no obvious reasons for the differences, but offer indirect evidence for explanations based on our knowledge of crime patterns and theories of racial differences in the commission of violent crime.

It is arguable that there are two types of homicide against black children. The first type involves domestic situations similar to those occurring for white children and Ontario children; the second type involves gang activity and perhaps drugs. We cannot control for these two possibilities directly, and our data only give us indirect clues as to the viability of the two types of homicide. For instance, our finding that older black children are often killed by nonfamily members, who are known to them and who use handguns, points in the direction of youth conflict.

Weapons also provide a further insight into certain cultural differences both between blacks and whites and between Ontario and Illinois. As expected, handgun use is lower in Ontario than in Illinois. Given this finding, it is surprising to find that the proportion of children killed with firearms in Ontario is greater than the proportion of white children killed with guns in Illinois. The Ontario children are mainly killed with rifles or shotguns, while the Illinois children are killed with handguns. This finding suggests that the stringent Canadian handgun laws protect Ontario children from being killed with pistols but not from being killed with other firearms.

On the other hand, the rate of handgun use against black children in Illinois is significantly higher than the rate for either of the other groups. Black offenders, especially younger offenders, do not seem adverse to the use of guns. Recent media reports suggest that long guns (assault rifles) are often used in drug-related killings and in sniper attacks in the housing projects of Chicago, which may explain the numbers of black children who are killed with these weapons. The long guns used in Ontario are almost certainly hunting rifles found in the home.

Miller (1983) suggests a different explanation for the Illinois findings. If the killings of white children mainly take place outside of Chicago, while the killings of black children mainly take place in Chicago, we could, she suggests, be dealing with two very different phenomena, determined by the lifestyles that are led in urban versus suburban or rural environments. In the case of the black children, we might find explanations in the structural theories mentioned above. In the case of the white children, we might look for explanations in the child-abuse literature.

CANADIAN CHILD HOMICIDE

In the remainder of this section, we examine the patterns of homicide against all Canadian children. The Illinois/Ontario comparison was guided by hypotheses suggested by the earlier literature on child-killing. Here we examine the same variables for all children killed in Canada to see if the Ontario findings hold true

FIGURE 7.1

RATE OF HOMICIDE AGAINST CHILDREN
CANADA, 1961–1990*

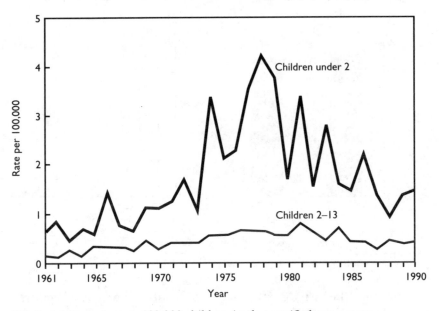

*Victimization rates per 100,000 children in the specified age groups.

for the rest of the country. The variables of concern include age-specific crime rates, gender, and social relationships between victim and offender, and types of weapons used. In addition, we will examine numbers of offenders and race of offenders and victims.

Figure 7.1 shows that homicide rates for victims between the ages of 2 and 13 rise slowly over the 1961–90 period but peak at only 0.8 per 100,000. The rate for those under 2 peaks at levels well above the average overall homicide rate. In 1978, the highest year recorded, the victimization rate for children under 2 is 4.2. The trend shows major fluctuations but generally is upward until 1978, after which it declines. The rate of killing young children has been higher than the rate of killing those 2–13 throughout the period. The rate of victimization against those 2–13 rises slightly to a peak in 1981 and then declines. The reason for the patterns are not obvious, but the rate against younger children, in particular, should be monitored closely.

A total of 876 cases involving child victims occurs in Canada between 1961 and 1990. This amounts to less than 10 percent of

PROFILE 7.1a

CHILD VICTIMS

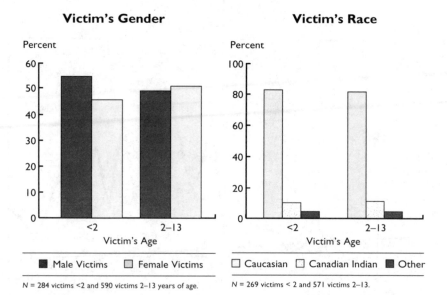

Victim's Gender

Percent

N = 284 victims <2 and 590 victims 2–13 years of age.

■ Male Victims   □ Female Victims

Victim's Race

Percent

N = 269 victims < 2 and 571 victims 2–13.

□ Caucasian   □ Canadian Indian   ■ Other

the total homicide in the country. About 33 percent of children killed in Canada are under the age of 2, while 67 percent are between 2 and 13. Victims are almost equally divided between male and female. Younger children are more likely to be killed by women, while older children are more likely to be killed by men, a finding consistent with the Ontario data. Almost 55 percent of victims under 2 are killed by females, while two-thirds of those 2–13 are murdered by males.[2]

Killers of younger children are themselves young. Fifty-seven percent of the under-2 group are killed by persons under 26 years of age. For those 2–13, 44 percent of the offenders are under 26 while 49 percent are between 26 and 44. Again, these data are very similar to the Ontario figures.

In the Illinois/Ontario study, we predicted that children, especially young children, would most often be killed by a parent. For younger (< 2) children in Canada as a whole, we find that 46 percent are murdered by their mother and another 34 percent by their father or stepfather. Of those 2–13, 25 percent are killed by their fathers or stepfathers and 29 percent by their mothers. All told, 86 percent of the younger group and 68 percent of the older group are killed by family members. For the older group, other

PROFILE 7.1b

CHILD VICTIMS

Suspect's Gender

Percent

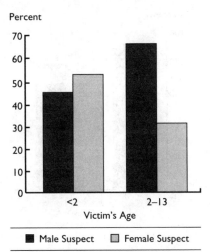

Victim's Age

■ Male Suspect   ▨ Female Suspect

N = 270 victims < 2 and 547 victims 2–13 years of age.

Suspect's Age

Percent

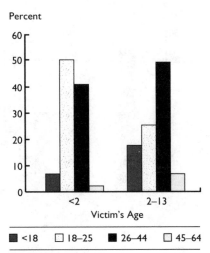

Victim's Age

■ <18   □ 18–25   ■ 26–44   □ 45–64

N = 270 victims < 2 and 543 victims 2–13 years of age.

Suspect's Marital Status

Percent

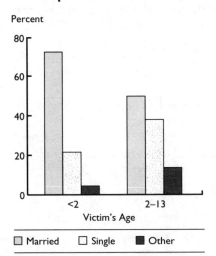

Victim's Age

▨ Married   □ Single   ■ Other

N = 268 victims < 2 and 541 victims 2–13 years of age.
Married includes common-law.

Suspect's Race

Percent

Victim's Age

▨ Caucasian   □ Canadian Indian   ■ Other

N = 257 victims < 2 and 532 victims 2–13 years of age.

PROFILE 7.1c

CHILD VICTIMS

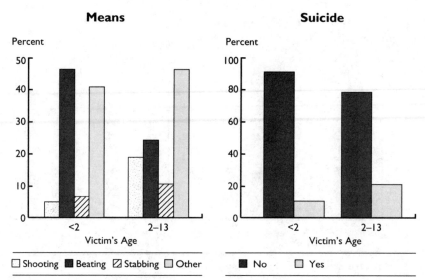

Means

Percent

<2 2–13
Victim's Age

☐ Shooting ■ Beating ▨ Stabbing ☐ Other

N = 279 victims < 2 and 578 victims 2–13 years of age.

Suicide

Percent

<2 2–13
Victim's Age

■ No ☐ Yes

N = 270 victims < 2 and 547 victims 2–13 years of age.

Place

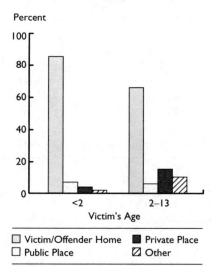

Percent

<2 2–13
Victim's Age

☐ Victim/Offender Home ■ Private Place
☐ Public Place ▨ Other

N = 277 victims < 2 and 571 victims 2–13 years of age.

PROFILE 7.1d

CHILD VICTIMS

Social Relationship Between Victims and Suspects

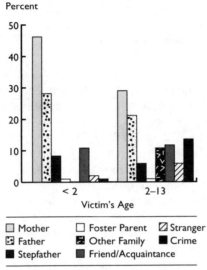

Percent

N = 270 victims < 2 and 547 victims 2–13 years of age.

family members are responsible for 11 percent of these deaths, while friends/acquaintances murder 12 percent, strangers 6 percent and 14 percent are killed during the course of another crime.[3]

On the basis of our discussion of battered children and children killed in other circumstances, we expected younger children to be less often killed with guns than older children. Indeed this is the case. Only 5 percent of children under 2 (none in Ontario) are shot to death compared to 19 percent of older children. On the other hand, 40 percent of those under 2 years of age and 47 percent of those 2–13 years of age suffer death through suffocation, strangulation, drowning, arson, and other means. (This, of course, contrasts with the adult homicide victim population, who are more likely to die by gun than by any other way.) Almost 47 percent of child homicide victims under 2 (compared to 24 percent of those 2–13) are beaten to death.

Homicide against younger children mainly occurs in the victim's home, as does homicide against older children; however, the probability of becoming a victim of homicide outside of the home is much greater for older than younger children. Most child killers are Caucasian (regardless of age of victim), and 11 percent are Canadian Indian. Virtually all of the cases are intraracial, again regardless of age of the victim.

The crimes involving those under 2 almost exclusively involve a single victim. About 80 percent of the homicides of children 2–13 involve a single victim, while 20 percent include more than one victim. Ninety-four percent of killings of children under 2 and 95 percent of those of children 2–13 are perpetrated by offenders who act alone.

Homicide against children can be differentiated by age of the victim. We have shown here and in the Illinois/Ontario study that killing of younger children is likely related to child abuse that has gone further than the parent intended, while it is likely that killing of older children is more deliberate. For the moment, these conclusions are interpolations based on earlier studies in the U.S. and on the indirect measures we have used here.

Children under 2 are killed by very young offenders. In Chapter 6, we showed that mothers who commit infanticide are barely more than children themselves. These offenders kill in panic, not knowing what to do with an unwanted child; their children are strangled, suffocated, and beaten to death, but rarely die by the gun. The killing of other young children is done in uncontrollable rage by mothers with low self-control who are often caught in an untenable life situation.

Older children may be killed by parents in fits of rage, but they are also killed by other relations and even die during the course of other crimes. They are murdered by friends during fights and by relatives in the course of arguments or violent anger. They are more likely than younger children to be the victims of shooting.

It is interesting to note that the rates of homicide against children decline somewhat after the age of 5 (Wright and Leroux 1991). This finding lends some credence to the routine activity notion. Children over 5 spend large parts of their day in school and out of the house. If they are, indeed, at risk from those with whom they live, then being away from those people alleviates any stress or tension in the home. The new daily activity of school takes children away from those whom we like to think are most likely to love and protect them, but in these instances are most likely to harm them.

THE ELDERLY VICTIM[4]

Accepted doctrine in criminology has been that the elderly experience low rates of victimization and high levels of fear of violent crime. Questions have been raised about the latter claim (see Ferraro and LaGrange 1988). In addition, it can be said that the vulnerability of the elderly does make them good targets. If a perpetrator knocks down an older woman and steals her purse, she is less likely to get up and give chase than a younger, more agile victim. At the same time, routine activities/lifestyle theory (Felson and Cohen 1980; Hindelang, et al. 1978) credits the low victimization rates of the elderly to their self-protective tendency not to venture out alone, thereby decreasing their vulnerability. In other words, by their actions the elderly reduce the probability of victimization. Victimization in their homes will likely occur at the hands of those who routinely occupy the same space—their family and/or close friends (Messner and Tardiff 1985). Some recent findings from American homicide studies contradict this predicted pattern.

The victimization literature consistently finds the elderly to be the least victimized age group in American and Canadian society (Centers for Disease Control 1986; Eve 1985; Goldsmith and Goldsmith 1976; Hindelang et al. 1978; Yin 1985; Canadian Urban Victimization Survey 1985, Fattah and Sacco 1990). It is argued that the isolation accompanying their lifestyle contributes to a lower rate of victimization (Canadian Urban Victimization Survey 1985). However, while such rates remain relatively low, recent studies show a rising rate of homicide against this age cohort (Copeland 1986; Wilbanks 1981/82; Kunkle and Humphrey 1982/83).

In a 1976 study, Dussich and Eichman delineate the effects of lifestyle on victimization of the elderly. They suggest that for vulnerability to attract an offender it must be obtrusive: offenders must be able to locate targets they consider prime for attack. For instance, an elderly person alone in an isolated area is "obtrusive and vulnerable." Generally, though, the lifestyle of most elderly people is unobtrusive, which by lowering their degree of blatant vulnerability should inhibit their victimization.

Following from this research, Messner and Tardiff (1985) and Cohen and Felson (1979) suggest that because the elderly (and the young) spend more time in their homes and interact primarily with "family" members, they more often than others will be killed by family members in or near their homes. Hence, while their routine activities protect them from strangers and predatory crime, they do not thwart family (and perhaps friends) who would prey on their vulnerability. Messner and Tardiff's (1985) analysis of age-specific homicide rates in the U.S. confirms only that the elderly and the young are more likely to be killed at home than elsewhere. At the same time, they are as likely to be killed by a family member as by a stranger (254).[5]

PROFILE 7.2a

VICTIMS AGED 65+

Victim's Gender

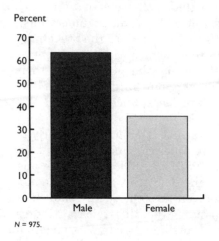

N = 975.

Victim's Marital Status

Married   ■ Widowed ☒ Common-law
☑ Separated □ Divorced ■ Single

N = 951 (excludes unknowns).

Victim's Race

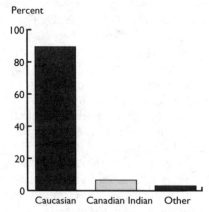

N = 920 (excludes unknowns).

PROFILE 7.2b

VICTIMS AGED 65+

Suspect's Gender

Percent

N = 813.

Suspect's Age

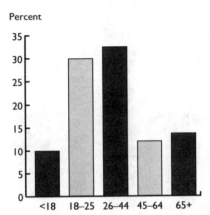

Percent

N = 810 (excludes unknowns).

Suspect's Marital Status

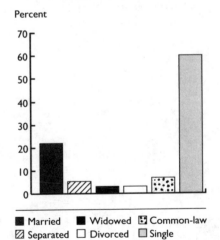

Percent

■ Married ■ Widowed 🖾 Common-law
🖾 Separated ☐ Divorced ☐ Single

N = 794 (excludes unknowns).

Suspect's Race

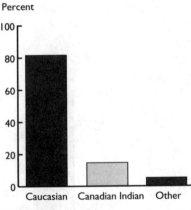

Percent

N = 778 (excludes unknowns).

PROFILE 7.2c

VICTIMS AGED 65+

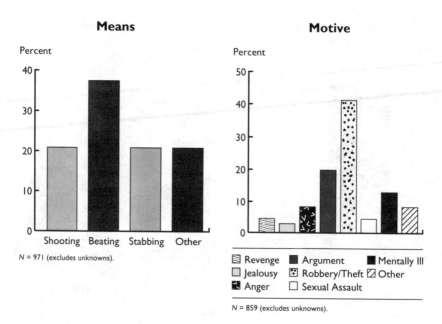

Means

Percent

N = 971 (excludes unknowns).

Motive

Percent

☰ Revenge ■ Argument ■ Mentally Ill
☐ Jealousy ⊡ Robbery/Theft ▨ Other
■ Anger ☐ Sexual Assault

N = 859 (excludes unknowns).

Place

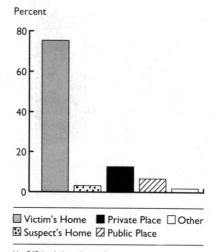

Percent

☐ Victim's Home ■ Private Place ☐ Other
⊡ Suspect's Home ▨ Public Place

N = 945 (excludes unknowns).

PROFILE 7.2d

VICTIMS AGED 65+

Social Relationship Between Victims and Suspects

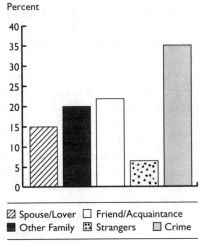

Percent

☑ Spouse/Lover ☐ Friend/Acquaintance
■ Other Family ▨ Strangers ☐ Crime

N = 813 (excludes unknowns).

Other research on routines of the elderly does not support Dussich and Eichman's hypotheses or Messner and Tardiff's findings. Copeland (1986) reports from research done in Dade County, Florida, that homicide among the elderly is more common than expected (though still relatively low), accounting for approximately 5 percent of all murders in that county during the previous five years. Contrary to both conventional wisdom and previous findings, he finds that homicide of the elderly most commonly involves robbery or burglary. Further, over 60 percent of the homicide of the elderly in Dade County occurs in their home, most often by gunshot wound but also commonly by blunt-force injury, sharp-force injury, and asphyxia (261).

Maxfield, using selected metropolitan areas from the U.S. Supplementary Homicide Reports, concludes that the "elderly are disproportionately victims of murder in connection with an instrumental felony" (1988:15). Such felonies include theft-based homicides. Fox and Levin (1991) find that the elderly in the United States are often victimized during theft crimes. Hence, findings of Maxfield, and Fox and Levin are consistent with the research of Silverman and Kennedy (1987), Kennedy and Silverman (1990), and Copeland (1986).

The vulnerability of the elderly, when outside of the home with no one to protect them, provides the minimum requirements for predatory crime, particularly theft. In the home, those people thought most likely to protect the elderly may in fact perpetrate violence. But the predictions of routine activities theory seem unable to account for Copeland's (1986) finding that frequently a stranger perpetrates homicide against the elderly in their homes. This contrasts with other age groups, for which victim and offender are most often family members or friends involved in arguments.

Among all victims in murder incidents in Canada between 1961 and 1990, the elderly suffer the lowest proportion (8 percent, N=975) of murder compared to other age groups (41 percent for those 26–45 and 20 percent each for those 18–25 and 46–64). However, this 8 percent is directly proportional to the numbers of elderly in the general population (Statistics Canada 1984). Unlike Wilbanks' (1981/82) data, Canadian national data reveal no upward trend in murder against the elderly. Over the thirty-year period, murder of Canadians averages 2.02 per 100,000, while murder of elderly Canadians averages 1.57 per 100,000 individuals over the age of 64. The rate for the elderly ranges from a low of 1.06 per 100,000 in 1962 to a high of 2.4 in 1976 and more or less declines between 1977 and 1990. In fact, the 1990 rate is lower than the 1961 rate.

More than 75 percent of elderly murder victimization occurs in the victim's home (compared to 53 percent of those under 18, 33 percent of those 18–25, 46 percent of those 26–44, and 58 percent of those 46–64). Most researchers suggest that younger individuals spend more time outside of the home and are therefore more likely to be victims in public places than are the elderly, who spend more time at home; hence, according to lifestyle theory, younger people will be murder victims more often than other age groups.

Building on the lifestyle hypotheses and the notion that the elderly spend more time at home than in other places, we suggest that the elderly victim of homicide will more often fall victim to someone known to them than to a stranger. Figure 7.3 indicates, as predicted, that the elderly are more likely to be killed by someone they know than by anyone else (58 percent). However, 43 percent of the elderly are killed by strangers (either during the course of another crime or not), a proportion almost twice as high as for those 46–64 years of age. Apparently, the elderly have more to fear from strangers than do other age groups.

As their probable greater vulnerability to physical violence suggests, the elderly are more likely than any other age group to die as a result of beatings than by any other means. Contrary to

FIGURE 7.2

ELDERLY MURDER VICTIMIZATION RATES, CANADA 1961–1990

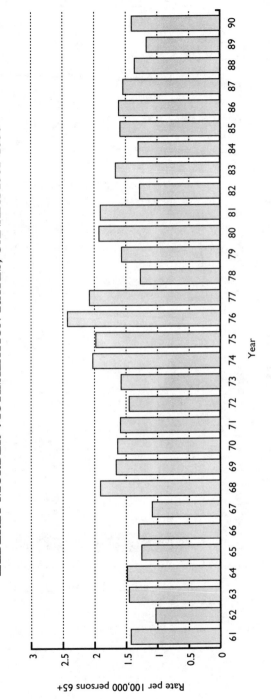

FIGURE 7.3

VICTIM/OFFENDER RELATIONSHIP BY AGE OF VICTIM, CANADA, 1961–1990

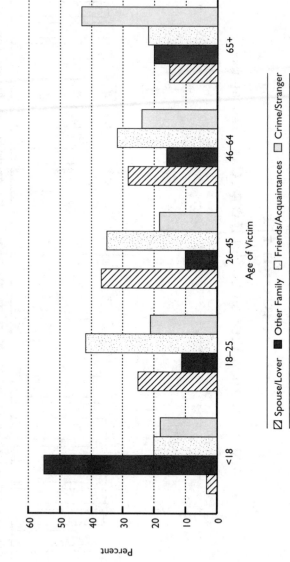

■ Spouse/Lover ■ Other Family □ Friends/Acquaintances □ Crime/Stranger

FIGURE 7.4

PRECIPITATING CRIME BY AGE GROUP OF VICTIMS,* CANADA, 1961–1990

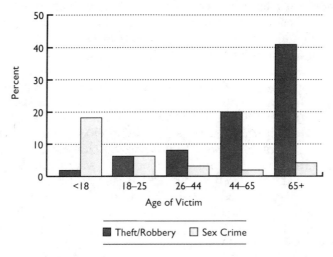

*Proportion of all homicides committed against each age group.

our prediction, there are a lower proportion of stabbings in this group than in any other age group except those under 18. The proportion of shootings is lowest for the elderly, with almost equal proportions of stabbing and other means following.

Routine activities theory suggests that the elderly are least likely of all age groups to fall to crime-based homicide, where a theft or robbery precipitates death. In fact, the elderly are more than twice as likely (41 percent) as others to be victims of theft-based murder[6] (this supports Copeland's (1986) findings in smaller, more local samples). Another 4 percent of murders with elderly victims involve sex-related crime.

To summarize, the elderly are victims of murder most often as a result of blunt force in their own homes. Although the location is as expected, beating rather than shooting or stabbing is the most prevalent means of murder commission against the elderly. Further, the elderly are victims of theft-based murder more often than anticipated; proportionately, they suffer this kind of murder far more often than any other age group.

What we can conclude from these findings is that, for the elderly, the home is as dangerous a place as a public place with regard to theft-based murders by strangers. It is also dangerous from the point of view of family offenders. These and earlier research findings are inconsistent with some of the predictions made by routine activities theorists. It is possible, however, to mesh theories and findings into a new formulation that retains the logic of the situational orientation of routine activities/lifestyle theory. Predictions that the elderly can become victims by isolating themselves at home are correct, as are those that suggest they will most often be killed by someone they know. However, this theory is inconsistent with the fact that a disproportionate amount of homicide of the elderly at home is at the hand of a stranger intent on committing theft. To explain this anomaly, we must re-examine the conceptual bases for our hypotheses.

Routine activities theory suggests that, at a minimum, the conditions for predatory crime require a convergence in space and time of motivated offenders, suitable victims, and a lack of victim protectors. Using these criteria to predict elderly victimization, researchers have concluded that being outside of their homes increases the target-likelihood for elderly persons as this exposes their vulnerability (frailty). Yin (1985) reports that the elderly are often victims of predatory street crimes, but their most usual routine activity is isolation in their homes, making them less vulnerable (accounting for the low general victimization rate). While we do not have direct measures of routine activities for victims of homicide, patterns in victimization surveys should apply. Data from the Canadian Urban Victimization Survey (CUVS) (1985) show that 90 percent of those over 65 and 63 percent of those under 65 report that someone is home for all or part of the day; 11 percent of the former compared to 37 percent of the latter report no one at home during the day; and the elderly report much more constrained evening activities than do younger persons.[7] In addition, measures of location and social relationship to offenders in homicide cases give some indirect clues about these routines.

Interpretations of routine activities have emphasized the activities of both offender and victim that generate the crime situation. For the elderly, the routine activity is to stay at home. In other words, the activity is inactivity—a state not generally considered by the routine activities theorists. The social isolation that virtually every researcher has thought lowers victimization rates is sometimes a liability. The activity of the burglar coupled with the inactivity and vulnerability of the elderly renders crime possible and, for some, perhaps irresistibly attractive. Reppetto's (1974) study of burglars and burglary shows that young burglars are more concerned with ease of dwelling entry than with the goods found within. Further, areas with low daytime occupancy rates are the most likely to be considered good targets. Warr

(1988) finds that opportunity characteristics that define the "good target" for burglary also define those for rape.

From this altered perspective, routine activities theory might now consider that the target of the crime is not the elderly person but rather the dwelling and its contents. Taking into account the work of Reppetto (1974), Miethe et al. (1987), Copeland (1986), Warr (1988), and Maxfield (1988), routine activities theory would now predict that the elderly person, living quietly alone in an area with low daytime occupancy, is not detected by the thief, or if so is not a threat because of his or her perceived vulnerability. In a confrontation, the elderly individual, if alone, may resist or not but is nevertheless beaten. While a younger person might recover, the elderly victim dies. Thus, for the elderly, the safety of the home is offset by the vulnerability to attack during a crime and the difficulty in recovery from beating.

Why are there such high levels of crime-based homicide against the elderly when compared to other age groups? Recent literature on the effects of injury on individual well-being provides clues. Findings on the impact of personal theft against the elderly support the view that they are especially vulnerable to the consequences of these acts, which are sometimes fatal (Dussich and Eichman 1976; Eve 1985; Hindelang et al. 1978; Kosberg 1985; Skogan and Maxfield 1981). The CUVS reports that, while the elderly are no more likely than younger victims to have suffered injuries as a result of victimization from any crime, the consequences of their injuries are typically more serious: "elderly victims who were injured were twice as likely as younger victims to have required medical or dental attention" (1985:2). Medical statistics substantiate the view that the death rate from injury is higher among the elderly than younger people, even though injury is the leading cause of death among the latter (Committee on Trauma Research 1985:19).

As we pointed out earlier, Warr (1988) suggests that one type of rape results from chance encounter. That is, a burglar inadvertently encounters a vulnerable woman and rapes her. This scenario is very similar to that suggested above for elderly victims of homicide. While Warr argues that this type probably does not account for a large proportion of all residential rape, it is likely (according to our findings) that death is the unanticipated outcome of many home burglaries of the unaccompanied elderly.[8] Following Warr, we can suggest that the elderly person whose dwelling's characteristics attract burglars is probably at higher risk of death through theft-based homicide than are those in less targetable dwellings.

Our explanation of elderly homicide fits a slightly modified version of routine activities theory. The lifestyle of elderly individuals who live alone makes some vulnerable to theft and injuries that may prove fatal (especially to them). Their isolation coupled with the offender's motivation to burglarize (or with the burglar's simple choice of target) create a potential homicide situation.

This reformulation does not undermine the activity-based portion of the lifestyle/routine activity theory most often used in recent research that can explain homicide against the elderly by a friend or family member. The value of the reformulation is that it explains the inconsistent research findings cited earlier by taking into account both inactivity and activity as precipitators of crime.

FEMICIDE: WOMEN AS MURDER VICTIMS

Women as victims of violence is an important contemporary topic. In this section, we propose to examine homicide data as they relate to female victims of murder. For much of the analysis, we contrast female victims with males. We have, of course, already referred to some of these issues in the chapters that dealt with spousal relationship and women as offenders.

Some authors have noted that the family is a nucleus of violence (Gelles and Straus 1988; Fattah 1991). We pointed out in Chapter 4 that proximity, coupled with intimacy, physical stature, domestically defined unresolved problems, and offenders with low self-control, can lead to violence. Because the proportion of family-related female victimization is so high, a discussion of the female victim of homicide is often inextricable from a discussion of family violence (Wilbanks 1982; Browne and Flewelling 1986). Alternatively, some authors attempt to examine female homicide victimization from the perspective of structural correlates such as women's participation in nondomestic productive activities (Gartner et al. 1987), labour force participation (Yang and Lester 1988), and female emancipation (Stack 1987). While an effect seems to be operative in some of these variables, the link between the theory and the measures is often tenuous.

Gartner and McCarthy (1991) examine motivational, opportunity, and alternative perspectives in attempting to explain femicide (female homicide victimization) in Toronto and Vancouver and find that none of the three is totally correct in its predictions. They report that femicide is time-dependent (that is, there are historically specific contexts and contingencies for homicide against women that change over time), but that it retains its "more intimate and private character ... compared to homicides of males" (1991:823). Marriage does not protect women from

PROFILE 7.3a

MALE AND FEMALE VICTIMS

Victim's Age

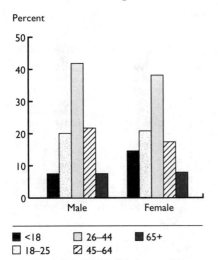

N = 8128 male victims and 4684 female victims.

Victim's Marital Status

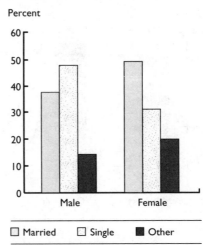

N = 8008 male victims and 4656 female victims.
Married includes common-law.

Victim's Race

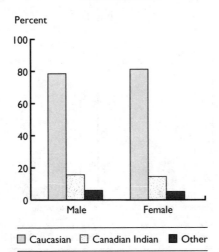

N = 7765 male victims and 4455 female victims.

PROFILE 7.3b

MALE AND FEMALE VICTIMS

Suspect's Gender

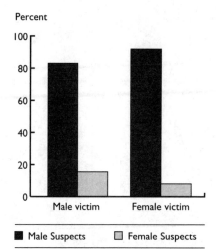

Percent

Male Suspects ■   Female Suspects ☐

N = 6683 male victims and 4073 female victims.

Suspect's Age

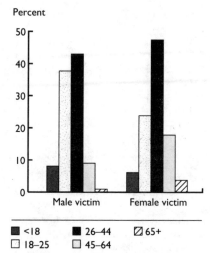

Percent

<18 ■   26–44 ■   65+ ☑
18–25 ☐   45–64 ☐

N = 6671 male victims and 4062 female victims.

Suspect's Marital Status

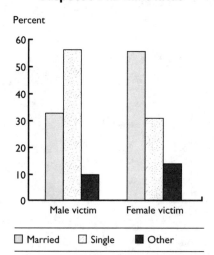

Percent

Married ☐   Single ☐   Other ■

N = 6501 male victims and 4021 female victims.
Married includes common-law.

Suspect's Race

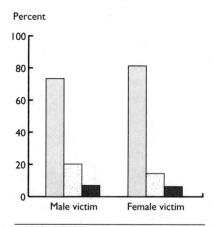

Percent

Caucasian ☐   Canadian Indian ☐   Other ■

N = 6455 male victims and 3908 female victims.

PROFILE 7.3c

MALE AND FEMALE VICTIMS

Means

Suicide

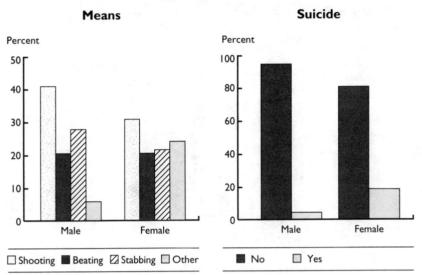

Shooting ☐ Beating ■ Stabbing ▨ Other ☐

N = 8106 male victims and 4616 female victims.

No ■ Yes ☐

N = 6683 male victims and 4073 female victims.

Place

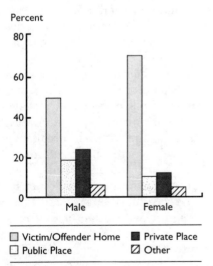

Victim/Offender Home ☐ Private Place ■
Public Place ☐ Other ▨

N = 7543 male victims and 4374 female victims.

PROFILE 7.3d

MALE AND FEMALE VICTIMS

Social Relationship Between Victims and Suspects

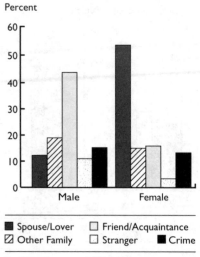

N = 6683 male victims and 4073 female victims.

homicide—in fact, the home is the most likely place for homicide to take place and intimate partners are most often the offenders. Interestingly, and contrary to some contemporary theorizing, after 1970, employed women are less at risk from homicide than women not in the workforce.

Women's routines are bound to play a part in their role as victim. The domestic scene outlines routinized behaviour as it relates to many women who are objects of violence. The violence occurs in the home and an intimate partner is the offender. The problems that precipitate the violence are domestic in nature. The offender is a low self-control individual and there is a high probability that the victim and/or offender consumed alcohol prior to the homicide. Unfortunately, we do not have direct measures of many of these variables, but we can extrapolate some of them indirectly through a description of the nature of homicide against women.

Women constitute about 40 percent of all murder victims over the thirty-year period we examined. The proportions vary somewhat over the years but have generally been in the one-third to 40 percent range. There is a media-fuelled public perception that violence against women is on the rise (*Maclean's* 1991). However, the rate of murder against women has been stable since the mid-1970s. Figure 2.3 shows that murder against women peaks at slightly over 2 per 100,000 women in 1975 and then stabilizes at rates between 1.5 and 2.0.[9] Male rates rise and fall much more dramatically than female rates, even when overall patterns are similar. In the early 1960s, male murder rates were about 50 percent higher than female rates, but, by the mid-1970s, the male rates were twice that of female victims.

The most notable difference between male and female murder patterns involves social relationship in the victimization patterns. Our data indicate that twelve percent of the males are killed by their spouse/lover, 19 percent by another family member, and 44 percent by a friend or acquaintance. Fifty-three percent of the female victims meet their demise at the hands of a spouse/lover, 15 percent are victims of nonspousal family members, and 16 percent are victims of friends/acquaintances. The proportions for males and females killed by a spouse are virtually identical to those found with a much larger number of cases in the United States (Browne and Flewelling 1986).

Figure 7.5 clearly differentiates male and female victims. For male victims, in recent years, over one-half of the murders involve friends and acquaintances, while less than 10 percent involve a wife as perpetrator. In contrast, the figure shows that the overwhelming proportion of female victimization over the thirty-year period has been spouse-generated. While that proportion has dropped from 70 percent of all murders against women in 1961 to 43 percent in 1990, it has remained the dominant type of murder against females throughout the period. As spousal murder has declined, the proportions of murder involving friends and murders involving other crimes have risen slightly.[10]

As might be expected from these patterns, when a female is a murder victim, 92 percent of the offenders are males.[11] Offenders who kill women tend to be a little older than those who kill males. Eighty-one percent of those who kill females are Caucasian, but 20 percent of the males and 13 percent of the females are victims of Canadian Indian perpetrators. Five percent of the cases with male victims and 8 percent of those with women victims involve more than one victim, but 19 percent of male homicides compared to only 5 percent of female homicides involve more than one offender; this finding is expectable given the social relationships that dominate each type of murder interaction (spousal for females and friend/acquaintance for males).

Male and female victims are very similar in terms of age distribution. Fifteen percent of the female victims are under 18, 21 percent are between 18 and 25, and 38 percent are between 26

FIGURE 7.5

TRENDS IN VICTIM/OFFENDER RELATIONSHIP BY VICTIM'S GENDER

Proportion of Female Victims by Social Relationship, Canada, 1961–1990*

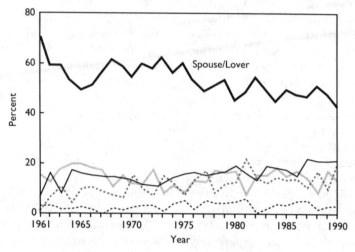

*Proportion of all homicides in which there was a female victim.

Proportion of Male Victims by Social Relationship, Canada, 1961–1990*

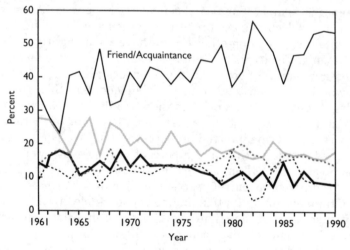

*Proportion of all homicides in which there was a male victim.

— Spouse/Lover — Other Family — Friends/Acquaintances ···· Crime ···· Stranger

and 44. Almost half of the female victims are married (legal or common-law), compared to 36 percent of the male victims. Forty-eight percent of the male victims, versus 31 percent of the female victims, are single. Close to 80 percent of male and female victims are Caucasian, but about 15 percent of each are Canadian Indians. A much higher proportion of murder against females than murder against males results in the suicide of the perpetrator (19 percent versus 4 percent); this, too, is an indicator of the very real differences between murders against women and those against men.[12]

A higher proportion of male murder victimization is the result of shooting (41 percent compared to 31 percent), but the major difference between the male and female categories is to be found in means other than shooting, stabbing, and beating. One-quarter of the crimes against females, compared to 10 percent of those against males, fall into the category of strangling, suffocating, and drowning.

Sixteen percent of murders against males and 6 percent against women involve a theft, whereas 1 percent of male murder victims and 12 percent of the females have been subjected to a sexual crime concomitant to the murder. Twice as many murders against women, compared to those against men, are attributed by police to the mental illness of the offender (11 percent versus 5 percent). Most murders against women occur in their own homes (65 percent compared to 40 percent for murders against men). Gartner and McCarthy (1991) find that the proportion of murders in the victim's home actually increases slightly over time. We do not have Canadian data to show where in the house the murder takes place, but, using Philadelphia data, Wolfgang (1976) shows that "the bedroom is a more lethal place for wives than for husbands. For the kitchen the reverse seems to be true" (1976:320). In Canada, 13 percent of the female victims compared to 24 percent of the males are killed in a public place.

In sum, contrary to some popular conceptions, femicide has not been increasing. Further, the proportion that is family-related—especially spousal—has declined over the thirty-year period, although it still remains very high. Risk of murder for women is still most likely related to being in a poor domestic situation.

Summary

Interest in elder abuse, child abuse, and female victims led us to examine these homicide victims. While the incidence of homicide is relatively low for children and the elderly, women make up 39 percent of homicide victims. Children are most often killed by a parent or another member of their family. Almost three-quarters of the children under 2 and one-half of those 2–13 are killed by a biological parent. Children are most often beaten or die through suffocation, strangulation, drowning, or "other" means. Older children are more likely to be shot than younger children. Our findings for child victims of homicide tend to confirm earlier research and suggestions regarding the relationship between child abuse and child homicide. Children are certainly most at risk from those with whom they have the closest relationships.

Research on elderly victims suggests that they would most likely be victims of people they know in their own homes. To some extent, our findings confirm these hypotheses, but the surprising finding is that the elderly are the most likely age group to be victims of homicide at the hands of a stranger in the course of a crime.

Assumptions of routine activities theory can be supported for the elderly victim of homicide only after some revision to the theory. Essentially, the elderly victim is vulnerable in his or her own home when a physically more agile offender invades the home with the purpose of burglary.

The homicide rate for female victims has remained relatively constant since about 1974. The proportion of homicide that is intimate-partner-related has stayed very high during the thirty years reviewed. The findings in this section are intertwined with our analysis of spouse/lover murder in Chapter 4 and are generally consistent with routine activities theory. Given the nature and "causes" of the victimization, it is possible that interventions may be more successful for murder against women than for other types of murder.

NOTES

1. Much of the literature review and focus of this section is taken from Silverman, Riedel, and Kennedy (1990), reprinted by permission.

2. In contrast, males dominate child-killing in Illinois regardless of age of victim.

3. In the Illinois/Ontario analysis, stranger and crime-based homicide were combined. Illinois reflected a smaller proportion of this kind of homicide.

4. Much of the literature review and focus of this section is taken from Kennedy and Silverman (1990), reprinted by permission.

5. Messner and Tardiff analyze the young and the old in their sample together, making it difficult to assess the effects of routine activities separately for each.

6. The next closest group in this category are 44–65, and only 20 percent of the homicides against this group are theft-driven.

7. These data were extrapolated from the Canadian Urban Victimization Survey Data Tape (Solicitor General of Canada 1985). The study was conducted in 1982, retrospective to 1981, but the data were not released until 1985.

8. As Warr (1988) points out, the problem of measuring motive hinders verification of this. Few data sets have direct or indirect measures of that psychological contingency, if, indeed, any can be developed.

9. The stability of homicide rates against women (over time) is also found in the United States (Smith 1987).

10. Contrary to the findings for Canada as a whole, for Toronto and Vancouver Gartner and McCarthy find that "femicides by intimate partners *did not* decrease relative to other types of femicide, even as women began to spend more time in a wider variety of public relationships" (1991:823).

11. When a male is the victim, 85 percent of the offenders are male and 15 percent are female.

12. This finding is similar to Wolfgang's (1976) finding for husbands and wives—19 percent of the husbands and 2 percent of the wives committed suicide following the homicide.

Canadian Indian Involvement in Murder

The connection between the elements of social inequality, social disorganization, and individual propensities toward violence is well illustrated in the case of Canadian Indians. Canadian Indians constitute 2 or 3 percent of the Canadian population but perpetrate 17 percent of the murder incidents committed in Canada. It is a well-documented fact that Canadian Indians are overrepresented in crime statistics and in our prison population (LaPrairie 1987; Sinclair 1990; Hamilton and Sinclair 1991; Havemann et al. 1985; Moyer 1987; Silverman and Nielsen 1992). How might one proceed to describe and explain Canadian Indian involvement in the justice system? We will review these and other issues related to Indian homicide in this chapter, which, it should be noted, incorporates arguments related to social structural disadvantage that were discussed in Chapter 3, because much of the violence in this group has been attributed to inequality and social disadvantage. The data analyzed, though, are the micro-level data drawn from the national data set on individual homicide events.

CANADIAN INDIANS AND MURDER IN PERSPECTIVE[1]

Those who research issues involving Canadian Indians in the justice system have used essentially two approaches. According to Havemann et al. (1985), the most fruitful explanation involves an examination of colonialism, industrialization, and modernization.

Canadian Indians are the most disadvantaged economic group in Canadian society and are large users of the welfare system. In the 1990s, one would not find any support for a thesis that suggests that the Canadian Indian culture per se promotes crime or violence. Instead, "the structure of power relationships resulting from colonialization is such that indigenous peoples are the under-class, i.e., the colonized" (Havemann et al. 1985). The relationship between indigenous peoples and the majority culture is viewed through the "exercise of economic power between developed and under-developed regions" (Havemann et al. 1985).

Havemann's theory has some basis in empirical fact because, historically, colonized people have experienced overinvolvement with the legal system. If colonized people are kept in underdeveloped areas, then their conflict with the legal system is likely to be even greater. Accordingly, "the legal system is an integral part of ... exploitation and plays a role in maintaining the position of the dominant political and economic groups" (Havemann et al. 1985). Colonized individuals are predisposed to failure when they confront a system that exists to promote and maintain the values of the majority culture.

Carol LaPrairie (1987) attempts to use the colonialization model in a somewhat different way than Havemann et al. (1985). LaPrairie accepts the explanation of the deprived social and economic position of native people in Canada. She suggests that the "emergence of the Indian reserve system and the under-development of reserves has created a social structure which produces a "culture" of poverty for native people in Canada" (1987:126). According to LaPrairie, colonialism has resulted in the demise of traditional economies and traditional male roles within the Indian cultural system; native women become targets of the frustration that is subsequently experienced by male natives—and the women strike back.

Among explanatory factors for Indian involvement in violence in the U.S. have been "such factors as acculturative pressures, impoverishment, alcohol usage and blocked assimilation" (Kupferer and Humphrey 1975). These analyses would be relatively easy to adapt to the Canadian case as very similar conditions exist for aboriginals in the two countries.

Figure 8.1 shows the Canadian Indian murder rate as compared with the total murder rate in Canada. The data are not as precise as we would prefer. Population denominators are extrapolated from census data. However, definitions of who qualifies as a Canadian Indian have not been consistent over time. At best, the findings can be considered an approximation of the Canadian Indian murder rate. Like the overall murder rate, the rate for Canadian Indians rises dramatically between 1961 and 1975. The

FIGURE 8.1

MURDER RATE FOR CANADIAN
INDIAN OFFENDERS, CANADA, 1961–1989*

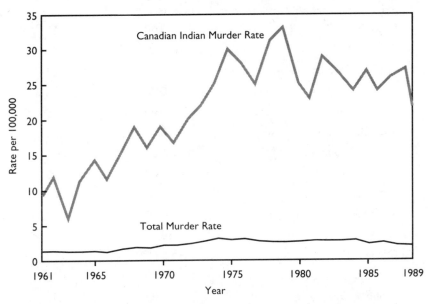

*Population bases for calculation of rates are extrapolated from census data.

rate peaks above 30 per 100,000 Canadian Indians in 1978 and 1979, more than ten times that of the rest of the population.

Canadian Indians have largely dwelt in underdeveloped areas. Sixty-five percent (approximately) of Canadian Indians live on reserves. The Canadian Indian murder rate, then, must be considered in the context of urban versus rural differences, regional variations, and the intra- versus interracial nature of murder. First, Canadian Indians are more likely to be involved in murder in nonmetropolitan areas (20.9 percent) than metropolitan areas (5.7 percent).[2] Second, regional differences in Canadian Indian murder are quite striking (see Table 8.1). We find, based on data from urban centres, that Canadian Indian murder rates may be ten to fifty times higher than those of the population as a whole (Kennedy et al. 1989). Although the reliability of some of these rates may be questioned because of small numbers in the numerator and denominator, as is the case in St. John, the numbers in the western Canadian cities are fairly stable for 1977–81. Saskatoon and Regina have Canadian Indian murder rates that

TABLE 8.1

Canadian Indian Homicide[1] and Total Homicide Rates Canadian Census Metropolitan Areas, 1977–1981.

CMA	Homicide Rates Native[2]	Total[3]
St. John's, NFLD	0.00	.52
St. John, N.B.	114.29	2.10
Halifax, Nova Scotia	0.00	1.01
Chicoutimi-Jonquière, Que.	0.00	1.24
Quebec City, Que.	0.00	.90
Trois Rivières, Que.	0.00	.72
Montreal, Que.	1.63	2.31
Ottawa, Ont.	0.00	1.09
Hamilton, Ont.	0.00	1.66
Kitchener-Waterloo, Ont.	0.00	.97
London, Ont.	30.78	1.48
Oshawa, Ont.	0.00	.78
St. Catharines, Ont.	0.00	1.38
Sudbury, Ont.	0.00	2.27
Thunder Bay, Ont.	9.46	1.81
Toronto, Ont.	12.30	1.57
Windsor, Ont.	0.00	2.68
Winnipeg, Man.	18.13	2.60
Regina, Sask.	57.04	3.77
Saskatoon, Sask.	57.39	3.24
Calgary, Alta.	41.71	2.19
Edmonton, Alta.	38.46	2.34
Vancouver, B.C.	27.65	2.73
Victoria, B.C.	23.05	1.11

[1] Much of the material in this table is extrapolated from Kennedy et al. (1989), reprinted by permission.

[2] This is calculated as a rate per 100,000 for the average number of native homicides between 1977 and 1981, divided by total native population in 1981 within the CMA.

[3] This is calculated as a rate per 100,000 for the average number of homicides between 1977 and 1981, divided by total population in 1981 within the CMA.

TABLE 8.2

Racial Characteristics of Homicide Victims and Offenders in Canada and Metropolitan and Nonmetropolitan Areas, 1972–1981

Canada

Victim	Offender	
	White	Native
White	2871 (96.5)	134 (19.7)
Native	105 (3.5)	545 (80.3)

Metropolitan

Victim	Offender	
	White	Native
White	1398 (97.4)	70 (50.7)
Native	37 (2.6)	68 (49.3)

Non metropolitan

Victim	Offender	
	White	Native
White	1473 (95.6)	64 (11.8)
Native	68 (4.4)	477 (88.2)

are about three times higher than rates in other cities, such as Winnipeg, and higher still when compared with those in Montreal and Toronto. These discrepancies suggest that the experiences of Canadian Indians in urban centres across Canada are not uniform, at least in terms of conditions that lead to lethal violence.

A third point is that the vast majority of Canadian Indian homicide is intraracial (see Table 8.2). The significant differences in the proportions of intraracial homicide for Canadian Indians and whites may be spurious. We find differences based on metropolitan/nonmetropolitan location and on regional location.

Compared to Canada as a whole, the percentages of intraracial homicides for whites are about the same in metropolitan areas, while those for Canadian Indians drop substantially. The fact that far fewer Canadian Indian homicides occur in metropolitan areas than in nonmetropolitan areas suggests that this homicide may stem more from the frustrations associated with poverty and discrimination than from direct conflict with individual members of white society. We conclude this chapter with an examination of the individual aspects of murders perpetrated by and against Canadian Indians.

CANADIAN INDIAN OFFENDERS

About 12 percent of Caucasian murders are committed by females, while 20 percent of Canadian Indian murders are committed by females. When Canadian Indian males kill, they kill other males about 70 percent of the time; when Canadian Indian females kill, 83 percent of their victims are males. This is not too different from the case of Caucasians where 62 percent of male-perpetrated killings involve another male compared to male involvement in about 76 percent of female-perpetrated killings.

When Canadian Indian females kill, about 45 percent of their victims are spouses or lovers, about 28 percent are friends/acquaintances, and only 7 percent are either strangers or people killed in the commission of another crime. Murder victims of male Canadian Indians are most often friends/acquaintances (39 percent). About 18 percent of their victims are spouse/lovers and another 26 percent are nonspousal family members. Ten percent of their killing is connected to a concomitant crime and 7 percent involves the killing of a stranger. Figure 8.2 compares social relationships between victims and suspects for Caucasians and Canadian Indians. Canadian Indians are more likely to kill a nonspousal family member, while Caucasians are much more likely to kill during a concomitant crime than are Canadian Indians.

About 63 percent of Caucasian killings occur in either the victim's or offender's home, while only 54 percent of Canadian Indian-perpetrated killings occur in those places (50 percent for male victims and 66 percent for female victims). Another area in which Canadian Indians differ from non-natives in terms of place of killing is "other private place," which is a nonresidential privately owned building. About 23 percent of Canadian Indian-perpetrated killings (versus 14 percent of homicides perpetrated by Caucasians) occur in another private residence, such as the home of a friend/acquaintance or relative, or in a community-owned property.

The highest proportion of Canadian Indian murders are committed by beatings and stabbings (almost equal proportions), fol-

FIGURE 8.2

VICTIM/OFFENDER RELATIONSHIP BY
RACE OF OFFENDER

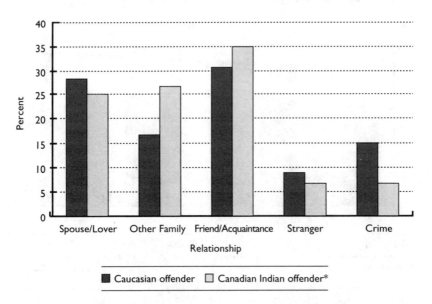

*Canadian Indian Data, 1961–1989.

lowed by shootings. This contrasts with Caucasian killings in which firearms are clearly the primary means, with stabbing and beating as second and third choices. Given the availability of firearms on Canadian Indian reserves, this is an intriguing finding that deserves further investigation. Part of the explanation for the finding is differential weapons use by gender of the perpetrator. Female Canadian Indians stab their victims in 61 percent of the cases. On the other hand, examining male Indian-perpetrated killings, beating (35 percent) is slightly more likely to occur than shooting (30 percent), followed by stabbing (25 percent) and other means (9 percent).

A Statistics Canada publication concerned with murders between 1974 and 1987 finds that "either the victim or the offender had been drinking alcohol in nearly two-thirds of the family murders among Canadian Indian people, while among the general population just one in five family murders involved alcohol." (*Globe and Mail* 1989). Alcohol involvement in all homicide is underreported. However, anecdotal evidence coupled with the

PROFILE 8.1a

CANADIAN INDIAN SUSPECTS

Victim's Gender

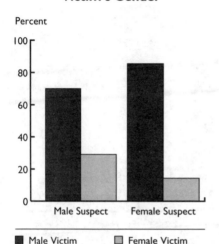

Percent

Male Victim Female Victim

N = 1421 males and 357 females.

Victim's Age

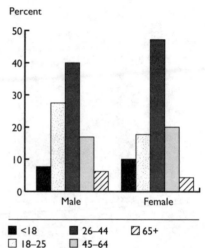

Percent

<18   26–44   65+
18–25   45–64

N = 1417 males and 357 females.

Victim's Marital Status

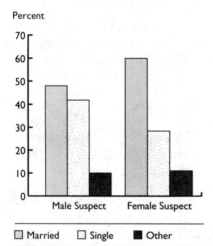

Percent

Married Single Other

N = 1410 males and 353 females.
Married includes common-law.

Victim's Race

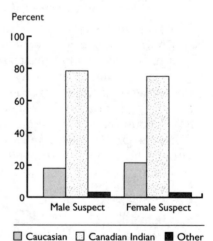

Percent

Caucasian Canadian Indian Other

N = 1386 males and 347 females.

CANADIAN INDIAN SUSPECTS

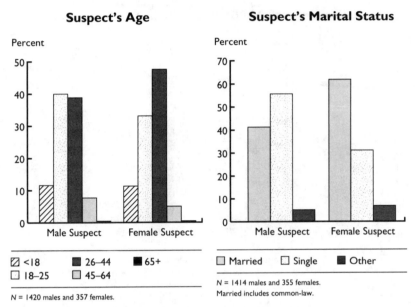

Suspect's Age

Percent

Legend:
- ▨ <18
- ☐ 18–25
- ■ 26–44
- ☐ 45–64
- ■ 65+

N = 1420 males and 357 females.

Suspect's Marital Status

Percent

Legend:
- ☐ Married
- ☐ Single
- ■ Other

N = 1414 males and 355 females.
Married includes common-law.

PROFILE 8.1c

CANADIAN INDIAN SUSPECTS

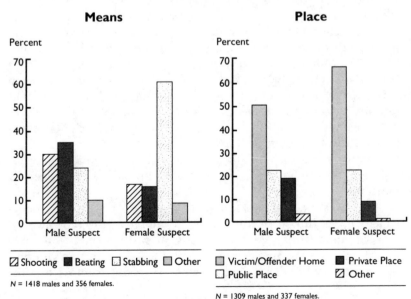

Means

Percent

Legend:
- ▨ Shooting
- ■ Beating
- ☐ Stabbing
- ☐ Other

N = 1418 males and 356 females.

Place

Percent

Legend:
- ☐ Victim/Offender Home
- ☐ Public Place
- ■ Private Place
- ▨ Other

N = 1309 males and 337 females.

PROFILE 8.1d

CANADIAN INDIAN SUSPECTS

Social Relationship Between Victims and Suspects

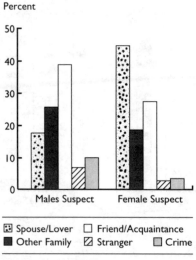

Percent

N = 1421 males and 357 females.

kind of report issued by Statistics Canada confirms the serious problem of alcohol involvement in Canadian Indian violence.

Canadian Indians commit murder in proportions far out-stripping their proportion in the general population. The data do not lend themselves to a precise analysis of the problems that precipitate the murders, but there is enough information about Canadian Indians to suggest avenues for future exploration. We showed earlier the high rates of Canadian Indian murder rates in urban areas. It is a best guess that the average Canadian Indian murder rate in recent years has been about 30 per 100,000,[3] which compares to about 3 per 100,000 for the whole population. In fact, the Canadian Indian rate is comparable to some of the U.S. murder data on black offenders. The amount of murder occurring in this group within Canada can only be described as alarming.

American sociologists discuss an isolated urban under-class that is linked to high rates of violence through poverty, lack of opportunity, and generally appalling conditions. We might well refer to one section of the Canadian Indian commu-nity as an isolated rural underclass that experiences similar conditions. Canadian Indians are among the most impoverished groups in Canada, a situation alleviated only partly through land claims settlements and other means. Indian youth, whom we examine next, are often unemployed or underemployed and consume prohibitive quantities of alcohol, which fuels violent behaviour.

CANADIAN INDIAN YOUTH OFFENDERS

Canadian Indian youth constitute 29 percent of all youthful murder offenders. They contribute about 2 percent of all of the murder incidents we examined. Eighty percent of all Canadian Indian youth perpetrators are male. Almost all of the younger group but only 56 percent of the older group indicate that they are students. Fifteen percent of the younger offenders kill a parent, while 8 percent of the older group kill parents. Eighteen percent of the younger group and 6 percent of the older group murders are killings of siblings. In total, 59 percent of the murder offences committed by younger Canadian Indian youth, and 38 percent of the older group's offences involve family members as victims.

Sixty-five percent of the victims of younger Canadian Indian offenders and 80 percent of the victims of the older offenders are male. Victims tend to be young. In the case of the younger offenders, 38 percent of the victims are under 18 and another 25 percent are between 18 and 25. For the older offenders, the proportions are 18 percent under 18 and 25 percent between 18 and 25. All of the victims of younger Canadian Indians are other natives (including one Métis victim), while 80 percent of the victims of older Canadian Indian youth are Canadian Indians and 19 percent Caucasians. None of these young offenders commit suicide following the murder.

About one-half of the murders committed by Canadian Indian youth occur in the offender's or victim's home, but 30 percent of the murders committed by the younger group occur in public places. Like other young offenders, 42 percent of younger Indian offenders shoot their victims, while in the older group shooting and stabbing are nearly equivalent (one-third each). While only one of the murders of the younger offender group accompanies another crime (theft/robbery), 14 percent of the older group's murders are related to theft/robbery, and 3 percent are connected to a sex crime. This contrasts with the Caucasian youth group in which much of the murder involves other crimes. The bulk of these murders are directed at only one victim, but 15 percent of the crimes perpetrated by the younger Canadian Indi-

PROFILE 8.2a

CANADIAN INDIAN YOUTH SUSPECTS

Victim's Gender

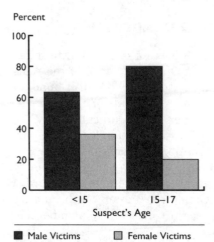

Percent

Male Victims Female Victims

N = 40 suspects <15 and 181 suspects 15–17 years of age.

Victim's Age

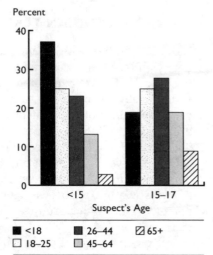

Percent

<18   26–44   65+
18–25   45–64

N = 40 suspects <15 and 181 suspects 15–17 years of age.

Victim's Marital Status

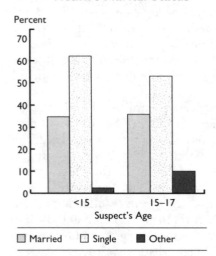

Percent

Married   Single   Other

N = 40 suspects <15 and 179 suspects 15–17 years of age.
Married includes common-law.

Victim's Race

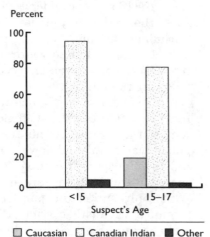

Percent

Caucasian   Canadian Indian   Other

N = 39 suspects <15 and 177 suspects 15–17 years of age.

PROFILE 8.2b

CANADIAN INDIAN YOUTH SUSPECTS

Suspect's Gender

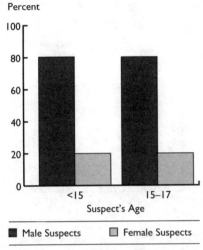

N = 40 suspects <15 and 181 suspects 15–17 years of age.

PROFILE 8.2c

CANADIAN INDIAN YOUTH SUSPECTS

Means   Place

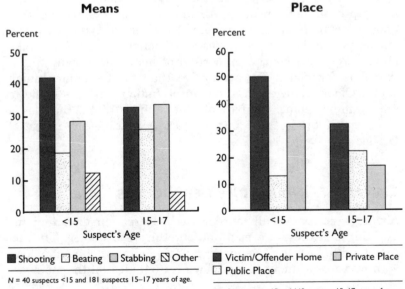

N = 40 suspects <15 and 181 suspects 15–17 years of age.

N = 36 suspects <15 and 163 suspects 15–17 years of age.

PROFILE 8.2d

CANADIAN INDIAN YOUTH SUSPECTS

Social Relationship Between Victims and Suspects

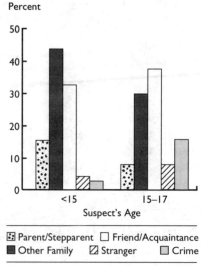

Percent

☐ Parent/Stepparent ☐ Friend/Acquaintance
■ Other Family ☑ Stranger ☐ Crime

N = 40 suspects <15 and 181 suspects 15–17 years of age.

ans and 19 percent of those perpetrated by the older Canadian Indian youth include more than one offender.

In keeping with Moyer's (1987) earlier study, we find that males predominate in all youth murder. Moyer concludes that "young female Natives were more than twice as likely as young female non-natives to be suspected of homicide" (1987:33). Like Moyer, we find that the proportion of homicides during "other crime" is far higher for non-native than for Canadian Indian youth. Older teenagers (Caucasian or Indian) are less likely to kill a family member than are offenders under 15; the routines of older youth bring them into contact with different potential victims.

CANADIAN INDIAN MURDER VICTIMS

About 15 percent of all murder victims are Canadian Indians. Two-thirds of these are men and one-third are women. The victims tend to be a little younger than Canadian Indian offenders, with 80 percent under 45 and few over 64. Most of the male vic-

PROFILE 8.3a

CANADIAN INDIAN VICTIMS

Victim's Gender

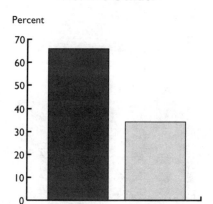

N = 1170 males and 608 females.

Victim's Age

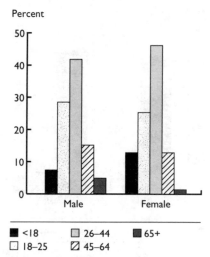

■ <18   □ 26–44   ■ 65+
□ 18–25   ▨ 45–64

N = 1166 males and 608 females.

Victim's Marital Status

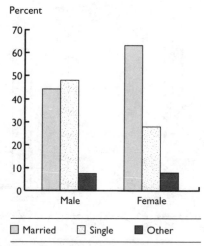

□ Married   □ Single   ■ Other

N = 1163 males and 607 females.
Married includes common-law.

PROFILE 8.3b

CANADIAN INDIAN VICTIMS

Suspect's Gender

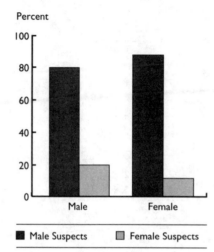

Percent

Male Suspects ▪   Female Suspects ▨

N = 1120 males and 560 females.

Suspect's Age

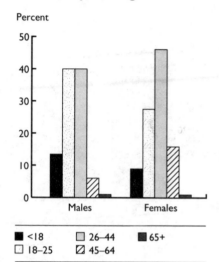

Percent

<18 ▪   26–44 ▨   65+ ▪
18–25 ▫   45–64 ▨

N = 1120 males and 558 females.

Suspect's Marital Status

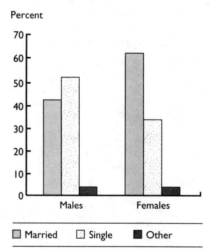

Percent

Married ▨   Single ▫   Other ▪

N = 1110 males and 558 females.
Married includes common-law.

Suspect's Race

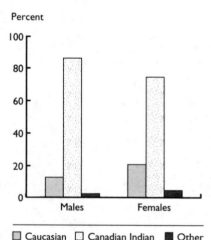

Percent

Caucasian ▨   Canadian Indian ▫   Other ▪

N = 1107 males and 547 females.

PROFILE 8.3c

CANADIAN INDIAN VICTIMS

Means   Place

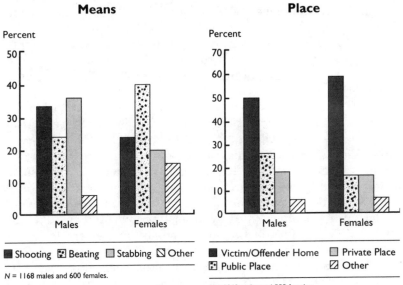

Shooting ▪ Beating ⬚ Stabbing ▢ Other ◫

N = 1168 males and 600 females.

Victim/Offender Home ▪   Private Place ▢
Public Place ⬚   Other ◫

N = 1063 males and 555 females.

PROFILE 8.3d

CANADIAN INDIAN VICTIMS

Social Relationship Between Victims and Suspects

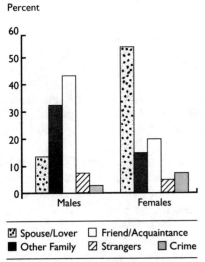

Spouse/Lover ⬚   Friend/Acquaintance ▢
Other Family ▪   Strangers ◫   Crime ▪

N = 1120 males and 560 females.

tims (48 percent) are single, while almost two-thirds of the female victims are married. One of the characteristics that distinguishes this group from their Caucasian counterparts is the proportion of the married group that is in a common-law relationship—19 percent of the Indian males compared to 8 percent of the Caucasian male victims, and 35 percent of the female Indians versus 13% of the female Caucasians. More than one-half of the female Indians are killed in a spousal incident, while most of the males (43 percent) are killed by friends/acquaintances. Family members are perpetrators in two-thirds of the female killings and 45 percent of the male killings. Few of the events involve strangers or other crimes.

Like almost all of the murders we have examined, males are perpetrators in 80 percent of the male deaths and 88 percent of the female killings. Offenders tend to be slightly older than victims. Those who kill male Canadian Indians are most often young (under 26) males. Killers of females tend to be a little older, reflecting the domestic situation in many of the killings. Very few of the offenders are over 64 years old. Canadian Indian males are most often killed by other Canadian Indians (86 percent), while one-fifth of Canadian Indian females are killed by Caucasians. The latter finding may reflect intermarriage.

Canadian Indian males are most often stabbed (36 percent) or beaten (33 percent) to death, while females are most often beaten (40 percent). Eleven percent of the female killings involve a sex crime (compared to 12 percent of Caucasian female victims). While most murders of Indians (male and female) occur in the victim's or offender's home, one-quarter of the male victims and 17 percent of the female victims are killed in "another private place"—often the home of a relative or friend.

SUMMARY

Canadian Indians are involved in murderous events in proportions that are about five times their proportion of the whole population. The rate of Canadian Indian murder (relatively stable since the mid-1970s) has been as high as ten times that of the rest of the population. These figures reflect elements of a persistent social problem.

Our analysis in the earlier part of this chapter indicates that the social conditions under which Canadian Indians in Canada live likely generate the conditions for violence. High levels of unemployment and poverty, coupled with feelings of despair and crowded living arrangements, result in high levels of tension. Alcohol plays a further (and significant) role in fuelling disputes.

A study of Cherokee and Lumbee Indians in North Carolina (Kupferer and Humphrey 1975) suggests ways in which we can further analyze the problems associated with native violence. The authors of the study attribute the different rates of violence found in the two groups to the different values each group places on aggression. The conservative Cherokee eschew violence and aggression and the modern Cherokee similarly do not extol aggression and fighting. In contrast, the Lumbee value courage and its demonstration through fighting when necessary. The Lumbee do not back down. The authors do not propose a "culture of violence," but their formulation of the management of aggression takes on the character of "conflict styles," outlining acceptable ways of managing interpersonal disputes. In fact, rates of violence follow the direction one would predict from the above description. There has been no similar geographic or band-centred analysis of Canadian Indian violence. Such a study might provide one link to a fuller understanding of the issues that precipitate violence among Canadian Indians.

While there have been many studies of Canadian Indians in the criminological literature, few have focused on trying to explain the violence that pervades the living conditions of many Canadian Indians. Understanding the conditions under which the violence occurs would facilitate positive intervention, preferably at the initiative not of government but of Canadian Indians themselves. Efforts to reintroduce traditional values to the younger member of bands is a step in the right direction.

NOTES

1. Portions of this section are drawn from Silverman and Nielsen (1992), reprinted by permission. For purposes of the analysis that follows, we will be concerned only with Canadian Indians. While other natives (i.e., Métis and Inuit) are involved in homicide, their rate of involvement is very low and would only confuse the analysis. Further, as Nettler (1982) points out, lumping "native" peoples together makes no theoretical sense.

2. It is difficult to compare rural and urban murder rates because there are significant methodological problems in estimating reliable rates for rural Canadian Indians based on census information, due to underreporting in these areas. In addition, given the remoteness of many of the Canadian Indian communities, we are not always sure that the information collected about murder is valid, or even if all murders are reported.

3. We cannot be precise with these figures because we have only ten years of data to guide us. The problem with these data is that the census seems to change its definitions of "native" with every census. Further,

in recent times, several reserves refused to participate in the census, and there are notorious problems of eliciting reliable data from a population that may be hunting or trapping while the census taker is doing his or her rounds.

C   H   A   P   T   E   R   9

Summing Up
WHAT WE FOUND AND
WHAT WE CAN DO ABOUT IT

As we have argued throughout this book, the violent act of murder often occurs as a byproduct of conflict between individuals who find it difficult to restrain their actions from becoming physically injurious. While we have concentrated on the individual components of murder through much of the book, we recognize a strong correlation between conditions in the economy (e.g., unemployment or other forms of social disorder) and murder. As was most evident in the chapter on Canadian Indians, such conditions give rise to many of the tensions that are precursors to interpersonal conflict.

The descriptions and analysis presented can at best indirectly expose the social and individual forces that result in murder. Nonetheless, these indirect measures give credence to many of the hypotheses generated by routine activities and social control theories, as well as the macro-level approaches. It is important to consider the total picture as we turn to our discussion of responses to homicide. Much of what we can do about murder rests with institutional plans for allocating more and better resources to lessen the likelihood of this event from occurring. We will examine these in some detail in the latter parts of the chapter. Let us first take some time to sum up what we have found.

SUMMING UP

Early in the book, we offered a detailed description of the legal definitions of homicide and murder as well as the related crimes of manslaughter and infanticide. While some criminologists would like to expand the definition of culpable crime to include acts that are not currently included in the Criminal Code (e.g., manufacturer negligence causing death), we have used the current Criminal Code definitions to guide our descriptions of murder. This is the definition that is used by the police when they make the decisions that generate the data we used for our analysis.

Our analysis shows how patterns have changed throughout Canadian history. There was a good deal of murder in Canada in the early 1930s, followed by a steady decline through to the mid-1950s. The rates do not reach 1930 levels again until around 1970. The most notable finding in this historical assessment is the enormous rise in the homicide rates between the early 1960s and the mid-1970s. These were times of turmoil. Canada was changing and one result of change was a rise in violence, including homicide. Since the mid-1970s there has been a levelling off and decline in homicide rates. While not perfect, there is some correlation between economic conditions and murder. Examining these trends, we also discover that male victims drive the rates; the female rate has been relatively constant since about 1974.[1]

We evaluate the relevance of a variety of contemporary sociological theories that seek to explain murder trends. One of the most elementary explanations is provided by Gottfredson and Hirschi (1990), who suggest that the act of murder requires little planning or foresight and is committed by poorly socialized individuals who lack self-control. To explanations based on lack of self-control must be added the contribution of drugs and alcohol, conflict-ridden situations, opportunity, and other forms of social dysfunction. Social relationship, proximity, and availability of weapons interact with low self-control in volatile situations. Individuals in these situations often lack conflict resolution skills but find themselves in "risky situations."

Other theories based on social control, socialization and development, as well as those dealing directly with aggression and violence, help to clarify behaviours that result in murder. Means of dealing with conflict and the ability to deal with conflict are central themes of the social control concepts. Conflict styles are influenced by socialization. Violence in some situations or in some subcultures may be considered a legitimate way of dealing with conflict. Again, social relationship and proximity are correlated with violent outcomes. The family is the place where violence is first learned (Straus 1987), and it is likely to mould future ideas about conflict resolution.

The routines followed by individuals are often good predictors of the likelihood of violent confrontations. Young males who spend long periods of time outside the home live lifestyles that can be called risky (Sacco and Johnson 1990: Kennedy and Forde,

1990a). Interactions that people maintain in their daily environments are important in predicting the types of conflict they are likely to encounter. These individual circumstances do not occur in a vacuum but are highly influenced by the social and economic environments in which people live.

Countries with higher levels of income inequality have higher murder rates (Krahn et al. 1986). The inequality that is a part of economic disparity seems to create situations ripe for violence (Blau and Blau 1982). The frustrations that come from poverty, unemployment, poor housing, and other socially disruptive conditions create tension in families and can result in violent outcomes. These structural factors can be mediated through community-level mechanisms of social control.

However, while we may talk about the correlation between murder and social inequality, unemployment, age relationships or gender, no one was ever directly killed because of social inequality. Killing takes place in emotionally charged environments or during the course of another crime. Frustrations with the economy may be an indirect precipitator of one individual's actions against another. One scenario suggests that frustrations with the economy may lead to psychological distress resulting in feelings of futility from which follow alcohol-precipitated violence and a culmination in murder. The best that the criminologist can do is say that, in certain circumstances, downturns in the economy will lead to the direct forces that influence the occurrence of murder. Criminological research can document the correlations between murder rates and various aspects of social structure (see Forde 1992), but it does not have the tools to attribute cause directly.

Having defined the issue and examined the explanations, our goal has been to introduce readers to the subject of murder in Canada in a thorough but uncomplicated way. To that end, we examined subgroups of offenders and victims. The contents of Chapters 4 through 8 showed what tangled web of factors influence murder. Wherever possible, we linked the findings to the theoretical issues provided by the theories.

We find that the proportion of murders committed in more intimate relationships has declined over time, while the proportion of friend/acquaintance killings has risen. This finding is different for female victims for whom spouse/lover murder has remained the dominant type for thirty years. Male offenders contribute most to the murder rate. Female offenders account for only about 12 percent of murders over the years, while females constitute about 40 percent of the victims in murder incidents. The female murder victimization rate has remained relatively constant since the mid-1970s.

In the spouse/lover category, far more wives are killed by their husbands than vice versa—in fact, almost half of all women killed are killed by their husbands. Husbands are more likely to shoot wives, while wives most often stab their victims. As predicted by routine activities theory, the vast majority of these incidents take place in the home. Proportionally more men who kill their wives exhibit remorse (indirectly measured by amount of suicide following murder) than do women who kill their husbands. We speculate that many of the latter are victims of serial spousal assault before the killing takes place. Spousal murder rates remain reasonably stable over the period examined.

Within the family, fathers and mothers also kill children. Child-killings account for a high proportion of offences by women but a much smaller proportion by males. Like other earlier studies, we find that very young children are killed by various methods of brute force, especially when mothers are the offenders. Offenders in these cases tend to be quite young. A high proportion of fathers and mothers commit suicide after killing one (or more) of their children. Serial violence is likely a precursor of many of these murders; lack of self control coupled with lack of problem-solving skills on the part of the offender are explanatory factors here.

Ninety percent of the offenders in nonspousal family murder are young males. When child and spouse victims are excluded from this group, we find that one-third of the offenders are Canadian Indians. The relationships in this category are close, and Canadian Indians (especially those living in rural areas or on reserves) are more likely in closer proximity to their extended families than are Caucasians.

As noted earlier, friend/acquaintance murder has been rising while other types have been falling as a proportion of all murder. There are at least three subcategories that can be examined—close friends, acquaintances, and business associates. The acquaintance category often describes internecine conflict between people who meet in public places, such as bars, where alcohol-fuelled conflict results in the death of one party. Again, offenders and victims are young, single males more often than any other sex/age combination. This subcategory has contributed most to friend/acquaintance murder since the mid-1960s and is the relationship that best describes the risky lifestyles we alluded to earlier. In Canada, business-relationship murder is relatively uncommon.

Stranger murder is rare in Canada. Overall, it accounts for only about 7 percent of all Canadian murder, and yet it is the kind of murder that generates the most fear in the public. Offenders are most often young, single males who kill in public places.

Victims exhibit a similar demographic profile to offenders. Essentially, stranger murders are likely distinguished by the lifestyles of both victims and offenders. There is little to differentiate these crimes from "casual acquaintance" interactions that lead to killing.

Robbery/theft and sexually related murders are overwhelmingly committed by young, single males. In the case of robbery/theft, victims are also most often males but tend to be much older than offenders. In the case of sexual crimes, the majority of victims are young females. We speculate that the target in both robbery/theft and sexual crime is chosen on the basis of the perceived gains and the vulnerability of the victims. While about half of each kind of crime occurs in the victim's or offender's home, more of the sexual offences happen in public places. Victims of theft/robbery are often shot, beaten or stabbed, while victims of sexual offences are more often killed by other sorts of brute force, strangulation and suffocation, for example. Our analysis indicates a slight rising trend for both robbery/theft and sex-related crimes over the thirty-year period. The descriptive analysis of these crimes is consistent with predictions generated by routine activities theory.

We portrayed mass murderers and serial killers in Canada as aberrations. These offenders clearly represent the smallest minority of murderers in Canada. They really do not clarify the theories for us, nor do the theories we have been using do much to explain their behaviour. The most satisfying explanations lie in the psychological realm. In some cases, it is claimed that warning signs go unheeded, but most of the facts indicate that authorities act appropriately within the restraints of the law. We observe these cases with a combination of fascination and horror, but we cannot easily apply the theories or remedies of sociology to them.

In Chapter 6, we explored three rather unique types of offender—women, children, and the elderly. One is gender-based—(only 11 percent of all murders are perpetrated by females) and two are age-based—794 children in our sample (under 18) committed murder, but only 2 percent of all murder incidents could be attributed to elderly offenders. The characteristics of each of these subgroups vary considerably.

Female offenders generally kill either their spouse or a child. This confirms hypotheses about proximity and some of the routine activities predictions. While our data do not directly address the issue, it is reasonable to assume that a fair amount of spouse killing happens after serial abuse by an intimate partner. Canadian law now considers this a legitimate defence to first-degree murder under certain circumstances. Younger children are often killed after serial abuse by one or both parents and clearly are more at risk than are older children. Killing by females has remained predominantly directed against family members over the years observed.

As the offender's age rises from under 13 to 17, the homicide rate rises dramatically. Almost one-half of the cases of younger children involve family members. Older children (15–17) also kill within the family but are more likely than younger children to have a stranger as a victim. About one-quarter of homicides by older children involve another crime. It is possible that we are dealing with inexperienced, poorly socialized individuals with low self-control, who, with the aid of a weapon, overreact to resistance. The most striking finding involving young homicide offenders is that three out of ten are Canadian Indian—a fact that calls out for further and intensive investigation of the structural variables (e.g., poverty and social isolation combined with socialization) that have helped to bring it about.[2]

As predicted by routine activities theory, two-thirds of the murders by the elderly involve a family member. Other predictions of the theory hold as well. Most of the victims are older females, while almost all of the offenders are males. Victims are most often shot, and the offender commits suicide following the event in one-third of the cases. These murders are an interesting but, again, anomalous type. They are clearly related to family (and perhaps health) issues.

Chapter 7 explored issues relating to elderly, young, and female victims. As in Chapter 6, demographics of age and gender defined the groups to be examined. Elderly victims were explored through the perspective of routine activities. Contrary to the theory and our expectations, the elderly are victims during robbery/theft murders in proportions far higher than any other age group. We hypothesize that they become victims during attempted break-and-enters into which offenders wrongly believe are unoccupied dwellings. Victims are commonly beaten and may succumb to injuries while a younger person might have survived. This scenario requires a slight revision of routine activities theory to take into account location and passivity as major factors in victimization. It also suggests some obvious target-hardening techniques (e.g., alarm systems) as a form of intervention.

Less than 10 percent of all murder victims are children. As we pointed out earlier, younger children are more at risk than older children and are more often killed by very young offenders (at least some of these cases involve infanticide). Older children, too, are often killed by parents or other people they know. The killing of younger children is likely related to child abuse, while the killing of older children more often involves other kinds of conflict. Younger children are more likely to be beaten to death. Theories involving self-control, frustrations with the structural variables, and poor socialization are best suited to these findings.

The murder rate for female victims has remained relatively constant since about 1974. The proportion of murder that is intimate-partner-related has remained very high during the thirty years reviewed. The findings in this section are clearly intertwined with our analysis of spouse/lover murder in Chapter 4. They are also generally consistent with routine activities theory, and given the nature and "causes" of the victimization, it is possible that interventions may be successful.

Chapter 8 showed the effects of poor socioeconomic conditions on those who live within them. Canadian Indians are the most disadvantaged group in Canada. They also have a murder rate that has been up to ten times the national average. The high murder rate for Canadian Indians also reflects a high proportion of Canadian Indian victims (almost 15 percent). In general, no matter which subgroups are considered, the great bulk of murders in Canada are intraracial.

It must be clear to the reader that it is difficult to provide direct tests of the theories we proposed earlier. Secondary data designed for purposes other than hypothesis-testing, including a limited number of variables, are not well suited to the task. Instead, we have tried to describe murder in Canada thoroughly, pointing out when the data seemed to confirm or reject parts of the theories. Needless to say, there is far more that can be researched about the crime of killing human beings.

WHAT CAN BE DONE?

Given some notion of the factors that interact to produce murder, what can be done about them? At a personal level, the conflicts that result in killings are often domestic or involve other intimates or are internecine in nature. Direct intervention does not seem likely in these situations. Among suggestions for dealing with interpersonal crime are: deterrence through the imposition of penalties on acts that may lead to violence (e.g., mandatory charging in cases of domestic battering); providing fewer opportunities for crime through stricter gun control and through the enhanced security of locations; adding resources to help those most vulnerable to the conditions leading to murder, either as offenders or victims; and ameliorating conditions in society that are most clearly linked to violent acts.

Some of the more hopeful responses to murder will be discussed in this chapter. The more broadly based changes needed in the social structure and economic conditions are difficult to produce. The extension of social programs to help those in need would be one way to reduce the crippling effects of poverty or chronic unemployment. Loosening up divorce laws should result in reduced tensions in marriages that have failed but which are legally constrained; however, as we have indicated, the forces at play in a poor domestic situation are often far more complex than divorce laws alone can remedy. Attempts to provide better housing and to address the serious drug and alcohol problems of the inner cities address the conditions under which conflict grows and murder results. Efforts to improve economic conditions and alleviate social disorder do not promise immediate results, but policy-makers cannot afford to ignore the circumstances and conditions that lead to violence in general and murder in particular.

Murder has always taken a central place in public debates about crime and has been an important focus of legal sanction over the years. There has been much debate about the usefulness of different forms of punishment in deterring this crime and in punishing the offenders. Discussion has also centred on using the law to prevent murder through such action as the introduction of increasingly stringent gun laws.

The type of deterrence discussed below involves efforts to change people's behaviour through threat. The more direct form of deterrence involves changing behaviour by limiting opportunities. For instance, deadbolt locks and alarm systems deter burglary. Is similar "target hardening" available to potential homicide victims? The answer is yes, but to a limited extent. Loosening divorce laws or establishing women's shelters, in effect remove the potential victim from the location of the offender and can be effective measures. Similarly, mandatory arrest of husbands who assault their wives removes the potential offender from the scene, at least temporarily; the final word on the effectiveness of this technique has yet to come (Gelles 1991).

We could similarly remove or reduce some of the correlates of homicide, such as alcohol. Whether it is a proximate cause or an excuse, alcohol is still intertwined with violent events; however the cost of attempting to remove it from our society (given that it is a part of cultural routine) is probably too great.

There have been recent efforts to draw attention to the importance of such extralegal factors as cited above in responding to homicide. The mobilization of resources to provide assistance to both potential offenders and victims is both a corroboration of and response to the idea that the social conditions that give rise to murder can to some extent be altered.

One view in criminology sees the offender as rational and deterred by the threat of punishment from legal sanction. This opinion is based on the idea that law is invariant and punishment is certain. A counterargument has been offered by criminologists who believe that crime occurs as a result of forces outside of the offender that influence his or her behaviour. While the first set of theorists—those who see offenders as rational—are very clear about the parameters of successful deterrence, those who see crime deriving from social disorder believe that the secret to crime prevention lies in changing the impact of negative forces, e.g., unemployment, poverty, or other types of social breakdown. The first perspective requires that we view the law as neutral, applied equally and fairly to all individuals.

It is the rational offender who serves as the focus of deterrence debates. Deterrence views the importance of legal threat as primary in reducing criminality. Yet, to follow the arguments related to social change, we know that the law is socially determined and reflective of social conditions.

The deterrence doctrine articulates the process whereby individuals are discouraged from committing criminal acts through the perception of legal sanctions as certain, swift and/or severe (Williams and Hawkins 1986). The deterrence that appears to work is built on the interweaving of morality spread through the institutions of society with the punishments that can be administered by the actions of the criminal justice system. The effectiveness of punishment depends on restricting the behaviour of the potential offender (specific deterrence), or on providing the threat that this restriction will occur (general deterrence). When people anticipate that others will disapprove of their arrest for committing a certain act, and they refrain from that activity because they fear the stigma of getting caught, general deterrence through legal sanction has taken place (Williams and Hawkins 1986).

Criminologists run into difficulty explaining crime on the basis of such factors as unemployment and social change, which seem to be only remotely related to individual actions. Deterrence enters the picture in the role that the community (family, etc.) can play in reducing the likelihood of certain crimes being seen as acceptable, and in responding through informal sanctions when the crime is committed and the offender identified. Individual characteristics and social conditions interact to create the situations that promote violence; deterrence of this type of outcome would seem to relate to a combination of formal and informal control factors.

Much of the contemporary debate on deterrence focuses on the social-psychological response to the punishment, particularly as it pertains to social stigma. Williams and Hawkins discuss the fact that individuals are not really afraid of the punishment per se, but they are afraid of the fact that others would judge them harshly for having received this punishment. The counterargument to this, based on the notion of the rational offender, is that individuals are deterred only through a punishment scheme that takes into account their innate propensity to offend (Wilson and Herrnstein 1985). Hence, the impact of punishment is direct and focuses on specific efforts to incarcerate and immobilize rather than on looking at community forces and their role in reducing criminality.

One offender has told us that he has a very different perspective on deterrence, punishment, and the criminal justice system than do criminologists:

> The violent offender as opposed to the threatener is seldom rational and punishment is totally irrelevant. Threat of punishment only deters those who wouldn't offend in the first place. It is cosmetic. To those of us angry enough to offend, punishment becomes a challenge that further angers; we rise to the occasion. When someone threatens us by negative forms of "control" the immediate reaction is anger and a desire to confront and destroy the source of the threat. We may seemingly retreat to circle behind or seemingly accept to lull our enemy, but we intend "winning eventually." "P" to many of us does not mean parole but rather payback. The confrontive, adversarial attitude of police and courts only furthers violent crime. Those of us with an archetypically warrior psyche tend to become more war-like when threatened or challenged. We have to learn to direct these emotions in a constructive fashion, but first we need to be aware of these emotions. The process has to be a helping one, not one of constant threat/confrontation.[3]

The debate about deterrence as it relates to murder is brought to a head in the debate about capital punishment. The world is divided in its use of capital punishment. The majority of countries still apply execution as a response to murder. Most of Western Europe is abolitionist, as is Canada. The United States is divided, with a legal system that allows states to determine whether or not to retain capital punishment.

In Canada, there has been a vigorous debate over the years about the need to retain or abolish capital punishment. There has always been strong public support for the death sentence, but despite this support, in the midst of the public debate in the mid-

1970s, Parliament decided to abolish capital punishment and replace it with a "life sentence,"[4] with no parole eligibility for twenty-five years. This law, enacted in 1976, was challenged in the late 1980s, but the challenge was turned back by a vote that supported the status quo.

A number of arguments are used to support or attack the death penalty. The strongest argument in favour of abolition is the fact that capital punishment appears to have little or no deterrent value (see, for example, Peterson and Bailey 1991). When the death sentence was abolished in Canada in 1976, homicide rates actually declined. Given the dearth of persuasive evidence on the extent or even the existence of the deterrence mechanism involved in capital punishment, we are hesitant to propose strict punishment regimes in order to contain criminality, especially if they are contrary to our views of what is humane and just. With the lack of deterrence, the costs of error and other issues related to cruel and unusual punishment become more potent (see United Nations 1986).

Based on our review of homicide trends and our conceptualization of the event, it should not be too surprising that capital punishment plays an insignificant role in deterrence. The conflict that spontaneously erupts into assault and a fatality is unlikely to be considered in the context of a possible execution for the offender. In most homicides, the offender is in a state of rage, not a state of mind that lends itself to the consideration of consequences (this is even more true for individuals with low self-control). Also, in response to those who argue that individuals who kill once will kill again, the evidence is that since 1963 only two people on parole and one on day-parole have murdered again (Solicitor General 1985:31). During 1983, 614 murderers were released on escorted temporary absences and 122 on unescorted temporary absences. The total number of permits issued for these individuals was 6726. Individuals failed to return six times for a success rate of 99.91 percent. In comparison, for other inmates who took 43,746 absences, 106 failed to return, for a success rate of 99.76 percent. (Solicitor General of Canada 1985:30)

The use of mandatory life sentences (nonparolable for twenty-five years) as punishment for first-degree murderers in place of capital punishment has raised concern that these long sentences will make the inmates more frustrated and thus potentially more dangerous to house in prisons. It would appear, however, that the Canadian experience with inmates serving these sentences is not causing the security problems anticipated, as these inmates tend to be the ones which are the easiest to manage in the institutions (Solicitor General 1985:26). Nonetheless, the question remains as to whether the twenty-five year nonparolable sentence is reasonable or justifiable on any theoretical grounds. Certainly, it is a longer sentence than that given for first-degree murder in much of the rest of the world where capital punishment has been abolished.

The rise in violent crime in the United States has led to a "get tough" position on crime, and many states have returned to the death penalty as a symbol of this toughness. Yet while there have been a few high-profile executions, generally speaking the rate of executions is very low, even in those states (e.g., Florida and Texas) where there is a determined effort to use this punishment. The low rate is partly attributable to delays that result from the need for careful scrutiny of each case and legal assurances that all appeals to the sentence are heard. This creates an expensive and time-consuming process; there are individuals in American jails who have been on death row for up to seven years with no immediate prospect of execution or reprieve.

Further, the rates of violent crime in the United States continue to climb regardless of the reinstitution of the death penalty. This has led abolitionists to argue that the deterrent value of the sentence is clearly lost when the punishment takes so long to administer, making a mockery of the criminal justice system. Proponents of capital punishment argue that without the death penalty crime levels would rise even faster, as offenders could commit crimes with the assurance that they could not be executed as a consequence.

If capital punishment does not deter, as its critics contend, does it have any positive effects? We are reluctant to call the effect positive, but it does satisfy many of those in the public that "justice" has been done. The people who feel this way confuse revenge with justice—an eye for an eye. No logical argument about deterrence will change their minds.

Also, capital punishment can be a mistake when the certainty of the killer is in some question. Fortunately in the case of Donald Marshall, he was not executed, but he did spend eleven undeserved years in prison. The risk of putting an innocent person to death is too great to contemplate the reinstitution of capital punishment in Canada.

The debate about capital punishment leads us to question the role of punishment in deterring murder, particularly as this crime continues to occur no matter what the penalty. The view that much more crime would occur without this punishment is fallacious. And yet it is clear that society cannot operate without sanctions on individual behaviour. Individuals must clearly perceive that there will be a cost to committing a crime, with this cost being communicated through the examples of others being punished. But as we have shown, much homicide is not a rational act but rather something done in rage or in the heat of passion—the very type of crime that cannot be deterred by threat of punishment (Williams and Hawkins 1986). As we said at the outset, homicide is many crimes. It is likely that some of those (e.g., robbery homicide) are more deterrable than others, but overall the deterrence effect is too negligible to justify the reinstitution of capital punishment.

LEGAL CHANGE, MURDER, AND OPPORTUNITY

The recent debate about constructive intent in Canada illustrates the point made in the early pages of this book concerning how a change in laws can affect the definitions of murder. The Supreme Court of Canada has decided that individuals who kill someone during another crime cannot be held accountable for first-degree murder unless intent to kill is proven. Critics of this decision argue that it undermines any potential deterrence to serious offenders involved in robbery, for instance, from using extreme force in the course of committing the crime. As a result of the Supreme Court decision, the courts have returned to a view of culpable homicide as murder that is planned and deliberate or is the direct consequence of an action, such as assault, that the offender understands could result in a death.

The Supreme Court decision shows how easily we can adjust definitions to remove certain actions from being classified as criminal or as fitting into specific categories. This reclassification is artificial, of course, in the sense that there is still a death to be accounted for regardless of how it is defined. Legal changes that reduce the possibility of the death occurring in the first place are obviously of greater interest to the public and the lawmakers. The role of law in preventing murder is exemplified in the case of firearms regulation. There is a continuing debate about gun control in this country. The public believes that stricter gun legislation will reduce the opportunity of potential perpetrators to obtain access to potentially lethal weapons.

Canada has had firearms regulation since the mid-1800s (Solicitor General 1983).[5] In 1977, the toughest legislation to date restricting ownership of firearms was introduced. Since 1978, in order to purchase a gun in Canada one needs a firearms acquisition permit (FAC). Firearms with no legitimate sporting or recreational use (e.g., sawed-off shotguns) are prohibited, as are fully automatic weapons. Handguns are restricted weapons in Canada. The new act also includes greater penalties for use of a weapon during a crime. The FAC was meant to "screen" dangerous persons from owning firearms in Canada (Solicitor General 1983).

Scarff (1983) reports that the general rate of homicide in Canada has been declining since 1975, and that the rate of gun use has followed that pattern. However, no dramatic change appears in the rates with the introduction of the new legislation. Weapons used in murder offences may be indicators of the interpersonal dynamics involved in an offence. Alternatively, they may serve as indicators of what was available to complete an intended or unintended act of violence. Restricting access to guns through legislation should have an impact on the pattern of weapon use across these events (Silverman and Kennedy 1992).

Mundt (1990) examined robbery, homicide, suicide, and accidental death rates to establish rates of firearm use in these crimes. Homicide by firearms in Canada has been more or less declining since 1974, and even the proportion of handguns used in robberies dropped a great deal in that period. The legislation passed in 1977 appears to have had little effect on the overall rates of violence. Mundt (1990) speculates that the legislation may have slowed the rise of violence that might have happened in its absence.

American research conducted by Kleck and Patterson (1989) identifies multiple indirect measures of gun-ownership levels. They conclude that "nineteen different major varieties of gun control appear to have no impact ... on any of the types of violence which frequently involve guns" (34). Murder patterns in Canada strongly suggest that forces in society other than legislation promoted the drop in firearms use in Canada since the mid-1970s. This conclusion is tentatively drawn on the basis of a downward trend in homicide by gun that started to occur before the legislation came into being. While shootings have generally declined, there has been a rise in handgun use when friends/acquaintances are involved. Finally, in spite of the fact that homicide by firearms is declining in Canada, guns are still the most popular means of killing (Silverman and Kennedy 1992).

Kleck and others attribute the null effect of legislation in the United States on gun use to a high-risk population retaining ownership of restricted weapons, and to poor enforcement of the laws. In Canada, the drop in gun use appears unrelated to changes in legislation. We must search for other factors to explain this decline.

First, legislation may have done little to affect the extent to which guns are used in crime simply because there was such a low level of gun ownership (particularly handguns) in the first place. A change in the laws would, therefore, have little effect on the availability of weapons. Second, the mobilization of resources for women (such as shelters) may have provided, as Browne and Williams (1989) argue is the case in the United States, a means of escape from dangerous relationships. Interestingly enough, the drop in gun use in intimate relations is accompanied by a drop in the rates of other weapon use (Silverman and Kennedy 1992). Gun laws affirm society's stand against the availability of lethal weapons and underline societal views that gun ownership is undesirable and potentially dangerous. The research, however, finds no direct correlation between legislative change and weapons use.

Despite this finding, there is a great deal of concern in society about the control of guns. Attention to this issue has been particularly focused with Marc Lepine's murder of fourteen women at the École Polytechnique at the University of Montreal. Lepine used a semi-automatic weapon to kill the women and then to kill himself. This event precipitated strong public sentiment to curtail the availability of multi-shot or assault weapons. There have been recent calls for the imposition of strict controls, through legislation, on the ownership of these firearms, which it has been argued increase the chances that violence will occur. The pro-gun lobby has attacked the restrictions on the ground that gun owners should be allowed to purchase multi-shot or automatic weapons for legal use (particularly in competition or sport shooting).

Bill C17, passed in Canada in 1992, allows for the ownership of these guns but puts strong emphasis on their control. Of particular note is the requirement that the guns be securely stored with strong punishment for noncompliance. The focus on restricting opportunity in the use of these guns draws attention to the danger they present (e.g., as a means of settling disputes) when readily available in households. The Canadian bill is both a symbolic reaffirmation of the need to restrict availability of firearms and a practical measure to control access to those weapons that are already in private hands.

RESOURCE MOBILIZATION

Some researchers believe that the social conditions upon which much murder is based can be adjusted in a way that may help to prevent these events from occurring in the first place. For example, Browne and Williams (1989) posit a relationship between legal and extralegal resources and the rate of female-perpetrated homicide. They point out that in the United States (as in Canada), women rarely kill; when they do, the victim is generally a male partner. Further, they speculate that the 25 percent reduction in female-perpetrated homicide in the decade since 1980 is the result of an increased awareness of the problems faced by women in dealing with violent spouses. This has led to the enactment of a number of different laws criminalizing family violence. In addition, there has been an increase in the amounts of funding available to support the construction of shelters and the provision of counselling to batterers.

The availability of resources that allow threatened women to escape or be protected from a partner's violence, Browne and Williams (1989) believe, should be associated with the decline in homicide (91). In their research, they actually do find a strong negative relationship between the presence of domestic violence legislation, high levels of resource mobilization, and the rate of female-perpetrated homicide. Browne and Williams have not been able to establish the degree of awareness that individuals have of the resources that are being made available; there is no clear measure of the accessibility of these resources, nor of how many people actually use them. Finally, it is not evident how responsive the resources are in meeting individual needs (91–92). What is clear from this research is that where these resources are available, the homicide rates are lower. The argument used by Browne and Williams points to the importance of mechanisms that can be used to reduce the conflict within relationships, and, if these get out of control, to provide alternatives to individuals to escape the potential dangers.

It seems plausible that if there are legal and extralegal solutions, such as resource mobilization, that can be used to reduce domestic homicide, there may be similar strategies that can be used to address other forms of homicide. According to the document *Healthy People 2000*, produced by the Centers for Disease Control (1990), homicide in the United States constitutes the eleventh leading cause of death, accounting for 20,812 deaths in 1987. As the authors suggest, it appears that violence has become the response of first recourse in many cases of emotional/mental distress and interpersonal conflict, as well as a tool of premeditated criminal acts.

The authors set a number of targets in the document to lower homicide levels substantially by the year 2000. For example, they observe that over 60 percent of the homicides that occur every year in the United States involve firearms. The rates per 100,000 population for deaths involving firearms have ranged in recent years as high as 15. The document recommends a reduction to no more than 12.6 by the year 2000. Among the suggestions the authors make to accomplish this goal is a coordinated effort involving public health, health care, mental health, criminal justice, social services, education, and other relevant sectors to develop effective preventive strategies. An important objective specified in the document is the curtailment of access to weapons. (The observation that many children routinely carry knives or guns to school sends a shudder up one's spine.) In order to monitor the success of programs in meeting this objective, the authors of *Healthy People 2000* recommend that data collection and tabulation be improved. In addition, they call for concerted efforts to identify the root causes of violence, including a focus on conflict management and the control of alcohol and drug abuse. Care for victims of violent behaviour, they suggest, should also be expanded to deal with the consequences of heightened conflict, and to teach people that there are ways to resolve interpersonal friction in nonviolent ways.

The above approach adopts a view that violence is part of a public health problem that requires similar strategies to those used in the detection and amelioration of infectious diseases. While the authors clearly acknowledge the social bases for the development of violence, their solutions to the problem are offered as health objectives. This provides a powerful mandate, as we expend great resources in our country to combat ill health and disease. Extending these resources to the treatment of violence would bring the weight of the medical professions behind the search for a solution to these problems. However, Harries (1990) expresses reservations about the use of a medical model in approaching the problem of violence, even though the consequences of violence may have serious implications for the delivery of medical services in certain communities. He states that public health as an institution has neither the extra resources nor the personnel (at the present time) to make a profound impression on the problem (189).

This does not mean that there is no role for public health officials to play in the effort. Violence is a product of a combination of forces that are counterproductive to the good health (both mental and physical) of members of the public, particularly those living in inner cities. What Harries says, pessimistically, is that the link of public health to disease to the exclusion of other threats to health may take a generation to overcome. Of concern to him is the fact (notwithstanding the objectives for a desired level of reduction in violence that are presented in the *Healthy People 2000* document) that the public health community has not produced a model that clearly demonstrates how public health methods will reduce homicide and assault, thereby leaving, by default, the remediation of these problems to the agents of law enforcement. This is insufficient. The police cannot be the sole agents of society in dealing with problems of violence.

In the meantime, the police are on the front line in responding to violence that sometimes turns fatal. It is the police who must deal with the problems encountered in domestic disputes, battles among acquaintances, and violence in public places. In addressing these cases, the police have begun to assume a proactive stance, arguing that by taking certain steps in removing opportunities for violence and by raising their own profile, individuals may be prevented or deterred from involving themselves in aggressive and violent acts. Strategies that have been recommended toward this end are practical ones. As we indicated earlier, in an attempt to respond to the increased amount of violence witnessed in the inner-city areas, the City of Edmonton police suggested to tavern-owners that patrons be forced to check their knives on entry to the premises. It is too early to tell if this simple strategy has had the effect of lowering the levels of interpersonal violence in these locations to any great degree; the strategy targets routine activities that are potentially hazardous and removes the means, if not the opportunity, to make them lethal.

An additional anti-crime strategy that has been suggested is an attack on "hot spots," i.e. locations where there is a continuous repetition of problems. These hot spots are often areas where individuals hang out or where they are attracted by the potential for "kicks" or "action." Bars, nightclubs, and other drinking establishments can provide this type of location, but so can shopping malls. By focusing attention on these areas through proactive patrol, citation for bylaw infractions, and other tactics, the police believe that they remove the opportunities for crime to occur. According to Sherman et al. (1989), the "attack on hot spots" is an important crime-prevention strategy that does not appear simply to displace potential offenders to other locations; rather, there is evidence from their research in Minneapolis that the removal of hot spots acts to reduce public crime and to diminish the chances that violence will occur in these and other areas.

Beyond an attack on hot spots, the police have begun to take a more proactive stand in communities in the belief that if they are more aware of the community needs and more familiar with the individuals in these areas, they will be better able to stop problems from getting out of control. Community policing strategies allow the police and the community to work together in problem-solving. With this cooperative approach, the difficulties that give rise to criminal violence may dissipate in the early stages of treatment. The police become an important agency in coordinating the community's attempts to deal with conflict and its eruption to violence. Community policing encourages the police to become involved in the community in a way that strict law enforcement does not permit.

The movement out of patrol cars and back into the heart of communities makes the police more aware of the sources of tension and the areas that most need attention. Familiarity with a neighbourhood and its inhabitants also allows the police to make better use of local resources in heading off anticipated problems. Proactive policing does not diminish the need for law enforcement but rather acknowledges that social interaction is complex and that sanctions that work to deter undesirable behaviour are often extralegal. The coordination of these informal mechanisms by the police increases the likelihood that the community will begin to take responsibility for managing problems that before were left to the criminal justice system. The result is not only a strengthening of community ties but also the development of a hybrid system that brings legal and extralegal forces to bear on individuals to contain their aggression and violence.

Proactive policing is illustrated in the new initiatives in policing to deal with family violence. Based on the research done by Sherman and Berk (1984) in Minneapolis, many North American police forces have introduced a mandatory charging policy that shifts the onus from the victim (in most cases the wife) to the police to lay charges where there is clear evidence of assault. This strategy has the intention of removing, through arrest, violent individuals from the home and then sanctioning them through sentencing, which most often takes on the character of probation with mandatory counselling. The importance of this initiative is that it makes offenders more keenly aware of the seriousness of their offenses and gives them the incentive to seek help in dealing with their problems. It also forces the police to take a more proactive stand in dealing with domestic disputes, which in the past may have been treated lightly or as "private matters" to be sorted out by the couple themselves. As Gelles (1991) points out, it is unclear how effective this and other police initiatives really are, but they seem to please politicians and other supporters of the programs.

Police in Edmonton have implemented several interventionist tactics in the downtown core that they credit with lowering the inner-city rate of violence. They pay special attention to the most crime-ridden areas and have been instrumental in having street lighting increased in the worst parts.[6] The Edmonton police also attribute such measures as the "no-knives" policy in hotels and making male washrooms more visible to a decrease in violence and fewer robberies. Lighting has been augmented on both the exteriors and interiors of hotels. A "mobile" check-cashing and bank-deposit facility has been set up, thus reducing the victimization potential of those who formerly carried all of their cash. Prostitution, Asian gang crime, and drug problems have been made special targets for police surveillance. Finally, substandard housing, where thefts and vandalism often occurred, has been closed down (Williams 1992).

Police have also been encouraged to seek out the assistance of other agencies in developing a coordinated response to the problems that they encounter in specific areas. There have been attempts in some cities to develop alternative dispute-resolution programs to handle problems outside of the criminal justice system. Experiments with community boards in areas such as San Francisco have facilitated ways in which people living in inner-city areas can address and resolve disputes without resorting to interpersonal violence.

The use of volunteers and the nonjudicial character of the mediation process make individuals more comfortable not only in bringing problems to community boards for resolution but also in living with the judgments of the mediators. The police are instrumental in making these programs work. Attempts to adopt local mediation committees as a means of problem-solving have met limited success in Canadian cities. There is some possibility, though, that the commitment of the police to the community policing model will lead to the development of community programs designed to head off small problems before they become big ones (see Kennedy 1990).

CONFLICT MANAGEMENT PROGRAMS

It may seem a little odd to talk about using alternative dispute resolution in dealing with murder, when the spontaneity of the act seems to mediate against conflict management. Often, murder occurs in the context of ongoing social interaction that gets out of control and leads to a lethal outcome. The pressures that develop in modern society from the effects of high levels of mobility, social detachment, poverty, unemployment, and family breakdown impact on the ways in which people conduct themselves toward others. The lifestyles of many people can be seen as risky creating opportunity for confrontation and violence. Not everyone has developed the skills to handle these types of problems. Further, there is often an effect that comes from the promotion, rather than the negative sanctioning, of conflict by third-party individuals who are present during the confrontation.

Deterring and preventing murder would seem to rest on the need to deter and prevent confrontational conflict. The opportunities for escalation of violence need to be removed, as do the means for making this violence fatal. Random violence is rare. Of much greater danger is violence that is routine and occasionally fatal. Members of society must become more aware of the steps that can be taken to keep these routines from developing, beginning with careful study of the opportunity and means to commit violence. Legal initiatives must be coupled with extralegal responses, including resource mobilization for the prevention and treatment of conflict and aggression.

Some efforts in this direction have been undertaken by Arnold Goldstein in his attempts to teach aggressive people negotiation techniques. For instance, he has introduced his techniques into the prison environment and attempted to teach aggressive inmates to negotiate instead of striking out every time some minor affront is perceived. Goldstein suggests that some individuals have so internalized the violent response that they cannot be taught nonviolent conflict resolution—a frightening thought. Other work has been undertaken by James Mercy to attempt to teach people in high-risk groups to handle conflicts in nonviolent ways (Meredith 1984).

In the future, we should consider developing the elusive integrated model of response to violence that Harries (1990) identifies as missing from our repertoire of programs that deal with different aspects of violence and victimization. It would appear to be a good exercise to set out goals for ourselves that should be met in the effort to reduce violence. However, establishing targets is not going to be very useful if we are unable to use all of the resources available to us to reach our objectives in a coordinated fashion. It is clear that violence has many different sources and many different "cures." Strategies for its prevention include education as well as punishment; reducing opportunities for violence, including access to weapons that turn violence into lethal outcomes; treating not only abusers of alcohol and drugs but also the victims of their violent behaviour; and changing public attitudes about the use of violence in resolving conflicts of whatever sort, in the schoolyard, in the home, or in public places. These strategies involve the action of many different agencies and all of the members of our communities, and include both legal and extralegal responses to violence.

Having described homicide and examined it in light of routine activities, social control and some structural considerations, it has been possible to offer some interventions that may ameliorate conditions that lead to homicide. Even using indirect measures, we have leant some support to these theories. Needless to say, whether dealing with mediation, resource mobilization, efforts to deter, or conditions of poverty and alcoholism, money is involved. Any society must decide how much violence it can tolerate, or, more appropriately, how much of its resources it can put into controlling violence. In truth, it would cost a great deal of money to reduce homicide even a little. There are only 600 or 700 homicides (of all types) per year in Canada. How much of our resources are we willing to commit to reduce this number? Given the nature of the crime and current social conditions, we are not sure that it would be possible to reduce the number of homicides by even fifty.

Efforts to ameliorate the social conditions that are correlated with violent crime, to clean up the inner cities, to reduce alcohol consumption, to reduce ownership of lethal weapons, and to intervene in domestic violence situations may have the most hope of limited success. There are choices to be made by policymakers.

NOTES

1. Some of the rise in 1974 and immediately thereafter is attributable to the inclusion of infanticide and manslaughter in the statistics since 1974. In most of our analysis from Chapter 4 on, we exclude those crimes.

2. Thornberry's (1987) framework would provide a good starting point for such an investigation.

3. From the files of Ray Enright.

4. The public often assume that a "life sentence" is synonymous with "life in prison." It is not. In many countries, a "life" sentence means twenty years and parole can come earlier than that. In Canada, it usually means a life sentence with no possibility of parole for ten years for second-degree murder and no possibility of parole for twenty-five years in the case of first-degree murder. Nonetheless, no matter how much time the offender spends in prison, the sentence is for life, meaning the offender will be under supervision (in prison or the community) for the remainder of his or her life.

5. Much of the discussion in the following pages is based on Silverman and Kennedy (1992), reprinted by permission.

6. Many studies have shown that higher levels of street illumination is an effective deterrent.

REFERENCES

Adelson, L. 1961. "Slaughter of the Innocents." *New England Journal of Medicine* 264, no. 26:1345–1349.

Adler, F. 1975. *Sisters in Crime*. New York: McGraw-Hill.

_____., G. Mueller, and W. Laufer. 1991. *Criminology*. Toronto: McGraw-Hill.

Akers, R., A.J. La Greca, and C. Sellers. 1988. "Theoretical Perspectives On Deviant Behaviour Among the Elderly." In B. McCarthy and R. Langworthy, eds., *Older Offenders: Perspectives in Criminology and Criminal Justice*. New York: Praeger, pp. 35–50.

Archer, D., and R. Gartner. 1984. *Violence and Crime in Cross-National Perspective*. New Haven: Yale University.

Avakame, Frank. 1989. *Black Homicide in Canada*. M.A. thesis. Edmonton: University of Alberta.

Avison, W.R., and P.L. Loring. 1986. "Population Diversity and Cross-National Homicide: The Effects of Inequality and Heterogeneity." *Criminology* 24:733–49.

Baron, S., and L. Kennedy. 1990. "Formal and Informal Deterrence in Punk Gangs: A Test of Social Control Theory." Unpublished paper. Edmonton: University of Alberta.

Baron, L., and M.A. Straus. 1988. "Cultural and Economic Sources of Homicide in the United States." *Sociological Quarterly* 29:371–90.

Barrett, T. 1990. "Greeve Death an Accident, Nienhuis Says." *Edmonton Journal*, February 17: B1.

_____. 1992. "Addict Gets Eight Years for Killing Friend." *Edmonton Journal*, March 1: C3.

Berkowitz, L. 1982. "Violence and Rule-Following Behaviour." In Peter Marsh and Anne Campbell, eds., *Aggression and Violence*. Oxford: Basil Blackwell, pp. 91–101.

Birnie, Lisa Hobbs. 1992. "Such a Good Boy." *Saturday Night* 107, no. 2:42–48, 65–71.

Blau, J., and P. Blau, 1982. "The Cost of Inequality: Metropolitan Structure and Violent Crime." *American Sociological Review* 47:114–129.

Box, S. 1981. *Deviance, Reality and Society*. 2nd ed. New York: Holt.

Boyd, N. 1988. *The Last Dance: Murder in Canada*. Scarborough, Ont.: Prentice-Hall.

Brantingham, Paul, and Patricia Brantingham. 1984. *Patterns in Crime*. New York: Macmillan.

Brodsky, Daniel. 1987. "Educating Juries: The Battered Woman Defence in Canada." *Alberta Law Review* 25, no.3:461–76.

Browne, A., and R. Flewelling. 1986. "Women as Victims or Perpetrators of Homicide." Paper presented at the Annual Meeting of the American Society of Criminology. Atlanta. November.

_____., and K. Williams. 1989. "Exploring the Effect of Resource Availability and the Likelihood of Female-Perpetrated Homicides." *Law and Society Review* 23, no.1:75–94.

Browne, W., and A. Palmer. 1975. "A Preliminary Study of Schizophrenic Women Who Murdered their Children." *Hospitals and Community Psychiatry* 26, no.2:71–72.

Brym, Robert J. 1986. "An Introduction to the Regional Question in Canada." In R.J. Brym, ed., *Regionalism in Canada*. Toronto: Irwin, pp. 1–45.

Burgess, A.W., C.R. Hartman, R.K. Ressler, J.E. Douglas, and A. McCormack. 1986. "Sexual Homicide: A Motivational Model." *Journal of Interpersonal Violence* 1, no.3:251–72.

Canadian Centre for Justice Statistics (Statistics Canada). 1988. *Relative Trends: Microcomputer Application and Database*. Ottawa: Statistics Canada.

Canadian Urban Victimization Survey. 1985. "Criminal Victimization of the Elderly." Bulletin no. 6. Ottawa: Solicitor General of Canada.

Centers for Disease Control. 1986. *Homicide Surveillance: High-Risk Racial and Ethnic Groups—Blacks and Hispanics, 1970 to 1983*. Atlanta: Centers for Disease Control.

_____. 1990. *Healthy People 2000*. Washington, D.C.: U.S. Department of Health and Human Services.

Cheatwood, Derral. 1991. "Doing the Work of Research: Wolfgang's Foundation and Beyond." Paper presented at the Annual Meeting of the American Society of Criminology. San Francisco. November.

Chimbos, Peter. 1978. *Marital Violence: A Study of Interspouse Homicide*. San Francisco, Calif.: R&E Research Associates.

Christoffel, K., and Stamler, J. 1981. "Epidemiology of Fatal Child Abuse: International Mortality Data." *Journal of Chronic Diseases* 34:57–64.

_____. and K. Liu. 1983. "Homicide Death Rates in Childhood in 23 Developed Countries: U.S. Rates Atypically High." *Child Abuse and Neglect* 7:339–45.

Cipparone, R.C. 1987. "The Defense of Battered Women Who Kill." *University of Pennsylvania Law Review* 135, no.2:427–52.

Cobb, Christopher, and Bob Avery. 1977. *Rape of a Normal Mind*. Markham, Ont.: Paperjacks.

Cohen, L.E., and M. Felson. 1979. "Social Change and Crime Rate Trends: A Routine Activity Approach." *American Sociological Review* 44, no.4:588–608.

Cole, K., G. Fisher, and S. Cole. 1968. "Women Who Kill: A Sociopsychological Study." *Archives of General Psychiatry* 19:1–8.

Collins, J. 1989. "Alcohol and Interpersonal Violence: Less than Meets the Eye." In N.A. Weiner and M.E. Wolfgang, *Pathways to Criminal Violence*. Newbury Park, Calif.: Sage.

Comack, Elizabeth. 1991. "Legal Recognition of the 'Battered Wife Syndrome': A Victory for Women?" Paper presented at the Annual Meeting of the American Society of Criminology. San Francisco. November.

Committee on Trauma Research. 1985. *Injury in America*. Washington, D.C.: National Academy Press.

Cook, P. 1987. "Robbery Violence." *Journal of Criminal Law and Criminology* 78: 357–76.

Copeland, A. 1986. "Homicide Among the Elderly: The Metro Dade County Experience, 1979–1983." *Medical Science and Law*, 28, no.4:259–62.

Cormier, B., C. Angliker, P. Gagne, and B. Markus. 1978. "Adolescents Who Kill a Member of the Family." In J. Eekelaar and S. Katz, eds.,

Family Violence: An International and Interdisciplinary Study. Toronto: Butterworths, pp. 466–78.

Coser, L. 1956. The Functions of Social Conflict. New York: Free Press.

Criminal Code. 1990. An Act Respecting the Criminal Law. RSC 1985. Chapter C46 and amendments through Sept. 1990. [The version used throughout this book is found in 1991 Pocket Criminal Code, Toronto: Carswell, 1990.]

Daly, M., and M. Wilson. 1988a. "Evolutionary Social Psychology and Family Homicide." Science 242:519–24.

_____. 1988b. Homicide. New York: Aldine de Gruyter.

Dietz, M.L. 1982. Killing for Profit: The Social Organization of Felony / Homicide. Chicago: Nelson-Hall.

Dixon J., and A. Lixotte 1987. "Gun Ownership and the Southern Subculture of Violence." American Journal of Sociology 93:383–405.

Doob, A., and J. Roberts. 1982. Crime: Some Views of the Canadian Public Toronto: Centre of Criminology, University of Toronto.

Dussich, J., and C. Eichman. 1976. "The Elderly Victim: Vulnerability to the Criminal Act." In J. Goldsmith and S. Goldsmith, eds., Crime and the Elderly. Lexington, Mass.: D.C. Heath.

Dutton, Donald, G. 1980. "Social Psychological Research and Relevant Speculation on the Issue of Domestic Violence." In C.T. Griffiths and M. Nance, eds., The Female Offender. Burnaby, B.C.: Criminology Research Centre, Simon Fraser University.

Easterlin, R.A., and M.O. Schapiro. 1979. "Homicide and Fertility Rates in the United States: A Comment." Social Biology 26:341–43.

Edmonton Journal. 1987. "Confused 16 Year Old Killed her Baby out of Fear." November 6: B2.

_____. 1991a. "Beaten Girl Remains in Critical Condition." February 19: B2.

_____. 1991b. "Man Shot Dead After Motorists Argue at Intersection." February 19: A3.

_____. 1991c. "Jail Term Reduced for Killing of Couple" (R. Henderson). May 1: A7.

_____. 1992a. "Victim Lives—City Couple to Face Trial for Murder" (M. Moysa). January 7: A1–A2.

_____. 1992b. "Victim's Sister Cries 'Satan' as Killer Dahmer Sentenced." February 18: A1.

The Edmonton Sun. 1988. "Murdered." August 5: 1, 4–5.

Egger, Steven A. 1990. Serial Murder: An Illusive Phenomenon. New York: Praeger.

Ellison, Christopher G., and Patricia L. McCall. 1989. "Region and Violent Attitudes Reconsidered: Comment on Dixon and Lizotte." American Journal of Sociology 95: 174–78.

Eve, S.B. 1985. "Criminal Victimization and Fear of Crime Among Non-Institutionalized Elderly in the United States: A Critique of the Empirical Research Literature." Victimology 10 nos.1–4:397–408.

Fattah, E. 1991. Understanding Criminal Victimization. Toronto: Prentice-Hall.

_____., and V. Sacco. 1990. Crime and Victimization of the Elderly. New York: Springer-Verlag.

Felson, M., and L. Cohen. 1980. "Human Ecology and Crime: A Routine Activity Approach." *Human Ecology* 4:389–406.

Felson, R., and H. Steadman. 1983. "Situational Factors in Disputes Leading to Criminal Violence." *Criminology* 21, no.1:59–74.

Ferguson, R. 1991. "Ten Year Term for Infant Son's Death." *Edmonton Journal* February 19: A10.

Ferraro, K.F., and R.L. LaGrange. 1988. "Are Older People Afraid of Crime?" *Journal of Aging Studies* 2, no.3:277–87.

Fiala, R., and LaFree, G. 1988. "Cross-National Determinants of Child Homicide." *American Sociological Review* 53, no.3:432–45.

Fischer, C. 1975. "Toward a Subcultural Theory of Urbanism." *American Journal of Sociology* 80:1319–1341.

Fishman, G., and I. Sordo. 1984. "Aging and Delinquent Behaviour: The Criminal Act and the Societal Response." In G. Shoham, *Israel Studies in Criminology, Volume 7.* Great Britain: Science Reviews Limited.

Forde, David R. 1992. *Homicide Rates in Canadian Cities: A Macrosociological Analysis of 1971, 1976 and 1981.* Ph.D. thesis. Edmonton: University of Alberta.

Fox, J., and J. Levin. 1991. "Homicide Against the Elderly: A Research Note." *Criminology* 29, no.2:317–27.

Gartner, R. 1990. "The Victims of Homicide: A Temporal and Cross-National Comparison." *American Sociological Review* 55, no.1:92–106.

_____., K. Baker, and F. Pampel. 1987. "The Sex Differential in Homicide Victimization." Paper presented at the Annual Meeting of the American Society of Criminology. Montreal. November.

_____., and B. McCarthy. 1991. "The Social Distribution of Femicide in Urban Canada, 1921–1988." *Law and Society Review.* 25, no. 2:287–312.

_____., and I. Piliavin. 1988. "The Aging Offender and the Aged Offender." In P.B. Baltes, D.L. Featherman, and R.M. Lerner, *Life-Span Development and Behaviour.* N.J.: Lawrence Erlbaum.

Gastil, R.D. 1971. "Homicide and a Regional Culture of Violence." *American Sociological Review* 36:412–27.

The Gazette. 1981. "Police have Solutions to only One-Third of Montreal Murders." July 15: A1.

Gelles, R. 1991. "Constraints Against Family Violence: How Well Do They Work?" Paper presented at the Annual Meeting of the American Society of Criminology. San Francisco. November.

_____., and M. Straus. 1988. *Intimate Violence.* Toronto: Simon and Schuster.

Gewerth, K.E. 1988. "Elderly Offenders: A Review of Previous Research." In B. McCarthy and R. Langworthy, eds., *Older Offenders: Perspectives in Criminology and Criminal Justice.* New York: Praeger, pp. 14–31.

Gillis, A.R. 1986. "Domesticity, Divorce and Deadly Quarrels: An Exploratory Study of Integration-Regulation and Homicide." in T. Hartnagel and R. Silverman, eds., *Critique and Explanation: Essays in Honor of Gwynne Nettler.* New Brunswick, N.J: Transaction.

Globe and Mail. 1989. "Near One in Four Family Murders Among Natives, Study Says" (S. Fine). October 4: A1, A10.

Goetting, A. 1986. "When Parents Kill their Young Children: Detroit 1982–1986." Paper presented at the Annual Meeting of the American Society of Criminology. Chicago. November.

———. 1989. "Patterns of Homicide Among Children." *Criminal Justice and Behaviour* 16, no. 1:63–80.

Goldsmith, J., and S. Goldsmith. 1976. *Crime and the Elderly*. Lexington, Mass.: D.C. Heath.

Goode, W. 1969. "Violence Among Intimates." U.S. National Commission on the Causes and Prevention of Violence. Task Force on Individual Acts of Violence. *Crimes and Violence* 13:941–77.

Gottfredson, M.R., and T. Hirschi. 1990. *A General Theory of Crime*. Stanford, Calif.: Stanford University Press.

Grant, B.J. 1983. *Six for the Hangman: Strange and Intriguing Murder Cases from the New Brunswick Past*. Fredericton, N.B.: Fiddlehead Poetry Books and Gooselane Editions Limited.

Hackler, Jim, and Kim Don. 1990. "Estimating System Biases: Crime Indices that Permit Comparisons Across Provinces." *Canadian Journal of Criminology* 32:243–64.

Hackney, Sheldon. 1969. "Southern Violence." *American Historical Review* 74:906–25.

Hagan, John. 1985. *Modern Criminology: Crime, Criminal Behaviour, and Its Control*. New York: McGraw-Hill.

———. 1986. "The Unexplained Crimes of Class and Gender." In Hartnagel, Timothy H. and Robert A. Silverman, eds., *Critique and Explanation*. New Brunswick, N.J.: Transaction Press, pp. 71–89.

———. 1989. "Enduring Differences: Further Notes on Homicide in Canada and the U.S.A." *Canadian Journal of Sociology* 14, no.4:490–91.

———. 1989. "Comparing Crime and Criminalization in Canada and the U.S.A." *Canadian Journal of Sociology* 14, no.3:361–71.

———. 1989. *Structural Criminology*. New Brunswick, N.J.: Rutgers University Press.

———. "The Pleasures of Predation and Disrepute." Review article of J. Katz, *The Seductions of Crime*. *Law and Society Review* 24, no.1:165–77.

———., A.R. Gillis, and J. Simpson. 1985. "The Class Structure of Gender and Delinquency: Toward a Power-Control Theory of Common Delinquent Behavior." *American Journal of Sociology* 30:25–38.

———., J. Simpson, and A.R. Gillis. 1987. "Class in the Household: A Power Control Theory of Gender and Delinquency." *American Journal of Sociology* 92:788–816.

Hamilton, A.C., and C.M. Sinclair. 1991. *The Justice System and Aboriginal People: Report of the Aboriginal Justice Inquiry of Manitoba*. Winnipeg: Queen's Printer.

Harding, J., and R. Matonovich. 1985. "Self-Study of Justice Research About Indigenous People: 1981–1984." Regina: Prairie Justice Research, School of Human Justice.

Harries, K.D. 1990. *Serious Violence*. Springfield, Ill.: Charles C. Thomas.

Hartnagel, T., and W. Lee. 1990. "Urban Crime in Canada." *Canadian Journal of Criminology* 32, no. 4:591–606.

Havemann, P., K. Couse, L. Forster, and R. Matonovich. 1985. *Law and Order for Canada's Indigenous People.* Regina: School of Human Justice, University of Regina.

Hickey, Eric W. 1991. *Serial Murderers and Their Victims.* Pacific Grove, Calif.: Brooks/Cole.

Hindelang, M.J., M.R. Gottfredson, and J. Garofalo. 1978. *Victims of Personal Crime: An Empirical Foundation for a Theory of Personal Victimization.* Cambridge, Mass.: Ballinger.

Hirschi, T. 1969. *The Causes of Delinquency.* Berkeley: University of California Press.

Hocker, Joyce L. and William W. Wilmot. 1985. *Interpersonal Conflict.* 2nd ed. Dubuque, Iowa: William C. Brown.

Holmes, R.M., and J. De Burger. 1988. *Serial Murder.* Volume 2 of *Studies in Crime, Law and Justice.* Newbury Park, Calif: Sage.

Howard, M. 1986. "Husband–Wife Homicide: An Essay from a Family Law Perspective." *Law and Contemporary Problems* 49, no. 1:63–88.

Huff-Corzine, L., J. Corzine, and D.C. Moore. 1986. "Southern Exposure: Deciphering the South's Influence on Homicide Rates." *Social Forces* 64:906–24.

Johnson, Holly. 1988. "Violent Crime." *Canadian Social Trends* 9:24–28.

Johnson, H., and V. Sacco. 1990. *Patterns of Criminal Victimization in Canada.* General Social Survey Analysis Series. Ottawa: Statistics Canada.

Jurik, Nancy, and Peter Gregware. 1992. "A Method for Murder: The Study of Homicides by Women." In Gale Miller and James Holstein, eds., *Perspectives on Social Problems.* Greenwich, Conn.: JAI Press.

Juristat. 1990. "Conjugal Violence Against Women." *Juristat.* Statistics Canada: Canadian Centre for Justice Statistics 10:7.

Kaplun, D., and R. Reich. 1976. "The Murdered Child and his Killers." *American Journal of Psychiatry* 133, no. 7:809–13.

Katz, J. 1988. *Seductions of Crime.* New York: Basic.

Kelley, Harold H., and John W. Thibaut. 1978. *Interpersonal Relations: A Theory of Interdependence.* New York: John Wiley.

Kennedy, Leslie W. 1988. "Going It Alone: Unreported Crime and Individual Self-Help." *Journal of Criminal Justice.* 16, no. 5.

_____. 1990. *On the Borders of Crime: Conflict Management and Criminology.* White Plains, New York: Longman.

_____., and D. Dutton. 1989. "The Incidence of Wife Assault in Alberta." *Canadian Journal of Behavioural Science* 21, no. 1: 40–54.

_____., David R. Forde, and Robert A. Silverman. 1989. "Understanding Homicide Trends: Issues in Disaggregation for National and Cross-National Comparisons." *Canadian Journal of Sociology* 14:479–86.

_____., and David R. Forde. 1990a. "Routine Activities and Crime: An Analysis of Victimization in Canada." *Criminology* 28:137–52.

_____., and David R. Forde. 1990b. "Risky Lifestyles and Dangerous Results: Routine Activities and Exposure to Crime." *Sociology and Social Research* 74, no. 4:208–11.

_____., Robert A. Silverman, and David R. Forde. 1988. "Homicide from East to West: A Test of the Impact of Culture and Economic Inequality on Regional Trends of Violent Crime in Canada." Discussion Paper 17. Edmonton: Centre for Criminological Research, University of Alberta.

_____, and R.A. Silverman. 1990. "The Elderly Victim of Homicide: An Application of Routine Activity Theory." *Sociological Quarterly* 31, no. 2:305–17.

_____., R.A. Silverman, and D. Forde. 1991. "Homicide in Urban Canada: Testing the Impact of Economic Inequality and Social Disorganization." *Canadian Journal of Sociology* 16, no.4:397–410.

Kiger, K. 1990. "The Serial Murder Enigma." In Steven A. Egger, *Serial Murder: An Illusive Phenomenon*. New York: Praeger, pp. 35–52.

Kleck, Gary, and Britt Patterson. 1989. "The Impact of Gun Control and Gun Ownership Levels on City Violence Rates." Paper presented at the Annual Meeting of the American Society of Criminology. Reno. November.

Kosberg, J. 1985. "Victimization of the Elderly: Causation and Prevention." *Victimology* 10, nos. 1–4:376–96.

Krahn, Harvey, Timothy F. Hartnagel, and John W. Gartrell. 1986. "Income Inequality and Homicide Rates: Cross-National Data and Criminological Theories." *Criminology* 24:269–95.

Kratcoski, P., and D.B. Walker. 1988. "Homicide Among the Elderly: Analysis of the Victim/Assailant Relationship." In B. McCarthy and R. Langworthy, eds., *Older Offenders: Perspectives in Criminology and Criminal Justice*. New York: Praeger.

Krohn, Marvin D., Lonn Lanza-Kaduce, and Ronald Akers. 1984. "Community Context and Theories of Deviant Behaviour: An Examination of Social Learning and Social Bonding Theories." *The Sociological Quarterly* 25:353–71.

Kunkle, S., and J. Humphrey. 1982/83. "Murder of the Elderly: An Analysis of Increased Vulnerability." *OMEGA* 13, no.1:927–34.

Kupferer, H., and J. Humphrey. 1975. "Fatal Indian Violence in North Carolina." *Anthropological Quarterly* 48, no. 4:236–44.

Land, Kenneth C., Patricia L. McCall, and Lawrence E. Cohen. 1990. "Structural Covariates of Homicide Rates: Are There Any Invariances Across Time and Social Space?" *American Journal of Sociology* 95:922–63.

LaPrairie, C. 1987. "Native Women and Crime: A Theoretical Model." *The Canadian Journal of Native Studies* 7, no. 1:121–37.

Lavigne, Yves, and M. Tenszen. 1991. "Depressed Father Shoots Self After Killing Wife, Three Stepsons." *Globe and Mail*, November 15: 1, 5.

Law Reform Commission of Canada. 1982. *Criminal Law: The General Part—Liability and Defences*. Working Paper 29. Ottawa: Minister of Supply and Services.

Lenton, Rhonda L. 1989. "Homicide in Canada and the U.S.A.: A Critique of the Hagan Thesis." *Canadian Journal of Sociology* 14:163–78.

Levi, K. 1989. "Becoming a Hit Man: Neutralization in a Very Deviant Career." In D.H. Kelly, *Deviant Behaviour: A Text-Reader in the Sociology of Deviance*. 3rd ed. New York: St. Martins Press, pp. 447–58.

Levin, J., and J.A. Fox. 1985. *Mass Murder: America's Growing Menace*. New York: Plenum.

Leyton, E. 1986. *Hunting Humans*. Toronto: Seal Books.

Luckenbill D.F. 1977. "Criminal Homicide as a Situated Transaction." *Social Problems* 25:176–86.

_____. 1984. "Murder and Assault." In R.F. Meir, ed., *Major Forms of Crime.* Beverly Hills, Calif.: Sage.

_____., and D.P. Doyle. 1989. "Structural Position and Violence: Developing a Cultural Explanation." *Criminology* 27, no. 3:419–36.

Lundsgaarde, H.P. 1977. *Murder in Space City: A Cultural Analysis of Houston Homicide Patterns.* New York: Oxford University Press.

Lupri, E. 1989. "Male Violence in the Home." *Canadian Social Trends.* Autumn. Ottawa: Statistics Canada.

Lystad, M.H. 1980. "Violence at Home: A Review of the Literature." In J.V. Cook and R.T. Bowles, *Child Abuse.* Toronto: Butterworths.

Macdonald, J. 1986. *The Murderer and His Victim.* Springfield Ill.: Charles C. Thomas.

Maclean's. 1981. "A Rhythm of Accusations." September 14:33.

_____. 1982a. "Why Police Pay Criminals" (Thomas Hopkins). February 1:22–25.

_____. 1982b. "Handsome Rewards for Show-and-Tell" February 1:26–27.

_____. 1982c. "$100,000 Soaked in Blood" (Malcolm Gray). January 25:19–21.

_____. 1989 "Montreal Massacre." December 18:14–22.

_____. 1991. "Women in Fear" (cover). November 11:26–32.

McNight, C., J.W. Mohr, R. Quinsey, and J. Erochko. 1966. "Matricide and Mental Illness." *Canadian Psychiatric Association Journal* 1, no. 2: 99–106.

Malinchak, A. 1980. *Crime and Gerontology.* Englewood Cliffs, N.J.: Prentice-Hall.

Markus, B., and B. Cormier. 1978. "A Preliminary Study of Adolescent Murderers." Paper presented at the Annual Meeting of the American Academy of Psychiatry and the Law. Montreal. October.

Marsh, Peter, and Anne Campbell, eds. 1982. *Aggression and Violence.* Oxford: Basil Blackwell.

Maxfield, Michael G. 1988. "Homicide Circumstances, 1976–1985: A Taxonomy Based on Supplementary Homicide Reports." Paper presented at the Annual Meeting of the American Society of Criminology. Chicago. November.

Maxim, Paul. 1985. "Cohort Size and Juvenile Delinquency: A Test of the Easterlin Hypothesis." *Social Forces* 63:661–81.

Mednick Sarnoff A., Terrie E. Moffitt, and Susan A. Stack, eds. 1987. *The Causes of Crime: New Biological Approaches.* New York: Cambridge University Press.

Megargee, E. 1982. *"Psychological Determinants and Correlates of Criminal Violence."* In M.E. Wolfgang and N.A. Weiner, eds., *Criminal Violence.* Beverly Hills: Sage.

Meloff, William, and Robert A. Silverman. 1992. "Canadian Kids Who Kill." *Canadian Journal of Criminology.* January: 15–34.

Mercy, J.A., and L.E. Saltzman. 1989. "Fatal Violence among Spouses in the United States, 1976–1985." *American Journal of Public Health* 79, no. 5:595–99.

Meredith, Nikki. 1984. "The Murder Epidemic." *Science.* December.

Messner, S. 1983. "Regional and Racial Effects on the Urban Homicide Rate: The Subculture of Violence Revisited. *American Journal of Sociology.* 88, no. 5:997–1007

_____. 1989. "Economic Discrimination and Societal Homicide Rates: Further Evidence on the Cost of Inequality." *American Sociological Review* 54:597–611.

_____., K. Tardiff. 1985. "The Social Ecology of Urban Homicide: An Application of the 'Routine Activities' Approach." *Criminology* 23, no. 2: 241–67.

Miethe, T.D., M.C. Stafford, and J.S. Long. 1987. "Routine Activities/Lifestyle and Victimization." *American Sociological Review* 52, no. 2:184–94.

Miller, L. 1983. "Murder in Illinois: 1973–1982." Chicago: Illinois Criminal Justice Information Authority (Order no. 84-18).

Moyer, S. 1987. *Homicide Involving Adult Suspects, 1962–1984: A Comparison of Natives and Non-Natives.* A final report to the Ministry of the Solicitor General of Canada. Ottawa.

_____. 1987. *Homicide Involving Juvenile Suspects, 1962–1984: A Comparison of Natives and Non-Natives.* A final report to the Ministry of the Solicitor General of Canada. Ottawa.

Moysa, M. 1991. "Man Told Room Mate of Killing, Trial Hears." *Edmonton Journal*, February 29: C1.

Mundt, R.J. 1990. "Gun Control and Rates of Firearms Violence in Canada and the United States." *Canadian Journal of Criminology* 32, no. 1: 137–54.

Nettler, G., N.D. "Nature of Crime and Criminal Law." Unpublished manuscript.

Nettler, G. 1982. *Killing One Another.* Cincinnati: Anderson.

Neuman, W.L., and R.J. Berger. 1988. "Competing Perspectives on Cross-National Crime: An Evaluation of Theory and Evidence." *The Sociological Quarterly* 29:281–313.

Newsweek Magazine. 1989. "Massacre in Montreal." December 18:39.

_____. 1992. "The Secret World of Jeffrey Dahmer." February 3:44–51.

Nye, F.I. 1958. *Family Relationships and Delinquent Behaviour.* New York: Wiley.

Osborne, J.A. 1987. "The Crime of Infanticide: Throwing Out the Baby with the Bathwater." *Revue Canadienne de Droit Familial* 6:47–51.

Parker, Graham. 1987. *An Introduction to Criminal Law.* 3rd ed. Toronto: Methuen.

Parker, R. 1989. "Poverty, Subculture of Violence, and Type of Homicide." *Social Forces* 67:983–1007.

_____., and R. Toth. 1984. "Family, Intimacy, and Homicide: A Synthesis of Theoretical Approaches." Revised version of a paper presented at the Annual Meeting of the American Society of Criminology. San Diego.

Peterson, R., and W. Bailey. 1991. "Felony Murder and Capital Punishment: An Examination of the Deterrence Question." *Criminology* 29, no. 3: 367–94.

Plischke, H. 1992. "Man Admits Knifing Stranger in Fight over Beer." *Edmonton Journal.* March 10: B3.

Polk, K. 1990. "Stranger Homicide: Has the Term Outlived its Usefulness?" Unpublished manuscript. University of Melbourne.

Pritchard, David. 1986. "Homicide and Bargained Justice: The Agenda Setting Effect of Crime News on Prosecutors." *Public Opinion Quarterly* 50:143–59.

Rae, R. 1981. "Canadian Crime Patterns: An Analysis of Provincial Data." Unpublished paper. Burnaby, B.C.: Simon Fraser University.

Ray, M., and R. Simons. 1987. "Convicted Murderers' Accounts of their Crimes: A Study of Homicide in Small Communities." *Symbolic Interaction* 10, no. 1:57–70.

R. v. Lavallee (3 May 1990), 21022 (S.C.C.) 335–72.

R. v. Whynot 1983. 37 C.R. (3d) 198, C.C.C. (3d) 449, 61 N.S.R. (2d) 33, 133 A.P.R. 33 (C.A.)

Reppetto, T. 1974. *Residential Crime*. Cambridge, MA: Ballinger.

Resnick, P.J. 1969. "Child Murder by Parents: A Psychiatric Review of Filicide." *American Journal of Psychiatry* 126, no. 3: 325–34.

_____. 1970. "Murder of the Newborn. A Psychiatric Review of Neonaticide." *American Journal of Psychiatry* 126, no. 10: 1414–1420.

Ressler R.K., A.W. Burgess, J.E. Douglas. 1988. *Sexual Homicide: Patterns and Motives*. Toronto: Lexington Books.

Riedel, M. 1987. "Stranger Violence: Perspectives, Issues, and Problems." *Journal of Criminal Law and Criminology* 78, no. 2: 223–58.

_____. 1992. *Stranger Violence: A Theoretical Inquiry*. New York: Garland Publishing.

Rowley, J., C.P. Ewing, S. Singer. 1987. "Juvenile Homicide: The Need for an Interdisciplinary Approach." *Behavioral Sciences and the Law* 5, no. 1:1–10.

Sacco, V., and H. Johnson. 1990. *Patterns of Criminal Victimization in Canada*. General Social Survey Analysis Series. Ottawa: Minister of Supply and Services.

Sampson, R.J. 1985. "Race and Criminal Violence: A Demographically Disaggregated Analysis of Urban Homicide." *Crime and Delinquency* 31, no. 1:47–82.

_____., 1987. "Urban Black Violence: The Effect of Male Joblessness and Family Disruption." *American Journal of Sociology* 93, no. 2:348–82.

_____., and W. Byron Groves. 1989. "Community Structure and Crime: Testing Social Disorganization Theory." *American Journal of Sociology* 94:774–802.

_____., and Janet L. Lauritsen. 1990. "Deviant Lifestyles, Proximity to Crime, and the Offender–Victim Link in Personal Violence." *Journal of Research in Crime and Delinquency* 27, no. 2:110–39.

Saunders, R.P., and C.N. Mitchell. 1990. *An Introduction to Criminal Law in Context*. 2nd. ed. Toronto: Carswell.

Savitz L., K.S. Kumar, and M. Zahn. 1991. "Quantifying Luckenbill." *Deviant Behaviour* 12:19-29.

Scarff, E. 1983. *Evaluation of the Canadian Gun Control Legislation* (Final Report). Ottawa: Programs Branch, Solicitor General of Canada.

Sellin, T. 1932. "The Basis of a Crime Index." *Journal of Criminal Law and Criminology* 23:335–56.

Sherman, L., and R. Berk. 1984. "The Specific Deterrent Effects of Arrest for Domestic Assault." *American Sociological Review* 49: 261–72.

_____., P. Gartin, and M. Buerger. 1989. "Hot Spots of Predatory Crime: Routine Activities and the Criminology of Place." *Criminology* 27:27–55.

_____., J. Schmidt, D. Rogan, and C. DeRiso. 1991. "Predicting Domestic Homicide: Prior Police Contact and Gun Threats." In Michael Steinman, *Women Battering: Policy Responses*. Cincinnati: Anderson, pp. 73–93.

Shichor, D. 1985. "Male/Female Differences in Elderly Arrests: An Exploratory Analysis." *Justice Quarterly* 2:399–414.

Silverman, R.A. 1990. "Trends in Youth Homicide: Some Unanticipated Consequences of a Change in the Law." *Canadian Journal of Criminology* 32:651–56.

_____., and Leslie W. Kennedy. 1987. "Relational Distance and Homicide: The Role of the Stranger." *Journal of Criminal Law and Criminology* 78: 272–308.

_____., and L. Kennedy. 1988. "Women Who Kill Their Children." *Violence and Victims* 3, no. 2: 121–35.

_____., and L. Kennedy. 1992. "Choose Your Weapon: Social Relationships, Firearms Regulation and Homicide." In A.V. Wilson, *The Dynamics of Victim–Offender Interaction*. Cincinnati: Anderson.

_____., and S.K. Mukherjee. 1987. "Intimate Homicide: An Analysis of Violent Social Relationships." *Behavioral Sciences and the Law*. 5, no. 1: 37–47.

_____., and Marianne Nielsen, eds. 1992. *Aboriginal Peoples and Canadian Criminal Justice*. Toronto: Butterworths.

_____., M. Riedel, and L. W. Kennedy. 1990. "Murdered Children: A Comparison of Racial Differences Across Two Jurisdictions." *Journal of Criminal Justice* 18:5.

Sinclair, M. 1990. "Dealing with the Aboriginal Offender: Indians and the Criminal Law." *Provincial Judges' Journal* 14, no. 2:14–23.

Skogan, W.G., and M.G. Maxfield. 1981. *Coping with Crime: Individual and Neighborhood Reactions*. Beverly Hills: Sage.

Smith, M.D. 1986. "The Era of Increased Violence in the United States: Age, Period, or Cohort Effect?" *Sociological Quarterly* 27:239–51.

_____. 1987. "Changes in the Victimization of Women: Is There a 'New Female Victim'?" *Journal of Research in Crime and Delinquency*. 24, no. 4:291–301.

_____. 1987. "The Incidence and Prevalence of Woman Abuse in Toronto." *Victims and Violence* 2:3.

Smith, S., R. Hanson, and S. Noble. 1974. "Social Aspects of the Battered Baby Syndrome." *British Journal of Psychiatry*. 125:568–82.

Solicitor General of Canada. 1983. *Firearms Control in Canada: An Evaluation*. Ottawa: Ministry of Supply and Services.

_____. 1985. "Questions and Answers on Capital Punishment." Unpublished manuscript. Ottawa: Government of Canada.

Stack, S. 1987. "The Effect of Female Emancipation on Homicide Trends—1950–1980: An Eight Nation Time Series Analysis." Unpublished paper. Auburn University.

Stanke, Alain. 1985a. "When the Boss Told Me to Kill It Seemed Logical. *Edmonton Journal*. April 21: B11.

_____. 1985b. "I Have Nightmares All the Time." *Edmonton Journal*. April 28: B11.

Statistics Canada. 1973. *Murder Statistics 1961–1970*. Ottawa: Information Canada.

_____. 1983. *Historical Statistics of Canada*. 2nd ed. Ottawa: Statistics Canada.

_____. 1984. *The Elderly in Canada*. Ottawa: Statistics Canada.

Straus, M. 1980a. "Victims and Aggressors in Marital Violence." *American Behavioral Scientist* 23, no. 5:681–704.

_____. 1980b. "A Sociological Perspective on the Causes of Family Violence." In M.R. Green, ed., *Violence and the Family*. Selected Symposium Series #47, pp. 7–31.

_____. 1987. "Primary Group Characteristics and Intra-family Homicide." Paper presented at the Third National Family Violence Research Conference. Durham, University of New Hampshire. July.

_____. 1988. "Primary Group Characteristics and Intra-family Homicide." Paper presented at the Annual Meeting of the American Society of Criminology. Chicago. November.

Terhune, K. 1970. "The Effects of Personality in Cooperation and Conflict." In P. Swingle, ed., *The Structure of Conflict*. New York.: Academic Press pp. 193–234.

Thompson, B.C. 1986. "Defending the Battered Wife." *Trial* 22, no. 2:74–78.

Thornberry, T.P. 1987. "Toward an Interactional Theory of Delinquency." *Criminology* 25:863.

Time Magazine. 1989. "The Man Who Hated Women." December 18.

Toby, Jackson. 1957. "The Differential Impact of Family Disorganization." *American Sociological Review* 22:505–12.

Totman, J. 1978. *The Murderess: A Psychosocial Study of Criminal Homicide*. San Francisco: R. & E. Research Associates.

Toupin, J. 1988. "Adolescent Murderers." Paper presented at the Annual Meetings of the American Society of Criminology. Chicago. November.

United Nations. 1986. *Crime Prevention and Criminal Justice Newsletter* Numbers 12 and 13 (November). Vienna: Centre for Social Development and Humanitarian Affairs.

Wahlsten, D. 1991. *Heredity and the Mind*. Unpublished manuscript. Edmonton: University of Alberta.

Walker, Lenore. 1979. *The Battered Woman*. New York: Harper and Row.

Warr, Mark. 1988. "Rape, Burglary, and Opportunity." *Journal of Quantitative Criminology* 4, no. 3:275–88.

Weisheit, R. 1986. "When Mothers Kill their Children." *The Social Science Journal*. 23, no. 4:439–48.

Wellman, B., and B. Leighton. 1979. "Networks, Neighborhoods, and Communities." *Urban Affairs Quarterly* 14:363–90.

Wilbanks, W. 1981/82. "Trends in Violent Death Among the Elderly." *International Journal of Aging and Human Development* 14, no. 3:167–75.

_____. 1982. "Murdered Women and Women Who Murder: A Critique of the Literature." In N. Rafter and E. Stanko, eds., *Judge, Lawyer, Vic-*

tim, Thief: Women, Gender Roles, and Criminal Justice. Boston: Northeastern University Press, pp.151–80.

_____. 1984. *Murder in Miami.* New York: University Press of America.

Williams, I. 1992. "Violent Crimes on the Decline in City Core." *Edmonton Journal* February 29: C1.

Williams, Kirk, and Robert L. Flewelling. 1988. "The Social Production of Criminal Homicide: A Comparative Study of Disaggregated Rates in American Cities." *American Sociological Review* 53:421–31.

_____., and Richard Hawkins. 1986. "Perceptual Research on General Deterrence: A Critical Review." *Law and Society Revie,* 20, no. 4:545–72.

Wilson, James Q. 1983. *Thinking About Crime.* New York: Vintage.

_____., and Richard J. Herrnstein. 1985. *Crime and Human Nature.* New York: Simon and Schuster.

Wirth, Louis. 1938. "Urbanism as a Way of Life." *American Journal of Sociology* 44:1–24.

Wolfgang, M.E. 1958. *Patterns in Criminal Homicide.* Philadelphia: University of Pennsylvania Press.

_____. 1976. "Family Violence and Criminal Behavior." *American Academy of Psychiatry and Law Bulletin* 4:316–327.

_____., and F. Ferracuti. 1967. *The Subculture of Violence.* London: Social Science Paperbacks.

_____., N.A. Weiner, W.D. Pointer. 1981. *Criminal Violence: Biological Correlates and Determinants.* Washington D.C.: U.S. Department of Justice, National Institute of Justice.

Wright, C. and J-P Leroux. 1991. "Children as Victims of Violent Crime." *Juristat.* Statistics Canada: Canadian Centre for Justice Statistics 11:8.

Yang, B., and D. Lester. 1988. "The Participation of Females in the Labour Force and Rates of Personal Violence (Homicide and Suicide)." *Suicide and Life-Threatening Behaviour* 18, no. 3:270–78.

Yin, P. 1985. *Victimization and the Aged.* Springfield, Ill.: Charles C. Thomas.

Zahn, M. 1991. "The Wolfgang Model: Lessons for Homicide Research in the 1990s." Paper presented at the Annual Meeting of the American Society of Criminology. San Francisco. November.

Zimring, F. 1981. "Kids, Groups and Crime: Some Implications of a Well-kept Secret." *Journal of Criminal Law and Criminology* 72, no. 3:867–85.

_____. 1984 "Youth Homicide in New York: A Preliminary Analysis." *Journal of Legal Studies* 13:81–99.

Name Index

Subject Index

Age: as exemption for penalties, 28; of suspect, 10, 11, 71, 73, 79, 83, 85, 88, 103, 117, 119, 121, 124, 143, 146, 157, 158–74, 184–85, 202, 205, 218, 221–24, 226, 228; of victim, 12, 13, 53, 71, 72, 77, 78, 82, 85, 87, 94, 103, 115, 116, 119, 120, 124, 142, 147, 159, 164, 167, 179–200, 201, 205, 219, 221, 222, 224, 226 (See also Suspects, children; Victims, children; Suspects, elderly; Victims, elderly)

Aggression, 46, 57, 123, 125, 229, 251

Alcohol and drugs, 12, 15, 49, 79, 85, 91, 95, 112, 118, 123, 161, 165, 204, 217, 220, 221, 247

Battered woman syndrome, 147–55 (See also Female killers)

Canadian Indians, 11, 13, 60, 72, 73, 75, 78, 79, 81–83, 85–88, 94, 171, 172, 188, 211–29, 234, 237; homicide rate, 212–16; socio-economic conditions, 211–12, 220–22; young offenders, 221–24 (See also Race)

Canadian Uniform Crime Reporting System, 32, 34

Canadian Urban Victimization Survey, 51

Capital punishment, 32, 240–42

Character contests, 90–92, 92–94 (See also Routine activities)

Charter of Rights and Freedoms, 18, 24

Child abuse, 123, 157–58, 188 (See also Victims, children; Family violence)

Child-killing (See Victims, children)

Children who kill (See Suspects, children)

Conflict management, 44, 48–50, 247; and relational distance, 49; conflict as, 50; programs, 250–51; third party mediation, 91

Crime-based murder, 107–38, 144, 161, 165, 188, 194, 197, 199, 207, 221, 224 (See also Relationships, crime-related)

Crimes of passion, 26, 27

Criminal Code of Canada, 17–31, 115, 149, 155, 232

Criminal negligence, 18

Culpable homicide, 7, 17–27, 243

Culpable killing (See Culpable homicide)

Date rape (See Sexual assault)

Delinquency, 46–47

Deterrence, 42, 45, 114, 125, 137, 138, 239–43 (See also Intervention; Prevention)

Divorce, 60, 75–76 (See also Marital status of suspect; Marital status of victim; Relationship, spousal)

Drugs (See Alcohol and drugs)

Educational achievement: of suspect, 10, 12, 85, 124, 146

Elderly killers (See Suspects, elderly)

Elderly victims (See Victims, elderly)

Expert testimony, 153–55 (See also Psychiatry)

Explanations of crime/homicide, 41–44, 47, 232–33

Family violence, 49–50, 200; against children, 49–50, 77, 156–57, 180 (See also Child killing; Battered wife syndrome)

Female killers (See Suspects, female)

Female victims (See Victims, female)

Femicide (See Victims, female)

Filicide (See Victims, children)

Formal control, 46, 59

Frontline, 131

Frustration, 54, 156–57

Gender: and socialization, 46; equality, 141–45; murder rates, 146; murder risk rates, 36–37; of suspect, 10, 11, 70–71, 73, 76, 77, 81, 83, 85, 88, 94, 98, 103, 117, 119, 121, 124, 128, 134, 141–58, 160, 161, 172, 185, 191, 202, 205, 216, 221, 223, 224, 226, 228, 232; of victim, 12, 13, 70, 72, 77, 78, 82, 85, 87, 94, 98, 103, 116, 119, 120, 124, 142, 147, 159, 161, 164, 167, 172, 184, 190, 200–207, 218, 221, 222, 224, 225, 228, 232 (See also Suspects, female; Victims, female)

Genetic predisposition. See Theories of murder, socio-biology theory

Green River case, 129

Gun control, 243–45

Healthy People 2000, 246, 247

Homicide: actus reus, 20–21; and domestic disturbances, 42; and economic conditions, 43, 58–59, 62, 231, 232, 238; as a process, 70; as opportunistic crime, 41–42; causes of, 10, 44, 57, 58; definition of, 7, 17–31; hot spots, 43; indirect cause of, 21; intent, 20–25, 30, 115, 157; likelihood of, 43 (See also Infanticide, Manslaughter, Murder)

Homicide rates: and birth cohorts, 62; and income inequality, 62, 181; and unemployment rates, 62; Canadian, 31–37, 62, 162–64, 183, 232; child homicide, 31–37, 180–81; international, 31, 181; young offender, 162–64 (See Statistics, murder)

Homicide research, 6, 89–90

Infanticide, 17, 27, 155–58 (See also Homicide; Victims, children)

Informal control, 45, 46, 59